Hermann Schoenfield

Higher Education in Russian, Austrian, and Prussian Poland

Hermann Schoenfield

Higher Education in Russian, Austrian, and Prussian Poland

ISBN/EAN: 9783743423725

Manufactured in Europe, USA, Canada, Australia, Japa

Cover: Foto ©Suzi / pixelio.de

Manufactured and distributed by brebook publishing software (www.brebook.com)

Hermann Schoenfield

Higher Education in Russian, Austrian, and Prussian Poland

UNITED STATES BUREAU OF EDUCATION.

CHAPTER FROM THE REPORT OF THE COMMISSIONER OF EDUCATION
FOR 1894–95.

HIGHER EDUCATION

IN

RUSSIAN, AUSTRIAN, AND PRUSSIAN POLAND.

WASHINGTON:
GOVERNMENT PRINTING OFFICE.
1896.

CHAPTER XV.

HIGHER EDUCATION IN RUSSIAN, AUSTRIAN, AND PRUSSIAN POLAND.

By HERMANN SCHOENFELD, Ph. D., *Professor of Modern Languages and Continental History in the Columbian University, Washington, D. C.*

TOPICAL OUTLINE.—*General summary of education.—Plan and arrangement.—Extent of Poland.—The Poles and the dismemberment.—Language.—Its structure. Sketch of the higher education in Poland during her independence: Ancient foundation of the University of Cracow; its early history.—Polish schools at the time of the Reformation.—Revival of higher education and downfall of Poland. Higher education in Russian Poland: The New University of Warsaw.—Constitution of the University of Warsaw.—Latest statistics of the University of Warsaw.—Report of the rector.—The four faculties.—Institute of veterinary surgery.—University library.—Archives.—Secondary education in Warsaw.—Musical education in Warsaw.—Secondary education in the country at large.—Wilno.—Archives of Wilno. Witebsk. Higher education in Austrian Poland: New University of Cracow.—Imperial Academy of Sciences.—The four faculties.—University library.—State archives.—University of Lemberg.—University library; Ossoliński library; Archives.—Imperial School of Technology in Lemberg; secondary schools.—Secondary schools in Galicia. Education in the ancient Polish provinces of Prussia: Polish origin of the University of Koenigsberg.—Lyceum Hosianum; secondary schools in Prussia; libraries.—Province of Posen, libraries.*

GENERAL SUMMARY.

The Kingdom, or rather Republic, of Poland [1] (Rzeczpospolita Polska) disappeared from the commonwealth of nations, after an existence of eight hundred years, at the end of the last century. The dismemberment of the Republic, which in the sixteenth century was the greatest power of eastern Europe and had for centuries served as a bulwark

---

[1] "Poland," says Lelewel, one of her greatest historians, "is a veritable and pure Republic, only invested with the forms of a constitutional monarchy." The principal character in the constitution of the Polish Government was a very decided separation between the executive power intrusted to the King, and the legislative power, superior to the former and exercised by the nation, i. e., the representatives of those citizens who alone enjoyed political rights, the nobility and the clergy. These deputies, nuntii, about 200 before the partition, and the senators, elected by the King, could assemble either separately or combined, thus forming but one Chamber, the Diet (Seym), generalem omuium terrarum conventum.

against the destructive invasions into Europe of the Mongolian, Tartar, and Turkish hordes,[1] was accomplished by Russia, Austria, and Prussia in three partitions (1772, 1793, 1795). The parts which once constituted the Republic of Poland are still integral parts of the three countries respectively. According to Morfill's words, "Its limbs, although distorted, are still instinct with life;" its language is still spoken by upwards of ten millions; its literature is the oldest Slavonic literature next to Bohemian, and surpasses in importance and scope all the other Slavonic literatures taken together, i. e., Bohemian, Servian, Croatian, Slavonian, Russian, Bulgarian.[2] Its institutions and laws have perished, some of them fortunately for the broad masses of the Polish people who had nothing but the patrimony of the disinherited, serfdom. Austria at once introduced into Galicia the Austrian civil code; in the Prussian Polish provinces the Prussian Landrecht prevails. Russia alone permitted to the Kingdom (tsarstvo) of Poland a shadow of self-government and many privileges. Alexander I conferred great privileges upon the University of Wilno, confirmed the Lithuanian statutes in the western and southwestern governments and the code of Napoleon in Poland proper from the year 1807. But all this was changed into Russian law by a ukase of June 25, 1840. Yet in spite of the difficulties and restrictions under which the dismembered country labors, there are several very active centers of Polish literature, culture, and education, foremost among them Cracow and Lemberg, thoroughly Polish, excellent universities in Austrian Galicia. The work of the Academy of Cracow, founded in 1872, is of such a high standard of excellence, its editions of the Polish authors of the golden age (1541–1606) are so valuable, the many learned reviews that appear in Polish, equal to the best in other civilized countries, present so much original research and material that it is only a question of time when Polish literature and culture as well as that of the other Slavonic countries will constitute an essential part of instruction in our universities to supplement the Germanic and Romance languages and literatures.

---

[1] In the reign of Boleslas V (1227–1279) the frightful Mongolian invasion took place (1241). Although gaining a Pyrrhus victory at the battle of Lignica (Liegnitz) in Silesia, they were diverted into Hungary after their force had been broken. Nothing since the battle on the Catalaunian fields can be compared with that carnage. In the fifteenth, sixteenth, and seventeenth centuries, the Poles went forth the champions of Christendom and rolled back the tide of Moslem conquest from Europe. Justly, therefore, Melanchthon, speaking on this subject, says: "The magnanimity of this nation is especially displayed in their continual wars against the Tartars for the tranquillity of all Europe. For centuries she has protected Europe against the Tartars and the neighborhood of savage Asia. Let us never forget these obligations to Poland, and let us recollect who are the people, and in what regions of the earth they were made instruments of Providence, and by protecting Europe, enabled her to preserve within her bosom humanity, religion, and those arts and sciences so beneficial to society."

[2] According to Estreicher (Bibliographia Polonica, Cracow, 1870), it represents two-thirds of the entire Slavonic literature.

The University of Warsaw, although Russified to a great extent since the late insurrection, is still rich in national Polish spirit, learning, and culture. The Polish press of Warsaw still turns out many valuable books, magazines, and reviews in all branches of literature and science.

Prussia has best succeeded in Germanizing her Polish possessions, slowly eliminating or weakening the Polish element, "carefully avoiding any of those reprisals which would cause a European scandal." But "der neue Kurs," under the enlightened young Emperor William II, has thoroughly reversed the old theory, if not the old practice. Coercion has been reduced to a minimum, yet the German language makes more rapid strides than ever and does not suffer under the fact that Polish is cultivated in family and school, especially in the religious education of the people, who are mostly Roman Catholics. It seems as if the idea had won ground in the highest authoritative circles of Prussia that a people with an almost equally old western civilization, abundantly rich literature, language, and history, can not be weaned and severed from it by persuasion, force or police measures. Thus, while the provinces of Posen, Upper Silesia, and old Prussia have a by far greater German population and more completely Germanized Slavs under the admirable Prussian school system, the educational influence of three years' military training,[1] and the general high standard of Prussia's judiciary and administrative institutions, yet the Polish language and literature are extensively cultivated among the people by the Catholic Church, in the public schools by Polish teachers during the limited time that is allotted to their language, and in the higher schools for their intrinsic value and because it is a fundamental necessity for understanding the historical origin and development of all the provinces between the Elbe, or at least the Oder, and the Vistula. Indeed, the colonization by the German element of all that land is nothing but a protracted struggle, beginning as early as Charlemagne's time and not finished yet by far, to subject, to absorb, or to annihilate the Slavonic, principally Polish, population that has expanded over the territory vacated by the German tribes during the first migrations of peoples. For Leopold von Ranke's statement, "Es sind zwei Völkerwanderungen, durch die der Umkreis der deutschen Gebiete aus dem inneren Germanien her bestimmt worden: die eine war nach dem Westen, die andere nach dem Osten gerichtet," is absolutely correct. But while the Germanic tribes had pushed themselves forward toward the west and south in powerful streams and in a comparatively short period of time, the backward

---

[1] I venture this statement, which may seem paradoxical to those who are wont to consider the German military service as a waste of time and energy, removing hundreds of thousands of men from temporary production. But any military instructor who, like myself, has had an opportunity of observing many Polish recruits who come to the army as analphabets and leave it with a good equipment of German education, an enlarged horizon and excellent training, will surely agree with me.

flood toward the east against the natural course of Slavonic immigration occurred slowly, gradually, through many centuries, often interrupted by long pauses, historically not determined. While during the first migration Teutonic pagans pushed beyond the boundaries of Germania, it was Catholic Christianity, the victorious Roman Church, the monks, who accompanied the progress of the Germans; later on it was the Reformation which led thousands and thousands toward the East. It is, of course, not to be forgotten that a second main incentive was the craving for material wealth and worldly power which made such invasions very bloody, cruel, and unjust, full of epic battles and adventures so graphically described in Mickiewicz's Konrad Wallenrod, concerning the struggle between the Lithuanians and the Teutonic knights.

There is no Polish university in these Prussian provinces it is true, but Posen and Bromberg (Bydgoszcz), Danzig and Thorn, even Breslau, the capital of Silesia, and all the Upper Silesian towns, not to speak of its mostly Polish villages, have still very strong Polish traits and traces. The concessions made to Polish education especially and Slavonic languages and literatures generally, the importance attributed to these branches in Prussia appear from the strong Slavonic departments not only at the eastern universities of Breslau and Königsberg, but also at the University of Berlin. It is a very characteristic fact that for the first time, so far as I know, a scholar in Slavonic languages, the famous Wladyslaw Nehring, has become rector magnificus of the University of Breslau (1893-94).

Prof. Karl Brugman, of Leipzic, in Die Deutschen Universitäten, edited by W. Lexis, says in regard to Slavonic philology in Germany: "Slavonic philology, that bloomed up in the countries of the Austrian Crown and is about as old as Germanic and Romance philology, can naturally not have such a broad ground in Germany as its sister disciplines. It has at present three full professorships, in Breslau, Leipsic, Berlin, occupied by Nehring, A. Leskien, whose principal merits lie in the domain of Slavonic grammar, and A. Brückner.[1] Besides the great successor of Miklósich (d. 1891), V. Jagić, who, besides an extraordinary many-sidedness in literary production, has done an exceedingly meritorious work in grammar as well as in editing revised texts and investigating topics of literary history, was at the University of Berlin for several years (1874-1880). The latter is the founder of the Archiv für slav. Philologie (founded in 1875), the central organ of that science."

As for the important rôle that the Slavonic element has been destined to play in German life, it appears from the history and literature of Germany, which are quite permeated with its influence, German historians never grow tired of showing the contrast of the two national characters; German poets and authors compare and contrast their

---

[1] In the research of the Baltic-Slavonic languages, the works of Leskien, A. Bezzenberger (Gottingue, Königsberg), and A. Brückner (Berlin) are foremost.

traits and peculiarities, their ideals of education and culture. No one has done it better from a German point of view than Gustav Freytag, himself born on the frontier of Upper Silesia and Russian Poland, at Kreuzburg, in his Soll und Haben, and especially in his classical historical novels Die Ahnen and Bilder aus der deutschen Vergangenheit.

PLAN AND ARRANGEMENT.

It is my particular task to give a report on the higher education in the different parts of Poland, and with special reference to the shaping of the methods of instruction and organization on the part of the three Governments, Russia, Austria, and Prussia, with a view to assimilating the Slavonic population to the Government policies, social traditions, and civilization of the three nations respectively.[1]

For this undertaking it is necessary, first, to define more accurately the limits of the Kingdom of Poland at the time of her prosperity and of her decadence, while yet independent among the European nations; second, to give a sketch of the development of her educational facilities in the way of higher institutions of learning and universities during the period of her independence. Only from a comparison of her educational conditions while independent can we ascertain and realize her progress or retrogression in higher education after her partition, the changes wrought for good or for evil, the assimilation to or reaction against foreign influences, the transmutation of political and social ideals, the participation of the different classes in an education which is partly not their own, inoculated with ideals conceived by her conquerors in order to bring her children to a gradual mental and intellectual as well as physical subjection.

EXTENT OF POLAND.

At the period of her greatest prosperity under the later Jagiellos, Sigismund I, Sigismund II Augustus (1507–1572), the short interregnum and the brief nominal reign of Henry of Valois (1575), and the valiant Stephen Batory (1576–1586), Poland extended from the Baltic to the Black Sea, touching it at Akerman; from Bohemia, Moravia, Austria proper, Hungary, and the Danubian principalities to Russia beyond the Dnieper. The greatest length of the country from north to south was 713 English miles, and from east to west 693 miles. It embraced an area of about 282,000 English square miles, and this area in 1880 had a population of 24,000,000.

For our investigation, however, which concerns Polish soil and

---

[1] The present monograph is a summary of a more extensive work on Higher Education in Poland now in course of preparation, and to be published later through the regular channels of trade. The author begs to acknowledge assistance from Senator Michael Kruszka, of Milwaukee, on Galician secondary schools, and receipt of valuable printed material from the pedagogical and geographical societies of Lemberg.

Polish people proper, we must exclude all the country which was not Polish in spirit and nationality, though at certain times it belonged to the republic by conquest. Thus that part of Kijowska which lies beyond the Dnieper, including the famous old city of Kief, one of the cradles of Russia, was ceded by the Crown to the latter country by the treaty of Andruszowo, 1667, and was never gotten back. Kief is consequently a purely Russian university, which will find no place in our treatise on higher education in Poland.[1]

Anatole Leroy-Beaulieu, in his unsurpassed work, The Empire of the Tsars and the Russians, has best expressed this idea, saying: "Separated from Great Russia at the time of the Tartar invasion, Little Russia was through five centuries subject to Poland and Lithuania, not to much purpose. Only the polished surface—the nobility of Kief, Volhynia, Podolia—became Polonized. It is owing preeminently to the Greek orthodox rite that the bulk of the people, the immense majority of the inhabitants of Kief and Ukraïna, have turned out quite as Russian as the people of Moscow." Leroy-Beaulieu's clever translator, Zénaïde A. Ragozin, shows in a footnote (I, p. 118) that the statistician, Tshubinsky, who has published some very detailed statistical tables on this very subject, has found out that the Poles could not muster 100,000 strong in the above three governments put together. Even making allowance for some exaggeration in the Russian documents, still so much remains that the figure of the genuinely Polish population is extremely low. In those three governments the number of Catholics, among whom there certainly are non-Polonized Little Russians, amounted to scarcely 400,000, or less than a seventh of the entire population (16.94 per cent). In these same three governments the number of Israelites rose to over 750,000. Unfortunately, Mme. Ragozin extends this calculation also to Lithuania and White Russia, i. e., to all the provinces annexed in one of the three divisions of Poland, without any statistical proof.

Smolenska also, with the important city of Smolensk, an object of strife between Lithuania, Poland, on one hand and Russia on the other, was transferred to Russia forever by the treaty of Andruszowo. Nor was Inflancka, or Livonia, with the old Hanseatic city of Riga, though acquired by Poland in 1561, ever Polish in spirit, or sympathy, or civilization.

Poland, in the strict sense of the term, also called the Crown of Poland (Korona), consisting of Great Poland (Wielkopolska) with the principal cities of Posen (Poznań), dating from the earliest period of the Republic, and Warsaw (Warszawa), which became the capital of the country as late as the reign of Sigismund III, and of Little Poland (Małopolska) with the famous old capital Cracow (Kraków), was united with Lithuania (Litwa) by the marriage of Jadwiga, the Polish

---

[1] We shall, however, learn later that this university, after the suppression of Warsaw, was the greatest resort of Polish students.

queen, with Jagiello, duke of Lithuania (1386); a more complete federation taking place at Lublin in 1569. The capital was Wilno; the official language of the country was White Russian, in which tongue its laws were promulgated. With this union Christianity was introduced. A Polish university was founded at Wilno by Stephen Batory under the care of the Jesuits (1578), which for centuries exercised its Polish and Roman Catholic influence upon the country, until it was suppressed by Emperor Nicholas I (1833) after the outbreak of the Polish insurrection of 1830, and the University of Kharkof founded in its stead.

As to a more accurate division of the Rzeczpospolita Polska in Palatinates (Województwa) for administrative and military purposes I may safely refer the reader to Morfill's Story of Poland (pp. 1–11), who follows Michael Bobrzyński's "Dzieje Polski w Zarysie," Warsaw, 1881, Vol. II, p. 363.

THE POLES AND THE DISMEMBERMENT.

This country was from time immemorial[1] inhabited by Slavonic tribes belonging to the great Indo-European or Aryan family of peoples. The early Slavs are said by the best historians to have been a peaceful agricultural people living under a patriarchal Democratic rule, without priests or kings, but the invasions of Asiatic hordes and the conflicts with the German tribes compelled them to adopt a sort of monarchical government. But the origin of Poland is fabulous;[2] history but begins with the reign of Mieczyslaw I and the introduction of Christianity in the Latin form under him (965), thus placing Poland at the outset in contrast to Russia, whose civilization was to be Greek in the Byzantine form.

Šafařik finds the first mentioning of this people in the Geography of Ptolemy, who lived in the second century A. D. They are here mentioned under the name of Bulanes. The generally accepted derivation of the name is from pole, field, plain, the country being one vast plain. Nestor, the old Russian chronicler, distinguishes between the Poliane Liakhove on the Vistula and the Poliane Rusove on the Dnieper, the dwellers on the Vistula plains and the dwellers on the Dnieper plains. Röpell, the excellent German historian of Poland,[3] has traced the devel-

---

[1] That is after having branched off from their original Iranian or Indo-European home in Asia, they immigrated into Europe at a period contemporaneous with or rather after the arrival of the Teutonic families. But an autochthoneus origin in Europe for the entire Indo-European race has been also maintained by such scholars as Penka and Schrader (Origines Ariacæ, Vienna, 1883), Sprachvergleichung und Urgeschichte (1885). Morfill has given a very excellent abstract, sifting the frequently conflicting views of the best Slavonic scholars on the Slavonic origin. (See Article "Slavs," Encycl. Brit., Vol. XXII, pp. 145–147.)

[2] Lelewel, the great Polish historian, has relegated all the period of Polish history from the earliest times to the reign of Mieczyslaw to the era of myths.

[3] The standard history of Poland by Röpell has been continued by Caro, both professors of the University of Breslau.

opment of the various divisions of society among the Poles back to their origin, showing how the nobility, szlachta (probably derived from the German word Geschlecht), became in course of time the Polish nation properly so-called, subjecting the cmetones (kmieci), an originally free class of peasants, and the peasants strictly so called (chłopi), to absolute bondage. When in the course of history also the power of the king was gradually diminished to a mere shadow by the pacta conventa, the military szlachta became the sole and almost absolute bearer of the power of the state. In this fact lies the germ of Poland's destruction, which became realized when the "Adelsrepublik," as Röpell calls it, had no other basis than a degraded aristocracy fallen from their old lofty patriotism, a national middle class being absolutely wanting, the trade of the country being almost entirely in the hands of foreigners, or people with foreign proclivities, Germans and Jews.[1]

So the dismemberment began. In 1772 Prussia took the Palatinates of Malborg (Marienburg), Pomeria (Pomerellen), Warmia (Ermelaud), Culm, except Danzig and Thorn and a part of Great Poland; Austria took Red Russia or Galicia, with a part of Podolia, Sandomir, and Cracow; Russia took White Russia, with all the part beyond the Dnieper. The territories seized by the three powers amounted to 13,000 English square miles, 416,000 inhabitants; 27,000 square miles, 2,700,000 inhabitants; 42,000 square miles, 1,800,000 inhabitants, respectively.

But in spite of many fruitless attempts to amend the new constitution, promulgated May 2, 1791, a second partition by Russia and Prussia took place in 1793, appropriating to Prussia the remainder of Great and a portion of Little Poland (22,000 square miles with 1,100,000 inhabitants), and advancing the Russian boundary to the center of Lithuania and Volhynia (96,000 square miles, 3,000,000 inhabitants).

In the third and last partition Austria participated, taking Cracow, with the country between the Pilica, the Vistula, and the Bug (18,000 square miles, 1,000,000 inhabitants); Prussia had the capital, with the territory as far as the Niemen (21,000 square miles, 1,000,000 inhabitants); Russia took the rest, amounting to 43,000 square miles, 1,200,000 inhabitants.

During the general European upheaval at the time of the Napoleonic wars waged against Prussia and Russia (1806–1807) and Austria (1809), when the Poles rallied round him a faithful army of patriots, Napoleon established the Duchy of Warsaw by the treaty of Tilsit (1807), chiefly out of the Prussian share of Poland, with a liberal constitution and the Elector of Saxony at its head. The duchy, under the guidance of Prince Joseph Poniatowski, wrenched western Galicia from Austria

---

[1] Of course the nobility of Poland differed entirely from the feudal nobility of the rest of Europe. The former sprang originally from among the country people. There were in Poland many villages, inhabited by a population of nobles only, who were as poor as the peasants, yet enjoying the same political rights with the wealthiest magnates.

(1809) after the defeat of the latter at Austerlitz. But with Napoleon's sinking star the grand allied army in 1813 put an end to its existence. After the cessions by Austria in 1809 the duchy contained 58,290 English square miles, with about 4,000,000 inhabitants.

The division of Poland was rearranged by the congress of Vienna in 1815. The original shares of Prussia and Austria were diminished. Prussia was to have Posen and what she had gained at the first partition. Austria was to have Galicia and the salt mines of Wieliczka, while the city and district of Cracow were to form an independent republic under the guarantee of the three powers, and were seized by Austria only in 1846 after a violent insurrection. The remainder of ancient Poland, comprising the chief parts of the recent Grand Duchy of Warsaw, reverted to Russia, and was to form a constitutional kingdom subject to the Czar.[1]

The country we have to deal with in our report, as finally arranged, is as follows:

Russian Poland, since 1867, for administrative purposes, is divided into 10 governments, viz:

Governments.	English square miles.	Population.	Governments.	English square miles.	Population.
Kalisz	4,400	774,759	Radom	4,762	644,827
Kielce	2,890	622,842	Siedlce	5,527	622,465
Łomza	4,677	538,588	Suwałki	4,847	603,174
Lublin	6,506	860,382	Warsaw	5,613	1,314,209
Piotrków	4,720	837,928			
Płock	4,209	538,141	Total	48,151	7,357,375

Prussian Poland, including Posen, most of Western Prussia, and several districts in Eastern Prussia; 26,000 square miles, 3,000,000 inhabitants.

Austrian Poland, including Galicia, Lodomeria, Bukovina, and Zipsetc; 35,500 square miles, 5,000,000 inhabitants.

If we exempt the German, the Armenian, the Ugro-Finnish, and Jewish elements, the bulk of the Polish population proper, according to the calculations accompanying the ethnological map of Mirkovich (1877), amounts to 4,633,378 in the Russian Empire; 2,404,458 and 110,000 Kashubes (Kassuben) living on the coast of the Baltic near Danzig, in Prussia, and 2,444,200 in Austria. Besides these there are 10,000 in Turkey. These figures give a gross total of 9,602,036. (Morfill, Story of Poland, p. 12.) This calculation is very moderate, and I am inclined to put it at a rather higher figure. Kropotkine, in his excellent article on Russian Poland in the Encyclopedia Britannica (ninth edition), numbers in Russia, outside of Poland proper, about 1,162,050 Poles in 1881.

---

[1] This Kingdom of Poland, or Congress Poland (Kongressówka), alone constitutes the whole of Russian Poland in the eyes of the Russians, who refuse to recognize as Polish the provinces annexed by Catherine II.

The prevalent religion among the Poles is the Roman Catholic, to which in Russian Poland 4,596,956 out of a population of 6,034,430 belonged (1870). Since the last insurrection a series of measures have been taken to reduce the numbers of the Roman Catholic clergy in Poland. In 1883 there remained 1,313 churches out of 1,401; 1,544 priests out of 2,322; 10 monasteries out of 29, and 8 convents out of 30; one diocese (Podlasie) having been abolished, and a new one established at Kielce, while several bishops had been sent out of the country. The whole situation remained unsettled until 1883, when the Pope recognized the new diocesan subdivisions introduced by the Russian Government. Poland is now divided into four dioceses—Warsaw, Sędomierz, Lublin, and Płock. (Kropotkine, Poland, Vol. XIX, pp. 309, 310.)

The Austrian Poles enjoy absolute religious freedom under their Apostolic Emperor of Austria, as well as a practical self-administration of their schools in an entirely national Polish spirit.

In Prussia, too, after the discontinuation of the "Kulturkampf," perfect religious peace has been restored. At the old bishopric of Posen-Gnesen (Poznań-Gniazno), founded by Mieczyslaw with the aid of St. Adalbert of Prague in 968, a Polish archbishop, Stablewski, has been inaugurated and confirmed by the German Emperor to further and enhance the union and harmony between the Roman Catholic Poles and their Lutheran German brethren. This was an act of far-reaching, ideal, and political importance—an acknowledgment of the Poles in Prussia and their claims as to freedom of language, religion, and a sort of home rule, of course within the principles of true Prussian citizenship and loyalty. The fact that a Polish archbishop occupies the seat of St. Adalbert, who for a short time was the second archbishop of Gnesen, before he went out to preach the gospel among the heathen Prussians[1] and suffered martyrdom, is a provisional solution of the Polish question, the more favorable to the Poles as it thoroughly reverses the former policy instituted against them.

On the whole, no retrogression of the Roman Catholic religion in Poland is going on outside of Russia. According to Lelewel the population of Poland in 1764 was subdivided as follows in the way of the different cults: Catholics, 7,000,000; United Greeks, 1,500,000; Protestants, 1,000,000; Orthodox Greek-Russian, 2,000,000; Jews, over 1,500,000; Mahometans, 50,000; Armenians, 30,000; Mennonites, 20,000; Jewish Caraïtes, 20,000.

While the Roman Catholic religion is normally growing in Prussian Poland, and especially in Austrian Poland, several millions of Russian Poles have since the last century been converted to the Orthodox Greek religion, owing to the political and social advantages arising therefrom and the prodigious spread of Orthodox Greek churches over the country.

---

[1] It is a curious historical incident that the heathen Prussians, who, with the Letts and Lithuanians, belonged to the Litu-Slavic family, for which Leskien has proposed the generic name "Baltic," should have given their name to that power which forms the bone and marrow of the German Empire.

LANGUAGE.

The language in which the vast and rich treasures of Polish literature are stored belongs to the western branch of the Slavonic tongue. To this branch belong (1) Polish: Masovian or Mazurian, Great Polish, Kashubish, and the upper Silesian dialects, which have very much degenerated (Wasserpolnisch). (2) Bohemian: Czechish, Moravian, and Slovakish. (3) Lusatian Wendish or Sorbish, which is gradually dying out and will soon be extinct like Polabish.

The dialect of Great Poland has become the literary language, rich and powerful, flexible and sonorous, no Indo-European language except Sanscrit presenting such a variety of inflections and sounds to mold it according to all emotions that may pervade man's breast. But this language has been deteriorated by foreign unassimilated elements that have crept in, just as German was impaired by the invasion of French in the seventeenth century. When large colonies of Germans began to settle in Poland after the Mongolian invasion (1241), which had widely devastated the country, and to build many German towns, and usurped nearly the entire trade of the country, for which the Poles never had either inclination or talent, a large stock of German words poured into Polish, giving it a strange alien aspect. As these Germans enjoyed, among many other privileges, their own laws also, the Jus Magdeburgicum, a "Sonderstaat im Staate," existed up to Casimir the Great's time, influencing also their judiciary organization.

With the reign of Sigismund III (1589–1632) the continuous wars and invasions of Poland and an all-pervading, very poor church Latin contributed considerably to bring about a degeneration in the Polish language and literature which threatened to suffocate the national idiom. The latter lost a great deal of its purity by the entrance of bad taste and macaronism. Theological dissertations in the manner of the decadence of scholasticism and affected panegyrics supplanted original invention and did the language itself untold harm. Yet a poet like Sarbiewski, who, according to Hugo Grotius, "did not only equal but surpassed Horace," and the poetess Elizabeth Druzbatska, show such purity of style and grace, such delicacy of thought and taste, that the inroad of all macaronism and pedantry in speech and literature could not stamp out the slumbering force of the Polish language. Still many unnecessary Latinisms disfigure the Polish language, which is not strange, since this macaronic period can be said to have lasted from 1606 to 1764. Yet, in flexibility, richness, power, and harmony, Polish is not excelled by any other language in Europe; its grammatical structure is fully developed and firmly established, its orthography precise and perfect. Morfill rightly quotes the poet Casimir Brodzinki's beautiful and expressive characterization of his native tongue:

Let the Pole smile with manly pride when the inhabitant of the banks of the Tiber or Seine calls his language rude; let him hear with keen satisfaction and the dignity of a judge the stranger who painfully struggles with the Polish pronunciation like a Sybarite trying to lift an old Roman coat of armor, or when he strives to articulate the language of men with the weak accent of children. So long as courage is not lost in our nation, while our manners have not become degraded, let us not disavow this manly roughness of our language. It has its harmony, its melody, but it is the murmur of an oak of three hundred years, and not the plaintive and feeble cry of a reed, swayed by every wind.

It would be impossible to give a fair idea of the grammatical structure of the language in a short survey of its phonetics, forms, and grammatical differences from the other sister languages. But a few hints at its nature may induce some reader to take recourse to one of the many excellent Polish grammars; besides, it may be considered necessary to have at least a vague insight into the language which was the basis of the educational system of a great realm and is still the medium through which education, culture, and the history and literature of a great past is inculcated in 10,000,000 souls.

Its structure.—The Slavonic languages, it should be first noticed, do not differ from one another to such an extent as, for instance, the Teutonic or even the Romance languages. A Slav[1] who knows his language to perfection will, I dare say, always be able to understand and to make himself understood among the other peoples of his race or at least of his subdivision (Southeast and West). The Low German dialect of Holstein and the Swiss dialect certainly differ very much more than Polish, Bohemian, and Lusatian.

The principal changes in the various Slavonic languages have been brought about under the destructive influence exercised by the vowel i and the semivowel j upon the preceding consonants. Thus many mutes were reduced to mere hissing sounds; hence comes this characteristic sibilation so frequent in the Slavonic languages, though not equally so in all of them.

The apparent heaping of consonants, especially at the beginning of syllables, by which so many are deterred from studying the languages, fearing the impossibility of pronouncing them, is really no heaping at all. Many of these consonants are liquid, and if not, they become liquid (mouillé) by very pure and sonorous vowels following them to modify any harshness that may arise. This prejudice against the harshness of the Slavonic languages has been largely created by the uncomfortable orthography in the Polish language, which frequently expresses one sound by a combination of two, nay, four consonants; thus Polish sz, cz, szcz are expressed in Russian by one sign. Though not harsh, Polish has more hissing sounds than any other Slavonic language.

---

[1] The name of the Slavs properly means illustrious, glorious; slava, slavitsa (old Slavonic), glory; slavinu, glorious; Lithuanian szlowe, glory, derived from old Slavonic sluti, to hear; church Slavonic slysza, I hear; sluch, the reputation; modern Russian slyszat; Polish sluchać, to hear, also in the sense of bene audire. Hence Russian Slavjaniu, slavjanskij; Polish Słowianin, Słowjanski; Czech Slovan, Slovansky, for Slav, Slavonic.

In regard to grammatical forms the Slavonic languages are infinitely superior to the Germanic and Neolatin languages. They are closer related to the synthetic languages, the nouns having no articles (but, of course, demonstrative pronouns), and the verbs being almost always conjugated without personal pronouns.

The Polish language has a most elaborate declensional system, comprising seven cases, by which the use of prepositions is limited and a great freedom of position of words insured in the sentences. Like Sanscrit, it possesses the nominative, genitive, dative, accusative, vocative, instrumentalis, locativus, wanting only the ablative. The noun has one of the three genders, but has lost the dual, which still exists in the Masovian dialect. It also has more diminutives and augmentatives than either Latin[1] or Italian.

The adjectives have diminutives and augmentatives besides the three degrees, as, for instance, *mały*, small; comparative, *mniejszy;* superlative, *najmniejszy;* diminutive, *malutki, maleńki;* zielony, green; *zielonawy*, greenish.

The verbs, by means of the so-called "aspects," have very delicate distinctions of meaning in the conditions of time, and even gender, quite unknown in the other modern languages. They have causative, iterative, inceptive, perfective, durative, participial, etc., forms, which contribute a great deal to the lucidity of grammatical constructions. Every root word thus becomes, according to the great philologist Schleicher, the germ of a largely ramified tree of derivative forms, each of which expresses a different sense. There is a creative vitality in their forms infinitely superior to the rigid, decrepit crystallization of the Germanic and Latin languages, as Schleicher puts it.

Less remote from Palæo-Slavonic than Russian, for instance, it has preserved some peculiar characteristics of the mother tongue, among them ą (pronounced like French sa*lon*) and ę (sa*tin*).

Łł is another consonant which does not exist in any other language.

It is similar to ll in Spanish, and has a peculiarly broad and thick sound.

The phonetic wealth of the language is expressed by 35 consonants, 9 vowels, and 1 letter j, which is considered to be a semivowel and semiconsonant.

The accent, except in foreign words and in compounds, which are exceedingly rare, is constantly on the penultimate—ródak, countryman; genitive, rodáka; dative, rodakówi.

In Polish words the syllable with the vowel which has the tonic accent is long; the other syllables are short. Thus the Polish language combines the advantages of the prosody of ancient poetry with those of the rhyme of modern; it possesses all the varieties of poetical forms from the Latin hexameter to the French Alexandrinian verse.

---

[1] That means a good deal when we consider such diminutive possibilities, like cista, cistula, cistella, cistellula.

The Polish language [says Schleicher] distinguishes itself among the other Slavonic idioms particularly by a varied and manifold softening of the consonants. This delicate expression of sounds, produced by the continual variations of the same consonants, makes this language very difficult for the foreigner; but in the mouths of educated Poles it is not harsh at all.

Among the Indo-European languages the Germanic languages possess not one softened (modified) consonant; the Romance laugnages but one—softened *n* (gu in French and Italian, ñ in Spanish); the Slavonic languages have several consonants of that kind. Polish, though harsher than several among them, has the most.

The total of words in the Polish language amounts to about 100,000, a great number among them being, as in the Neolatin languages, composed of verbs or nouns preceded by prepositions. The words composed of substantives and verbs or two substantives, so common in German, are very rare in Polish. Almost all the feminine substantives and adjectives in Polish, as in the other Slavonic and in the Neolatin languages (except French) have the termination a; and the great number of Polish words terminating with vowels serve to soften the harshness of the language indisputable in other respects.

On the whole, however, we may adopt Schnitzler's statement:

Original, flexible, sonorous as it is, Polish is as rich in forms as it is in words, so that it easily expresses all the ideas to be conveyed and adopts all possible sounds. One may say that Polish is a scholarly language, which has been elaborated, polished, refined by numerous authors, some of whom, men of first order, are justly counted by the Poles among their titles of glory and as a compensation for their political disasters.

Such an account of the most striking characteristics of the language may appear as a digression from my theme, but the language spoken by the people is the very skeleton upon which the structure of their education is built. And as their language is practically unknown with us, it seems to me an indispensable preliminary step to my treatise on the higher education in Poland.

SKETCH OF THE HIGHER EDUCATION IN POLAND DURING HER INDEPENDENCE.

The introduction of Christianity into Poland under Mieczyslaw, or Mieczko, to use the abridged form of his name, took place as already stated, in its Latin form. The Latin alphabet was adopted, and the Latin language became the sacred language of the nation. From the church, Latin soon penetrated everywhere, into the schools, the administration, the tribunals, and the domain of history and letters.

The exclusive use of Latin as the literary language during several centuries arrested in Poland all progress and all development of the national language, and, worst of all, debarred the broad masses of the people from participating in the literary movement of the time. But, on the other hand, the knowledge of Latin was soon followed by reading the books of the clerical and secular authors who rapidly spread over Poland. Thus the bad results of "Latinomania," of which some Polish writers so bitterly complain, were partly compensated by the intense literary aspirations of the higher classes.

Mieczko's successor, Boleslaw the Great (992–1026), in order to spread Christianity more effectively among the Poles, invited some Benedictine monks from France and founded monasteries on Lysa Gora, at Sieciechowa, and Tynec, and around the monasteries schools of various kinds arose, just like the "Klosterschulen" in Germany under Charlemagne.

<small>From the eleventh century on [says Leonard Chodzko] libraries were established in Poland. In 1166 the historian Matthew Cholewa, bishop of Cracow, incessantly quotes the Digesta and the Institutiones Romanæ, which had been discovered in Italy about 40 years before. Also quotations from the Roman historian Valerius, all traces of whose works have since been lost, are found in the Latin chronicles of that Polish bishop. The Polish schools and libraries in the twelfth century were in the same flourishing condition as those of the Latin races.</small>

Jan Dlugosz (Longinus), the famous canon of Cracow (1415–1486), in his most important Latin chronicle, extending from the earliest periods of his country's history to his own time, speaks of Polish schools that were said to have existed in Poland during the eleventh century.

At the end of the thirteenth and the beginning of the fourteenth centuries the young Polish students frequented the universities of Padua, Bologna, and Paris, in which several of their compatriots, as Nicolas of Cracow, Jan Grot de Huplé, and Przeslaw, were installed as professors and even rectors.

There was even a dim, flickering light of natural science awakening in Poland, inasmuch as the mathematician Ciolek (Vitellio), who lived in the second half of the fourteenth century, became one of the originators of the science of optics.

The reign of Casimir the Great (1333–1370) marks the dawn of a new era in the literary, educational, and political history of Poland. This King, who at the diet of Wislica, in 1347, had the celebrated statute of Wislica enacted—the first monument of Polish jurisprudence, and a code destined to rule the Kingdom according to principles of higher statesmanship[1]—is the founder of the University of Cracow.

Ancient foundation of the University of Cracow; its early history.— The city of Cracow had become prominent as the capital under Ladislans Lokietek (lokiec, an ell), who was the first monarch crowned there. Under his great son and successor, Casimir III, Cracow (also Danzig) became a member of the Hanseatic League.

In 1364 the foundation of the University of Cracow was laid in the

---

[1] The most eminent Polish jurist, Francis Wolowski, states concerning the statute: "One is struck with astonishment at the thought that this first Polish code, remarkable by its wisdom and the clemency of its dispositions, precedes by nine years the celebrated golden bull of Emperor Charles IV of Germany, which in relation to its penal legislation still breathes to a high degree the barbarities of the Middle Ages." In the statute there is a strong attempt to raise the wretched condition of the "misera contribuens plebs," which procured for Casimir the title of honor of "the peasants' king" (Król chłopów).

village of Wawel (now Kazimierz, the suburb of Cracow). Podczaszynski maintains its creation in 1347, which date would make it the oldest university of the north and east of Europe. But Lelewel, the best authority, has put it in 1364,[1] and Friedrich Paulsen, in his admirable Wesen und Geschichtliche Entwickelung der Deutschen Universitäten (Die Deutschen Universitäten, W. Lexis, I, Berlin, 1893), states:

> Prague and Vienna are the first founded German universities, the former[2] established in 1348 by the house of Luxemburg, the latter in 1365 by the house of Habsburg, both on the eastern side of the German domain of culture, apparently for the reason that Paris was near enough to the west, with which the oldest church institutions on the Rhine, especially Cologne, were closely connected. Only toward the end of the century did the west of Germany follow with the universities of Heidelberg (1385) and Cologne (1388, discontinued 1794), Middle Germany with Erfurt (1392, discontinued 1816). The dissolution of the University of Paris, owing to the great church schism, brought about the foundation of these three universities.

In Cologne, the old seat of scholastic education, Albertus Magnus and Thomas Aquinas, as well as the Minorite, Duns Scotus, had excelled. To replace Prague, lost to the Germans by the Hussite troubles, the University of Leipsic was founded in 1409, that of Rostock for the Baltic countries in 1419.

This digression is made to show that Poland was not behind Germany in her aspirations, at least for educational excellency, and was well nigh the first to found a university.

Organized after the model of that of Paris, the University of Cracow propagated in Poland all the sciences cultivated at that time in France, grammar, logic, metaphysics, the physical and mathematical sciences, jurisprudence, politics, morals, astrology, and music, i. e., a studium generale of the three faculties—law, medicine, and philosophy.

Thus, like the German universities, and preceding all but one, Cracow derived its origin from Paris, the first great university of the Occident, "ex diluvio scientiarum studii Parisiensis." Yet the independently created universities of Italy, especially that of Bologna, originating in a law school, must have exercised their influence upon Cracow. While, then, the oldest universities of France, Italy, Spain, and England date back to the thirteenth and with their roots to the twelfth centuries, the oldest Polish and the German universities take a contemporaneous start in the second half of the fourteenth century.[3]

---

[1] Perhaps he accepted as date the year 1364 because in this year Pope Urban V raised it to the rank of other similar institutions in Europe.

[2] The university was divided among four nations—Bohemians, Poles, Saxons, Bavarians. The spirit of rivalry among them was strongly manifested in the quarrels which took place between the national and the German party. A privilege granted to the Germans and revoked by Charles IV on the 6th of October, 1409, produced such discontent that all the German students left Prague, which caused the foundation of the University of Leipsic.

[3] At the same time a reform of education was begun among the lowest strata of the nation. Primary schools were established throughout the country admitting the children of the peasants as well as those of the nobles.

Of course, the University of Cracow had its vicissitudes and drawbacks. There was at first a lack of professors, and consequently no definite results of teaching were obtained. Under Casimir's successor, Louis of Hungary (1370–1382), the university came to a standstill, and the Polish students passed over to Prague, where they formed one of the four nations. The French and Italian universities were also frequented by many Polish students who later on obtained fame in their fatherland. But the plan of Casimir in regard to the University of Cracow was fully carried out by Queen Jadwiga and Ladislaus Jagiello of Lithuania. The statutes of the university were approved by Pope Boniface IX, its revenues raised by the Queen in 1397, and the institution transferred to the center of the city in 1400. Throngs of students from all Poland, Hungary, and Germany assembled there and carried its fame in all directions.[1]

Under the Jagiellons (1386–1548) the Polish language, so long displaced by Latin, began to reconquer its ancient privileges. It owed its success especially to the Hussites, who had entered Poland in order to recruit in favor of their doctrines from all ranks of society that could be reached only by means of the national language. The Polish humanists and reformers[2] also used Polish in their liturgies, printed in the vernacular catechisms, sermons, religious songs, employed it in their controversies, and thus forced their adversaries to reply in the same idiom.[3]

Printing began at a very early time in Poland (Estreicher, Polish Bibliography, Cracow, 1870). As early as 1475 we find a Silesian-Polish imprint in a Latin work, Statuta Synodalia. In 1476 appeared a work by Turrecremata (Torquemada), Explanatio in Psalterium, published in Cracow. Since that time the printing press has not stopped in Poland.

In 1491 Swiantopelk Fiol printed at Cracow a book of prayers in Slavonian, with Cyrillic letters. In the beginning of the sixteenth century, Haller, a citizen of Cracow, established the first regular book trade, employing at first foreign presses, namely, those of Leipsic and Nuremberg, but afterwards establishing his own printing office at Cracow. Haller rendered great services to the progress of literature in Poland by publishing himself many works, and by supporting other printers with advances of money and types, so that many new printing offices were soon opened at Cracow.

---

[1] Huss's fellow-martyr, Hieronymus of Prague, was called to Cracow in 1410, in order to help at the reorganization of that university.

[2] Kallenbach, Les Humanistes Polonais, Fribourg, 1891.

[3] A very interesting and most important transaction between Poland and Bohemia was the public disputation held at the University of Cracow in 1431 between the Hussite deputies of Bohemia and the Roman Catholic doctors of the university. The disputation was carried on in the presence of the King and the senate. Dlugosz, who relates that memorable transaction, says that the conferences were almost continually held in Polish. The fact alone that heretical tenets were suffered to be publicly discussed at the university is sufficient to prove the state of toleration at that time prevailing in Poland.

The first Polish book, a life of St. John Chrysostom, by St. Bonaventura, translated by Opec, was printed at Cracow in 1522, by Vietor; and in 1536 the Catechism of Luther was also published in Polish. The liberty of the press, established by royal ordinance in 1539, was sustained in spite of all attempts to suppress it during the fierce religious struggles raging at the time in Poland as well as in western Europe. Printing establishments were even increased in all parts of Poland, for the Reformers tried to spread their doctrines by the press, and their Catholic opponents to refute them by the same means.

The followers of the Greek Orthodox Church in Poland, whose spiritual center was in Kief and its famous Greek seminary until 1667, when lost to Muscowy forever, had also several presses of their own.

The religious struggles, fatal as they were in many respects, yet had a powerful influence on the development of the national intellect. Theological controversies compelled those concerned in them not only to be well versed in the Scriptures and the works of the church fathers but also in the ancient languages, Polish dialects, and many other kindred branches of human learning. Works not only of a religious and controversial but also of a literary and scientific character went forth in great numbers from the presses established in various parts of Poland. There were even many private presses established by nobles in their own houses; thus the Tarnowskis, Radziwills, Chodzkiewicz, and several other magnates possessed printing establishments. Bandke, in his History of the Press in Cracow, even enumerates 46 towns outside of Poland where the productions of Polish authors were also printed.

This glorious elevation of liberty of the press and education did not, however, last undisturbed. Under the reign of Sigismund III a kind of censorship was introduced by a royal decree of the 14th of October, 1621, prohibiting the printing or even the custody of any works whatsoever, but particularly those of a sacred character, without a license from ecclesiastical authority. The resolution adopted by the synod of Warsaw under the primate Lubienski (De non imprimendis absque revisione et approbatione libris, ac revidendis ad minus semel in anno bibliothecis bibliopolisque), which not only confirmed this royal decree, but extended the censorship by establishing an inquisitorial revision of libraries and booksellers' shops, became from that time a law, and its application was stringently adhered to. Under this law, which soon extended its sway over books of the past, excesses were committed, and a good number of the best productions of the golden age of Polish literature must have been irrevocably lost, and many became so scarce that even at our time some valuable unique copy is now and then found hidden away in the dust of old Polish libraries.

This short account of the Polish printing press may perhaps appear as a digression from our theme, but the universities and high schools of that time were so closely connected with the new printing facilities that they can hardly be appreciated without the latter, being the most powerful engine for the dissemination of the truth and of all learning.

Thousands of students gathered at the University of Cracow in the fifteenth century from Ruthenia, Russia, Germany, Hungary, and Moravia. The first Ruthenian, Latin, Hebrew, Greek, and Hungarian books proceeded from its printing press. At the beginning of the sixteenth century it extended all over Poland. The number of books printed in Poland during the sixteenth century amount to 10,000 at a low calculation. More than 500 printing presses had been up to the end of the eighteenth century active in about 100 towns of the realm, 90 in Cracow alone.

One of the most interesting buildings in Cracow is the old Jagiello Library, with its quaint quadrangle. Here is stored a fine collection of books and many of the rarest treasures of the Polish press, early editions of the native authors. "In an album preserved in the library, with the names of visitors inserted, may be seen the autograph of Henry of Valois, Marini, Mniszek, the bride of the False Demetrius, and that of Anna Jagiellonka, the wife of the glorious Stephen Batory" (Morfill). All these treasures were turned to the advantage of the Jagiellon University.

Among the most famous students of this university at that period we must count the above-mentioned historian and chronicler, Jan Dlugosz; Jan of Glogau, who introduced Aristotle's philosophy into Poland, on which he wrote several works; Michael of Breslau, Jan of Oswięcim and scores of others. But none gave to his country such a luster of splendor and fame as Nicolas Copernic (Copernicus), born in 1473 at Thorn (Toruń), Prussian Poland, died the 23d of May, 1543. The great French scientist, Arago, says of his death: "Il s' éteignit en tenant dans ses mains défaillantes le premier exemplaire de l'ouvrage qui devait répandre sur la Pologne une gloire si éclatante et si pure." A statue of Copernic, by the finest Danish sculptor, Thorwaldsen, adorns one of the public squares of Warsaw.

It is true Poland and Germany still dispute with each other the honor of producing him, a common fate of all great men in olden times; but this much is sure, that his father, a Polish subject, was a Slav, though perhaps Germanized, his native town having recently belonged to the order of the Teutonic Knights. His mother, as her name—Barbel Watzelrode—indicates, must have been of German extraction. Brought up under the guardianship of his uncle, Lucas Watzelrode, subsequently prince-bishop of Warmia, he matriculated at Cracow in 1491, and there studied mathematics, optics, and perspective. Leaving Cracow without taking a degree, he enrolled himself in 1496 in the "Natio Germanorum" of Bologna University as a student of canon law. The year 1500 he spent at Rome, where he lectured on astronomy and "observed an eclipse of the moon" on the 6th of November. The following year he began the study of medicine at Padua, medicine being at that time essentially dependent on astrology. In 1505 he left Italy never to return to it, and settled in Prussia.

He is the founder of modern astronomy. The Copernican system is, mainly, the shifting of the center of the solar system from the earth to the sun, and the consequent explanation of the alternation of day and night by the earth's rotation on its own axis, and of the change of the seasons by the earth's revolution around the sun. For the rest, the glory of developing the lines so broadly laid down belongs to Kepler, Galileo, and to Newton, who finally marked out the form of modern theoretical astronomy.

Under Sigismund I (1507–1548) political struggles with the Tartars and Turks and the rising power of Russia strangely contrasted with literary achievements. His second wife, Bona Sforza, daughter of the Duke of Milan, though personally hurtful to her adopted realm on account of her intrigues and avarice, yet had a beneficial effect upon the country by the introduction of painters and artists of various kinds and Italian refinement to embellish the Polish court.

The new doctrines of the Reformation made their appearance in the country. The centrifugal forces began to tend in different directions; the Protestant towns of secularized Prussia, and still more the Polish towns proper that had adopted Lutheranism, gradually became estranged from Poland at the time when royalty was being weakened more and more, and the nobility with their unmeasured privileges spread the sphere of their influence ever farther.

But in the clash and conflict of diverging tendencies lay the germ and ferment of a higher educational and intellectual life. The influence of the Renaissance began to be felt in Poland, and when the classical models of Greece and Rome pervaded the national spirit of the Polish republic of letters the national language assumed an exquisite purity; its golden age and classical period began (1541–1606). But the University of Cracow had somehow degenerated, and King Sigismund, in order to raise its standard, in 1535 ennobled all the doctors and professors of the same, uttering the following grand words: "Satius enim est gestis propriis florere quam maiorum opinione uti nec minor nobilitas est ea quæ propriis virtutibus comparatur" (Morfill, Poland, p. 82).

But trouble soon began again. It may not be uninteresting as a piece of history of culture in Polish university life of that time to speak here at some length of an event by which the beginning of the reign of Sigismund Augustus was marked, and which, although insignificant in itself, was important from its consequences.

In 1549 a woman of ill repute, being publicly insulted by some students of the university who stood before the door of All-Hallows College, called to her assistance the servants of Czarnkowski, prebendary of Cracow and principal of this college. A scuffle ensued, in which some students were killed. This occurrence produced a universal commotion amongst all the students of the university, who entered

Missing Page

time in a very flourishing condition, under the direction of Frankendorf, the most eminent of Melanchthon's pupils. This school was already the favorite resort of many Polish students. The later royal family of Leszczynski was one of those who generally educated their children in that establishment. Many went also to the newly erected University of Königsberg, in Prussia, which was a Protestant stronghold under the duke, Albert of Prussia, who had adopted the reformed creed. No wonder, then, that most of them returned to Poland imbued with Protestant doctrines and as zealous propagators of such in their Catholic country.[1]

Yet, in spite of drawbacks and religious struggles, the progress of Polish literature and literary achievements went on.

Nicholas Rej (1505–1569)[2] opens the long list of great Polish poets, though his best work, Zwierciadło albo żywot poczciwego człowieka (The Mirror; or, The Life of an Honorable Man) was written in prose.

Martin Bielski wrote in Polish the Annals of the History of Poland and a Universal Chronicle, the first universal historical work that appeared in Europe. Great historians, philologists, jurists, scientists, and the most illustrious Polish poet, Jan Kochanowski, make us well understand that the sixteenth century was the golden age of Polish literature.

Another cause of this marvelous development is that merit was a veritable title of nobility. Talent could attain any office, however elevated.

> Every bishop, every senator, every high magistrate [says Leonard Chodzko] owed at that time his elevation to his talents, and the son of a noble, a burgher, or a peasant found the same admittance. The historian Kromer, son of a peasant, and the poet Dantiscus, son of a brewer, rose consecutively to the bishopric of Warmia with the title of prince-bishops. Erasmus Ciołek, natural son of a wandering musician, became bishop of Płock. Janicki, son of a cartwright, obtained the poet's crown from the hands of the Pope. Cardinal Stanislas Hosius, one of the presidents of the Council of Trent, was born in Wilno, of very obscure origin.

We can infer from this what the condition of the schools in Poland at that time must have been.

Not only did the lower and middle classes produce highly educated men, but the nobles also rivaled in culture and education at a period when the nobility in France and Germany, with the exception of men like Franz von Sickingen and especially Ulrich von Hutten, were sunk in ignorance. The famous French historian, De Thou (Thuanus), speaking of the embassy of Polish nobles who came to offer the crown of Poland to Henry of Valois in 1572, says:

> The most remarkable thing was their facility in expressing themselves in Latin, French, German, and Italian; these four languages were as familiar to them as their own tongue. There could be found only two men at the court who could respond in Latin, the Baron of Milhau and the Marquis of Castelnau-Maurissière. These had

---

[1] V. Krasinski, The Reformation in Poland, London, 1838, Vol. I, pp. 155–159.
[2] V. Krasinski, The Reformation in Poland, Vol. I, p. 161.

Missing Page

was just about founding a university in Livonia, which thirty-five years later was lost to Sweden.

In Poland and Lithuania, however, Catholicism from this time on had the upper hand and molded the education of the country.

The University of Wilno was founded by Batory as the chief seat of the Jesuits in Lithuania, in the center of a population a large majority of which was Protestant and Greek. A great opposition arose against its foundation. Prince Radziwill, palatine of Wilno and grand chancellor of Lithuania, as well as the vice-chancellor, Eustachius Wollowitz, refused to fix the seal of the State to the charter for the university; but the King disregarded their representations. Also the diet of 1585 protested against the erection of the University of Wilno, and of the Jesuit college in the newly conquered town of Polock, deeming the sole authority of the monarch insufficient and unconstitutional. But the influence of the King prevailed over the opposition of the diet and the privileges of these foundations were at last confirmed. The University of Dorpat was founded by the Swedish King Charles XI, and became a bulwark of German learning. Only in these days is it becoming thoroughly Russianized; it has now even lost its old name, the Russian name for it being Jurjew.

But with the reign of Sigismund III (1587–1632), the continuous wars and foreign invasions, the bloody religious, external, and internal strifes, which retarded civilization in all eastern Europe for centuries, made a speedy end to that great period in Polish literary history. Foreign elements came up to take charge of the public instruction in the country in spite of the opposition of the University of Cracow. Briefly, the old maxim of "Inter arma Musæ silent" proved true again. The above-mentioned period of decadence, the macaronic period, set in, barely illuminated by a few superior lights. Polemical divinity, the principal subject of instruction in the schools, made the students lose their time in dialectic subtleties and quibbles. About 1618 the censorship was established in Poland, though contrary to a royal decree of 1539, which had proclaimed the liberty of the press. The first index librorum prohibitorum was published by the bishop of Cracow in 1617. The University of Cracow had a hard struggle with the Jesuits, who worked hard to get possession of this ancient seat of learning. They tried to establish a high school of their own at Cracow, which would have facilitated the final accomplishment of the object. This occasioned a violent quarrel between the Jesuits and the university, which was supported on that occasion by all the monastic orders. The issue was decided in favor of the university by the Diet of 1628, and a papal bull of 1634 prohibited its renewal.

The Jesuit schools spread over Poland, and the superintendence of national education was in their hands. Broscius (Brozek), rector of the university of Cracow, and the most learned man of his time in Poland, in a work published in Polish, about 1620, under the title Dialogue

Missing Page

high degree of prosperity by the immigration of many thousands of Protestants, who fled to Great Poland after the defeat of the "winter king" Frederick, palatine of the Rhine, at the battle of Weissenberg. Besides the ancient languages, universal history, geography, the Polish and German languages, mathematics, natural history, and other sciences were taught in that school, conducted by men of the highest learning, as Rybinski, Andreas Wengierski, the great naturalist Johnstone, and John Amos Comenius.

The latter, perhaps the greatest educator of all times, born in 1592, at Komna, in Moravia, whence he derived his name, driven out, as Protestant minister, from Bohemia and Moravia by the edict of 1624, finally settled at Leszno, in Poland. Having become professor of Latin and pastor of the Bohemian Church, he published, in 1631, his Janua Linguarum Reserata, i. e., The Gate of Languages Unlocked, which rapidly and deservedly gained for its author a prodigious reputation. Had Comenius only published this one book, Bayle rightly remarks, he would have immortalized himself and the Slavonic race. This work, translated into nearly all European languages, and even into Arabic, Turkish, and Persian, was composed for the use of the school of Leszno, published in that town, thus connecting it with his immortal name. It is impossible to give even an outline of Comenius's life and works here, but no educator should forego studying the masterly work of Kvaczala (now professor in the University of Dorpat) on Comenius, who was called by the Governments of Sweden and England, Transylvania and Holland, to reform their respective schools. After a residence of four years at the court of Sigismund Ragoczy, prince of Transylvania, he returned to Leszno and superintended its school till the destruction of that city under the reign of John Casimir. He fled to Silesia, and after long wanderings through Germany finally settled at Amsterdam, where he died in 1671.

The model school of Leszno was frequented by Protestant youths not only from every part of Poland but also from Prussia, Silesia, Moravia, Bohemia, and even Hungary. It justified its celebrity by an excellent organization and a continuous improvement of the methods of instruction. Comenius opened a new road on that important field, while the University of Cracow, the Jesuit colleges in Poland, and all the Catholic and Protestant schools in Germany and Poland alike lost themselves in the old scholastic methods of wasting the precious time of professors and pupils.

While the great Comenius improved the methods of education, nay, revolutionized them, Jan Johnstone, a Pole of Scotch descent, composed for the same school his Historia Universalis Civilis et Ecclesiastica, etc., ab orbe condito ad 1633—Leyden, 1633 and 1638; Amsterdam, 1644; Frankfort, 1672—continued till that year, and many works on natural history, monumental for their time, making him "unsurpassed in learning by any of his contemporaries."

Thus Leszno acquired a European reputation by its great men and its printing office, from which issued many important works in Polish, Bohemian, German, and Latin, and which was also provided with Greek and Hebrew types. But these literary establishments of Leszno were involved in the sad destruction of that town in 1656.

But the Protestants of Grand Poland, assembled at the synod of Parcice, resolved to rebuild their old and famous school by subscription. It was really reopened in 1663 and a classical seminary attached to it. Yet, owing to the fact that the family of Leszczynski had passed to the Roman Catholic Church, that a great part of its property was lost, and that the Protestant supporters of the town were generally ruined by war, it never attained its high standard again, although it has passed all the vicissitudes of the stirring history of the country, and exists to this very day, incorporated into and leveled to the present admirable school system of Prussia in her province of Posen.

The Bohemian brethren had also a higher school at Kozminck, established as early as 1553, which enjoyed for some time a great reputation. It dwindled down, however, toward the end of the sixteenth century, into a primary school, of which the Bohemian brethren possessed several in Great Poland, as, for instance, at Poznania, Barcin, Ostrorog, Wieruszew, Lobceniza, etc. The instruction given in such schools consisted, in addition to religion, of reading, writing, arithmetic, and Polish grammar, the rudiments of Latin, and in some places of German. The Helvetian confession, which prevailed in Little Poland, had 14 higher schools in that province, including the palatinates of Red Russia, Volhynia, and Podolia. The most celebrated of them were those of Dubiecko and Lubartow. The latter, established and supported by Firley, palatine of Cracow, enjoyed for some time an extraordinary popularity, and was frequented by many Catholic youths as well. But all these schools had only temporary prosperity, and were soon ruined by the want of permanent endowments, the voluntary contributions by which they were sustained diminishing or ceasing with the frequent conversion of their supporters to Catholicism. Thus the school of Paniowce, in Red Russia, founded by Jan Potocki, and apparently of some importance, since it had the privilege of an academy and possessed a printing press, was abolished by Potocki's son, who returned to the Catholic Church. As for primary schools, we may safely assume that every larger congregation had one.

In Lithuania, too, there were quite a number of colleges belonging to the Helvetian Church, supported by the Protestant magnates of the Radziwills, who, although professing the Roman Catholic religion, continued to protect the foundations of their ancestors, and some of them last to this very day.

But, on the whole, it may be asserted that this period also in the Reformed world of Poland was rather barren in regard to the highest education and learning. The many petty but harassing religious antagonisms between the parties within the church itself hemmed the progress of the Catholic University of Cracow, whose students frequently indulged in excesses; the Jesuit colleges, and the Protestant schools likewise. Many of the best Poles, nobles and divines, had to obtain their education in foreign universities, and, as an indispensable preparation for their academical studies, they were taught foreign languages, to make the foreign literatures accessible to them. In this foreign education, which was brought about by the downfall of the Polish schools of higher order, lies at the same time the reason why these schools could not recover till about the middle of the eighteenth century. The suppression of the anti-Trinitarian or Socinian schools in Poland, especially that of Rakow, which was conducted by scholars, Poles as well as foreigners, who enjoyed a European reputation; that of Lubartow, which belonged to the wealthy magnate family of Kazimirski, and many others; the abolition of their printing offices, prohibiting their restoration under the penalty of civil death, and the banishment of the professors—all left a deep gap in the system of Polish schools of high order.

Revival of higher education and downfall of Poland.—To Stanislas Konarski, a priest of the congregation of the Patres pii, belongs the high merit of reorganizing public instruction in Poland, of nationalizing it after the denationalization brought about by the macaronic period, and of giving a new stimulus to Polish literature. He found worthy assistants in the bishops Joseph and Andreas Zaluski, who established at their own expense a public library of 200,000 volumes at Warsaw, which they made public in 1747. When Stanislas-Augustus Poniatowski ascended the throne in 1764, a general movement of renaissance in Polish literature took place, which was zealously accelerated by the King. He also founded at Warsaw the "school of cadets," the nucleus of the now famous university. In order to encourage teachers and students by his presence, he used to come to the examinations held at that school, and had a familiar intercourse with the professors, whose erudition and works he liberally rewarded by the highest offices. After the suppression of the Jesuit order by papal decree, he employed their confiscated property and extensive estates to found and endow schools. Under his reign a commission of national education was established in 1775 to administer and perfect public instruction. This institution was, according to Forster, the first supreme magistracy of the kind in Europe, which sustained the reformed universities of Cracow and Wilno and hundreds of new schools by the funds obtained from the estates of the Jesuits, who had been expelled from Poland after the suppression of the order by Pope Clemens XII.

There is only one other State—namely, Prussia—which, after the destructive defeat of Jena and Auerstädt in 1806 and the subsequent loss of all her provinces on the left side of the Elbe, tried to compensate the material loss by an ideal gain, by the foundation of the University of Berlin in 1810. Just in the same way, Poland, after the first dismemberment, in 1772, organized the said commission of education in 1773[1] and made it a government institution in 1775.

Of course the influence of the philosophy of the eighteenth century, the so-called period of enlightenment, and the progress in the system of teaching, the study of Montaigne, Komenski, Locke, Basedow, and Pestalozzi, and the spread of the influence of the encyclopædists had everywhere slowly created a sentiment in favor of good schools; in Poland, during the time of her misfortune, more than anywhere else the conviction took possession of many minds that good schools and higher education were necessary for the salvation of the country and for the moral and material progress of the nation. The King deemed it to be the duty of the Government to promote and aid schools of all grades for the promotion and extension of education, and the vice-chancellor of Lithuania, Joachim Chreptowicz, introduced a bill in the Polish diet of 1775 to make the commission of education a government institution. The act gave to the commission the exclusive right to control and govern all the Polish universities, colleges, academical colonies, and all the public schools. The commission was composed of the ablest men; among them were Andrew Zamoyski, Count Ignatius Potocki, Prince Adam Czartoryski, Prince Michael Poniatowski, bishop of Płock; Julian Niemcewicz, the famous poet; Gregor Poramowicz, Pater Kopczynski, and Pater Hugo Kollątai, the latter being the soul of the commission, an able and aggressive statesman, a highly cultured and liberal-minded man, a democrat in the best sense of the word. The commission held semiweekly sessions.

The country, so far as it was not annexed, was divided into six school districts. Each district had higher-grade and lower-grade colleges. The universities of Cracow and Wilno were reformed, and a teachers' seminary (normal college) added to each. Each district had inspectors of the schools and methods of teaching; libraries and museums were founded at the universities and colleges; gold and silver medals were coined to stimulate industry by awarding them to the best scholars; talented young men, after graduating from the home schools, were sent to the western and southern European countries to perfect themselves still further and to acquire more knowledge about other nations, their institutions, customs, and character.

The diet of 1793 extended the powers of the commission of education, and placed also the female institutes under its control. After the second partition the Government lost control of almost all its functions and the commission passed out of existence in 1794.

---

[1] In July, 1873, the hundredth anniversary of the commission of education was celebrated at Lemberg (Lwów), capital of Galicia, Austria. In commemoration of that event the "charter of the commission of education" was reprinted in thousands of copies; it was to be the first volume of the "Pedagogical Library" of Lwów.

It is indeed remarkable that Poland, in the short period of her precarious existence, 1775-1793, made far greater progress in learning and produced more works of merit than during the whole period that macaronism dominated public education, a period which lasted nearly a century and a half. This progress of learning began also to exercise a most salutary effect on the state of the church in Poland, which had immensely suffered from the protracted struggle between the Catholics and the Dissidents.

But the Republic was doomed to annihilation. Yet, as if to illuminate its downfall, one of the most fruitful periods of scientific and literary elevation set in,[1] accompanying the restoration of schools, high and low. Krasicki (1735-1801) was surnamed the prince of poets. His immense genius excelled in the most varied fields of poetry. His Myszeis (mysz, mouse; Myomachia) is a mock-heroic poem, consecrated to the war of King Popiel[2] against the mice of his kingdom. The oddities of the court of King Popiel and the quarrels, strifes, and intrigues of the mice are ingeniously and bitterly sarcastic allusions to the court and Polish nation of the time. It is in its kind—comparable to Sebastian Brant's Narrenschiff and Rabelais's satiric works—one of the best mock-heroic epics and the finest monument of Polish literature in the eighteenth century. His fables, too, are one of the master works of Polish literature. Niemcewicz is especially famous by his historic songs, which have been set to music by the Polish composers. Numerous other great literary men, like the historians Naruszewicz, Krajewski, Jezierski, etc., the jurists Skrzetuski and Ostrowski, the publicist Hugh Kollątaj, etc., glorified the political downfall of the country. Stanislaus Staszic, born in 1755, a genuine patriot, after the establishment of the short living Congresspoland, at the Congress of Vienna, was named minister of public instruction, in which position he improved the existing schools and established new ones, and raised the University of Warsaw to a much more important position. He also founded an institute for the deaf and dumb and a school of engineering, thus laying the corner stone for the later developed schools of technology in Russia. It is his merit to have advanced the intellectual condition of the country in its political decline.

Another patriot, who devoted himself to the education of the Polish

---

[1] It is difficult to see how Morfill can find the period of Krasicki and Niemcewicz and the literature which the political decay of the eighteenth century produced as "harmonizing with its decadence." This statement is as unwarranted as to call Krasicki a "Polish embodiment of a French abbé;" "his epic on the war of Chocim no epic at all;" "his lighter pieces and mock heroics as pleasing."

[2] The legend of King Popiel, very similar to that of Bishop Hatto (cf. the mice tower on the Rhine), goes as follows: "King Popiel was a vicious man, and had become so hateful to the nation that a conspiracy, headed by his uncles, was entered into against him. He treacherously poisoned his enemies and left their bodies to the beasts of the fields. But numberless rats sprang from their bodies and consumed the king and his family."

nation, raised the Academy of Cracow to a high standard, bringing about a great progress in the education of the country, was Hugh Kołłątaj. But his efforts to remedy the political evils of the country were thwarted by the blindness of his opponents.

Thus all the brilliancy of the period in literature, history, and education served only to illuminate the end of Poland. From this time on education in Poland has to go through all the phases and political changes of the three countries of which she forms integral parts.

HIGHER EDUCATION OF RUSSIAN POLAND.

On April 25, 1795, Stanislaus Poniatowski resigned the crown of Poland at Grodno, and therewith the history of the country under Russian, Austrian, and Prussian rule begins. Emperor Paul treated his Polish subjects with great regard and kindness. His successor, the romantic Emperor Alexander I, also allowed, to a large extent, self-administration and the use of the native language, and in 1803 conferred great privileges upon the University of Wilno.

The crushing defeat of Prussia by Napoleon and the inglorious Tilsit treaty brought to a part of Poland once more a shadow of independence. By virtue of Article V of that treaty the duchy of Warsaw was created in 1807 under the Elector of Saxony, Frederick Augustus. It was composed of almost all the Polish provinces taken from Poland by Prussia in 1772, 1793, and 1795; it had about 2,200,000 inhabitants and an area of about 101,500 square kilometers, embracing six departments—Posen, Kalisz, Płock, Warsaw, Łomza, Bydgoszcz (Bromberg). In consequence of Napoleon's war of 1809 against Austria, in which the duchy participated, the latter was increased by all the land between the Vistula, Bug, and Pilitza, i. e., Cracow, Sandomir, Lublin, and other cities and territories.

This establishment of a national government in the new duchy of Warsaw had a favorable influence upon public instruction. The commission of education was resurrected, and Count Stanislaus Potocki placed at its head. The name was changed first to "chamber of public education," then to "directory of public education," and after the creation of the "congressional Kingdom of Poland," under Russian government, to "commission of enlightenment." Warsaw was endowed with a law school (1808), to which was added in 1811 a school of administrative sciences and a school of medicine. Each province of the duchy was to receive a district-college, every village its primary school.

But the invasion into Poland of the confederate armies in 1813 made an end to the attempted reforms. Still the literary movement and the ascendency of public instruction went on; historians like Lelewel and Albertrandy flourished, numerous literary societies were formed, and the cities and academies rivaled in preeminence as to certain branches. Thus the school of Krzemieniec was superior to that of Warsaw in poetry; Wilno excelled by its school of medicine; while in Warsaw the

Society of the Friends of Sciences contributed very much to encouraging and developing the literary movement. Mickiewicz planted the standard of romanticism in Poland; he is the Polish Victor Hugo. His Konrad Wallenród (1828) and Malczeski's Maria, a song of the Ukraine (1826), are pearls of epic and lyric poetry unsurpassed in any literature.

Thus the intellectual progress of the Russian part of Poland ever went on and the political dependence did not weigh too heavily upon the country. Russian Poland was to form a constitutional kingdom allied to Russia by personal union, somewhat like Sweden-Norway. The constitution allowed the country was even too liberal, as compared with autocratic Russia, to last very long. Poland was to be governed by responsible ministers, a senate, and a legislative chamber. A national army under the national White Eagle, a separate budget, a free press, and personal liberty, as well as the free use of the Polish language in private and official life were guaranteed; but this good will would and could not last. In 1819 the anti-Russian movement, which steadily increased, made a censorship of the press necessary, contrary to the terms of the constitution; some of the students of the universities of Wilno and Warsaw were imprisoned and tried for high treason.[1] At last the University of Warsaw and a great number of schools and private institutions of learning were suppressed by ukase of November 9, 1831, and the school of cadets at Kalisz by ukase of January, 1832. An ukase of February 15, 1832, decreed that the library of 150,000 volumes, engravings, and the cabinet of numismatics should be transferred from the University of Warsaw to St. Petersburg. The ukase of February 26, 1832, known by the name of "organic statute," destroyed all the stipulations of the Vienna treaty and declared "Poland is an integral part of the Russian Empire; its inhabitants must in the future form with the Russians but one and the same nation. The ministry of public instruction is abolished." All educational institutions of Poland were placed under the control of the department of the Interior in St. Petersburg. Here the school system of Poland begins to become absolutely Russianized in form, spirit, and contents; and it can not be said that, in spite of many hardships, the efforts of the Russian Government were unwise, impracticable, though hostile to the Polish education of the Polish nation.

In place of the closed university a "general college" was opened for the purpose of teaching law and classics. The nobility and bureaucracy had separate philological provincial colleges, while the other classes ("le tiers état") were educated in the so-called "real-gymnasia" with a more technical training. According to the ukase of Czar

---

[1] In 1830 Warsaw had the following higher educational institutions: The university with about 600 students; three classical gymnasia (lycea); one polytechnic school, founded in 1825; one agricultural college, founded in 1816; one school of forestry, founded in 1816; one musical conservatory; four seminaries; three female high schools with 830 pupils.

Nicolaus I in 1840 the purposes of education in Poland were to arouse the love of religion and monarchical government and the acquisition of special technical knowledge.

Mr. W. A. Day in his Russian Government in Poland (Longman, Green & Co., London, 1867), the best and most impartial book on the subject, based on the best and most reliable Russian sources, speaks about the educational events of that epoch in substance in the following way:

Warsaw and Wilno were the seats of two universities, where men of the Polish race had long been educated; they possessed libraries and collections, the relics of old times, the memorials of an age when Copernicus taught and Sobieski ruled. These institutions were regarded by the Emperor as memorials of that past which it was his mission to crush out. If he suppressed them, he thought he would destroy two of the rallying points of disaffection and revolt, so his mandate went forth, and the universities were closed.

The libraries and collections they had contained were transferred to St. Petersburg and Kief, and Poland and the western provinces were deprived of their accustomed means of education. No longer possessing them in their own neighborhood, the nobles of the Kingdom were compelled to send their sons to the distant universities of Kief, Moscow, and St. Petersburg. Some of the poor students, who were unable to afford the cost of an education, were supported at these universities on condition that after leaving it they should pass several years in the public service. Thus, far away from their own land, the Emperor anticipated that they would forget the misfortunes of their country, that they would cease to look back on its past history with vain repining, and that they would devote all their energies to the service of the Empire.

The result did not answer his expectations; in many instances it prevented the poorer proprietors from affording a liberal education to their sons, and frequently the wealthier classes refused to part with their children, as they objected to the long and remote separation rendered necessary by their distance from the Russian universities. And the wealthier proprietors were unwilling that their sons should enter the public service and they therefore sent them very frequently to some German university to receive their education, and left them to gather it as best they could in the course of foreign travel.

Education was thus in a measure checked by this act of power, but nevertheless large numbers of Polish students went to the principal Russian universities, where, instead of losing their nationality, it became more than ever confirmed.

Sometimes in periods of political excitement they banded themselves together as a distinct and separate body, neither sharing in the sports nor sympathizing in the pursuits of the other students. Thus, in the university of St. Petersburg they formed one-third of the whole body of students, and in that of Kief they were comparatively even more numerous; in the former they partially and in the latter they altogether refused to associate themselves with the Russians. Oftener, however, they took the lead in daring political speculations, supported the most advanced liberal theories, and endeavored there to prejudice their Russian fellow-students against all the forms of an autocratic Government.

The policy of the Emperor Nicolaus on the subject of education was consistent with the measures adopted in other branches of the administration.

The study of the ancient history of Poland was forbidden or permitted only in the feeble or garbled treatises of Russian scribes, as though every battlefield had not its memory, as though every tomb in the churches, every banner that moldered on their sacred walls, did not teach some passage of her history. The works of foreign authors were rigorously forbidden, and secret commissions punished their study with imprisonment and exile. The visits of foreigners were as much as possible discouraged, and they were subjected to numberless vexatious restrictions, having their speedy departure for their object.

The process of Russification was inaugurated with great skill and executive talent, however painful the systematic policy of destroying an old, historic, and rich civilization might be to the Pole or any other nationalist.

The first act of that process was an act of charity. The poor Polish orphans and waifs, whose parents had perished during the bloody revolution of 1830 or had been deported, were taken under Russian care and protection to be educated in order to become useful Russian soldiers. On the 24th of March, 1832, Prince Paskewitsh issued the following order:

> It has pleased His Majesty the Emperor that all abandoned male children, orphans, or paupers in Poland be incorporated into the cantonal bataillons, and that accordingly they be taken in a body (enlevés en masse) and sent to Miúsk, where they will be disposed of according to the regulations of the generality of His Majesty.

Also the children of the Polish schools of charity, the orphans of the Child Jesus, were taken care of by the Russian administration. An ukase of June, 1832, prohibited the use of the Polish language before those tribunals of Russian Poland which lay outside the Kingdom proper.

The 15th of August Pope Gregory XVI addressed an encyclical to the bishops of Poland (alike in spirit to a recent encyclical of Leo XIII to the Polish bishops in Russia) to submit themselves to their magnanimous Emperor Nicolaus I as their legitimate sovereign. An ukase of June, 1838, prescribes that history and the exact sciences be taught in the Gymnasia (Lycea) in Russian. By virtue of decrees rendered in 1843 and 1845 in regard to the public instruction in Poland, superior and secondary instruction were limited to the technical sciences. To pursue the courses of classical and philosophical instruction the Polish youths must betake themselves to the Russian universities proper. The communes were authorized to abolish old and incompetent schools according to their best judgment; thus 239 primary schools were closed in the decade of 1845–1855. The revolutionary movement in 1846–1848 forced the Russian Government to new measures of restriction. But a new stimulus was given to the cause of education when the noble Emperor Alexander II, in 1856, appointed Marquis Wielopolski minister of civil government of Poland.

At the accession of Alexander II to the throne, education in Poland was at a very low ebb. The suppression of the University of Warsaw left no establishment in the Kingdom where a superior education could be procured. In all the Kingdom there were only eight gymnasia or institutes for nobles where a secondary education was given, and by law the professors in these institutions were obliged to teach the sciences in the Russian language, though practically this enactment was not always observed, for it was difficult to find professors who could speak Russian, and still more difficult to find scholars to comprehend them.

The elementary public instruction was in a better condition. The number of elementary schools was 1,000, and there were 20 district and "real" schools. Yet even under these improved conditions, in 1860 only 137,417 persons (28 per 1,000) in Poland had obtained a superior education; 825,470 (170 per 1,000) could write and read; 3,877,579 (802 per 1,000), or more than four-fifths of the population, could neither write nor read.

In 1857 the Government had taken the first step toward the establishment of a university in Warsaw by endowing a faculty or academy of medicine there. A further step was taken in 1861, when the Emperor directed the commission of public instruction to elaborate a project of law in order thoroughly to reform the organization of public instruction in the Kingdom. The aim of this scheme was to enable men of every religion and condition to study special sciences there, and allow the common people to acquire all elementary knowledge necessary for them.

The law consequently elaborated was sanctioned by the Emperor, and put in force from March 20, 1862, and consisted chiefly of the following particulars:

Catholic priests and proprietors of towns and villages were allowed to found, at their own expense or at that of the place where they were established, elementary schools for teaching the Catholic religion, reading and writing in the Polish language, and arithmetic, and they could appoint as masters of such schools all individuals having the qualifications required by law for enabling them to take such office. In addition to these, one or more elementary schools were to be founded in each commune at the expense of the Government; these schools were to be placed under the surveillance of the Catholic priests and certain inhabitants of the commune, elected by the commune itself, and to be subject to their inspection and local administration.

The district schools were to be divided into "general" schools for general instruction; "training" schools for preparing masters for elementary schools, and special or "real schools" for teaching agriculture, trade, and other special subjects.

In addition to the 7 existing gymnasia, 6 more were directed to be added, and instead of the Institute of Nobles a lyceum was founded as an establishment where a supplementary or superior class to those existing in the gymnasia might be taught. The scholars might belong to any religious denomination, and the cost of instruction was only 16 rubles a year.

A polytechnic institute was founded in Pulova, and the plan of the University of Warsaw was sketched out. It was to be composed of four faculties—medicine; philosophy, or phyics and mathematics; jurisprudence; history and philology. To the university two seminaries were to be attached for preparing masters for gymnasia and district schools. The polytechnic institute was to be composed of five sections—mechanics, civil engineering, mining, agriculture, and forestry. Students of all religious persuasions were admitted to the university, and the cost of instruction was only 20 rubles a year.

The national language, history, and literature were to be taught in all the schools; the Polish language was alone employed in giving instruction, and the Russian language was only taught in the superior and secondary schools.

Such were the institutions founded in consequence of the decree of March 14, 1861, by the noble and liberal-minded Emperor Alexander II, and his right hand in Poland, Wielopolski. These institutions were intended to pave the way to others of a yet more liberal and national tendency, and to the eventual introduction of a system of constitutional government in Poland, for extended education is the surest preparation for the responsibilities of power.

But the insurrection of 1863 stopped the beautiful free development of a national education in Poland. Yet even under these changed conditions, the fruits of the educational movement were not lost, although partly lost, to Polish nationalism.

Marquis Wielopolski, although animated by sincere patriotism, with great knowledge of his country and the wishes of his countrymen, was nevertheless probably the most unpopular man in Poland. Yet his merits in the improvement of education in Poland were extraordinary. Under him the schools were reorganized and rapidly increased. The university was partly reestablished in 1861 under the name of "Principal School," in 1862 the Marymont Institute was changed into the Polytechnic Institute, and in 1869 the former was raised to the standard of the other Russian universities, all instruction being, however, unfortunately conducted in the official Russian language.

The new University of Warsaw.—On June 8, 1869, an imperial ukase was issued to the Ruling Senate (Pravitelst vuyuschiy Senat), reading as follows:

Having recognized the advantages of erecting in the place of the now existing Principal School at Warsaw an imperial university, enlarging it in accordance with the local conditions and the legislation on the basis of which the other universities are constructed, we authorize the drawing up, by the minister of public instruction and in the committee for the affairs of the Tsarstvo of Poland, the plans for the establishment and the statutes for the University of Warsaw, and transmitting them to the Ruling Senate, we decree that—

(1) On the basis of these plans and regulations there be established in place of the Principal School at Warsaw at the beginning of the ensuing academic year 1869–70 the Imperial University of Warsaw.

(2) For the support of this university there be turned over the sum of 132,100 rubles, which is at present given for the maintenance of the Principal School, and the remaining sum of 79,680 rubles, needed for the budget of the university, shall be added from the imperial treasury.

(3) The balance necessary for the maintenance of the university in this current year of 1869 in consequence of the change of its status shall be entered into the accounts of expense of the ministry of public instruction.

In the following year (1870) the total of 211,718 rubles required shall be put under the proper heading in the financial accounts of the ministry of public instruction.

(4) All the plans for the construction of the university in place of the Principal School at Warsaw shall be submitted to the minister of public instruction.

The Ruling Senate shall not cease to work for the completion of the proper plans.
ALEXANDER II.

TSARSKOE SELO, *June 8, 1869.*

The University of Warsaw, like all the Russian universities, belongs, according to Friedrich Paulsen, to the German type of university, which also includes Austria, Switzerland, the Netherlands, and Scandinavia. The word of J. Delyanoff, Russian minister of public instruction, will be unassailable:

We endeavor in everything that concerns educational affairs to accept Germany as a model, and this is very good. Our universities are established after the German type. Germany is the country of higher civilization; its universities stand on a considerable height.

A commission of all the curators of the Russian universities and 7 professors, under the chairmanship of the curator of Dorpat, George von Bradke, in 1862 undertook the modification and advancement of the law of 1835 concerning the universities, not its change. In 1863 the "improved" bill of that commission became law under the minister of public instruction, A. Golownin, who deemed it essential and necessary to make the autonomy of the universities the basis of the law. It consequently transferred the direct administration of the universities to the rector and the academic council, "which shall decide all the affairs either definitely or subject to the confirmation by the curator of the university. The academic council is the center of the internal administration, the highest resort, to which all the other organs are subjected."

Briefly, all this meant self-government of the universities, to the exclusion of the State and governmental power.

Golownin's successor, Count D. Tolstoi (1866-1880), soon recognized the necessity of organic changes. The attitude of the students; their excesses of a political nature; disturbances, especially among those of the university, the medico-surgical academy, and the school of technology at St. Petersburg, forced the minister to fix their position legally in harmony with the other higher organs of the State power (1867); collisions in the academic council brought about instructions in regard to the duties and rights of the rector (1868); extremely undesirable results at the reelection of professors, who needed a majority of two-thirds of all the votes of the academic council, caused the abolition of this arrangement.

It was just at this critical juncture that the University of Warsaw was established with the old principal school as its nucleus, and it was but natural that it should receive regulations of its own, especially adapted to the necessities, from a Russian standpoint, of a university of the Tsarstvo of Poland. The other Russian universities received their general statute only in 1884, which decisively transferred the acting power from the academic council and the faculties to the organs of the State, the curator, the inspector, a kind of police supervisor, and the rector.

The constitution of the University of Warsaw.—The constitution of the university is given in 11 chapters and 138 sections,[1] of which it may be desirable to make the following brief extracts:

The University of Warsaw consists of the 4 faculties, the historico-philological, the physico-mathematical, the legal, and the medical faculties. It is under the supreme supervision of the minister of public instruction and belongs to the circuit of the curator of Warsaw. He supervises the relations of the university with the minister and the supreme imperial power, decides questions which are not reserved to the minister, and has especially to maintain order and discipline within the university. The immediate administration of the same belongs to the rector, the academic council, the directors, and the faculties.

The Russian language is obligatory in conducting all instruction as well as in all official documents of the university.

The rector is nominated by the minister of public instruction from among the full professors and confirmed by the Emperor. He has the immediate administration of the university and is superior to the officers of the same. The academic council, in which all full and associate professors, under the chairmanship of the rector, have a seat and vote, bestows, at the request of the respective faculties, academic dignities, and has an advisory power with the curator or the minister in the affairs of instruction and inner administration of the university.

---

[1] Ustav Varshawskago Universiteta, pp. 33.

As to the general features of the Russian universities, their institutions, reforms, administration, I may safely refer the reader to the Report of the Commissioner of Education, 1890-91, pp. 195-242, prepared by Miss Frances Graham French.

The constitution of the universities at St. Petersburg, Moscow, Kharkov (Charkow), Kazan, Kief, Odessa, is established by the imperial universal statute of August 23, 1884, and by a great number of regulations issued by the minister of public instruction. The University of Helsingfors (Finland) has its own statutes of 1852. The University of Tomsk has so far only a medical faculty, though the other faculties are now in preparation. The statutes of the old German University of Dorpat (Jurjew) and the formerly Polish University of Warsaw do not differ very much from the universal statute except in several incisive points, especially adapted to the purpose of making them centers of Russian learning par excellence. The university of Warsaw under the present curator, Apuchtin, is the center of the educational district of Warsaw, which is one of the 14 educational districts into which the Empire is divided (St. Petersburg, Moscow, Kazan, Orenburg, Charkow, Odessa, Kief, Wilno, Warsaw, Dorpat, Caucasus, Turkestan, West Siberia, and East Siberia). According to the original plan of this division during the reign of Alexander I, at the head of each district a university was to stand, but it is wanting as yet in the districts of Wilno, Orenburg, Caucasus, East Siberia, and Turkestan. All the universities, and in fact most of the schools, of the Empire are under the ministry of public instruction; only certain special schools are under separate ministers. The total contribution for education from the various ministries was 43,884,534 rubles in the budget for 1893.

The board of directors, which consists of the deans of the four faculties and the inspector, is charged with the economic administration, and exercises a judiciary power over the students. The disciplinary power is, first of all, in the hands of the inspector, a police officer without scholarly qualification, who, at the proposal of the curator, is nominated by the minister, and, although dependent on the rector in his activity, reports not directly to the rector but to the curator. With his assistants and servants and with the secretary for the affairs of the students he has to watch over the conduct of the students within the university buildings and, so far as possible, also outside of them. If the good order or good morals are disturbed in the university he has to employ proper measures to restore order.

The university has the right to import books from abroad without censorship as well as the right to publish books without preventive censorship upon the responsibility of the faculties. Each faculty consists of the dean, the full and associate professors, the docenten, and the lectors. The deans are elected at the meetings of their faculties from the number of the full professors for three years, and, if there are less than 3 such professors in the faculty, also from the number of the [extraordinary] associate professors. They must be confirmed by the minister of public instruction.

The historico-philological faculty of the University of Warsaw was originally established with 11 professors and 6 docenten.

The instruction in the Polish language as well as in the other modern foreign languages may be given by lecturers in their native tongue.

The following studies were to be obligatory: (1) Philosophy, (a) logic, (b) psychology, (c) history of philosophy; (2) Greek, (a) Greek language and interpretation of authors, (b) history of Greek literature, (c) Greek antiquities; (3) Latin (divisions like Greek); (4) grammar of the Slavonic languages; (5) Russian and the other Slavonic languages and the history of Russian literature; (6) history of general literature; (7) Slavonic philology, (a) Slavonic languages—Polish, Czech, Servian, etc.; (b) Slavonic antiquities; (8) general history; (9) Russian history.

In the physico-mathematical faculty the academic chairs were originally distributed among 10 professors and 5 docenten: (1) Pure mathematics; (2) mechanics (a) analytical, (b) practical; (3) astronomy and geodesy; (4) physics; (5) chemistry, (a) applied, (b) theoretical; (6) physical geography; (7) botany, (a) morphology of plants, (b) anatomy and physiology of plants; (8) mineralogy, geognosy, and paleontology; (9) zoology, (a) anatomy and systematics of animals, (b) anatomy of men and physiology of animals; (10) technical chemistry; (11) agronomical chemistry.

The law faculty was to have 10 professors and 3 docenten: (1) Encyclopedia of law, (a) encyclopedia of the legal and political sciences, (b) the history of the philosophy of law; (2) history of Russian law; (3) history of the Slavonic legislations, with a view to the other ancient and modern legislations; (4) Roman law, (a) history of the Roman law, (b) dogmatics of the Roman civil law, (c) Byzantine law; (5) public law, (a) theory of public law, (b) public law of the various foreign states, (c) Russian public law; (6) civil law and theory of pleading; (7) penal law and procedure; (8) police law; (9) finance law, (a) theory of finances, (b) Russian finance law; (10) international law; (11) political economy and statistics.

The medical faculty was to consist of 16 professors, 10 docenten, and 3 demonstrators (prosectors), and was to be provided with the necessary clinics and laboratories. One lector, for Russian, German, French, English, and Italian, respectively, was to be appointed.

As to the academic degrees, conditions, and appointments of the docenten and professors at the University of Warsaw, there is no difference from the other Russian universities. I can therefore refer to the Report of the Commissioner of Education, 1890-91, pages 237 to 242. As to salaries, they were fixed in the imperial ukase of 1869 at 5,000 rubles for the rector, 3,000 rubles for the full professors and the inspector, 2,000 rubles for the associate professors, 1,200 rubles for the docenten and demonstrators, 2,000 rubles for the lector in Russian, and 800 rubles for the lectors in the other modern languages. For the cabinets and laboratories 7,650 rubles were appropriated; for the clinics, 8,000 rubles; for the edition of the university journals and gazettes, 800 rubles.

The matriculation of male students only, connected with many formalities, can take place only at the beginning of the winter semester in the case of such young men as are in possession of a certificate of maturity from a regular gymnasium under the supervision of the minister of public instruction. In the historico-philological and physico-mathematical faculties of the University of Warsaw only pupils of the religious seminaries, after passing an entrance examination, can be matriculated. Also, other friendly disposed persons besides the students can, under certain conditions, be admitted to the courses. Passing over from one Russian university to another can take place only with the permission of the board of directors of the latter institution. When applying for admittance, the student has, with his other certificates, to file his photograph with his own signature. He has to procure from the inspector every semester a new passport and entrance card to the university. The student pays to the university 50 rubles per semester (in the other Russian universities, 25 rubles) and a fee of 1 ruble per weekly hour for the semester (about 15 to 20 rubles). There is, however, an extraordinary liberality in remitting these fees, and even in granting scholarships, to needy but worthy students. These scholarships (stipendia) mostly enjoin the obligation upon the student of remaining in the State service for a certain number of years after graduation. Students' societies, deputations, collective petitions, and addresses are forbidden. The punishments that can be inflicted upon students are like those in the German universities—admonition, prison (in the so-called "carcer"), removal from the university (consilium abeundi), and relegation without the right of passing over to another Russian university.

The complete academic course comprises, for medical students, 10 semesters; for those of the other faculties, 8 semesters. Controlling examinations take place at the end of every semester. After completing his course, the student may obtain scholarships for two or three years, in order to prepare himself for the higher degrees. The requirements of scholarship and attainments are minutely described in the regulations, confirmed by the minister of public instruction. The final medical examination presupposes a preliminary examination in natural sciences after 4 semesters (like the tentamen physicum in Germany). There are two academic degrees—that of magister and of doctor—which are a necessary preliminary for obtaining a professorship in a Russian university.

To the original regulations of June 8, 1869, eleven appendixes (priloshenia) were added, to extend and improve the teaching and administrating power of the university. These additional decrees were promulgated by the minister of public instruction or the curators of the Warsaw circuit of education from March 18, 1881, to December 27, 1891.

The need of a thorough Polish literary education having been strongly felt, it was at last decided by the committee on Polish affairs to leave it with the minister of public instruction to appoint a professor for Polish literature at a salary of 3,000 rubles. The Emperor having given his consent on January 12, 1882, it was reported by the curator on February 1, 1882.

The regulations concerning the rights of the rector as chairman of the academic council were fixed, the payment of fees by the students arranged, the university library provided with librarians and assistants, the astronomical observatory and meteorological station established, the numismatic cabinet and the museum of antiquities founded; briefly, the university put in working order in every respect.

Latest statistics of the University of Warsaw.—According to the statistical data given by the rector of the University of Warsaw, there were on the 1st of January, 1894—

Professors, ordinary, including the rector	48
Professors, extraordinary	12
Privat-docenten, prosectors (demonstrators in the medical faculty, and lecturers, i. e., instructors in modern languages (the only ones who need not be Russian subjects)	20
Total	80

Of the 47 chairs founded at the establishment of the university and distributed over the 4 faculties, there were 4 vacancies during the last scholastic year—agricultural chemistry, encyclopedia of the law and political sciences, legal medicine, and the clinical chair of therapeutics.

Number of students

During the scholastic year 1889-90:	
Historico-philological	53
Physico-mathematical	143
Law	389
Medical	579
Total	1,164
During the scholastic year 1890-91:	
Historico-philological	53
Physico-mathematical	138
Law	378
Medical	621
Total	1,190
During the scholastic year 1891-92:[1]	
Historico-philological	47
Physico-mathematical	135
Law	379
Medical	612
Total	[2]1,173

[1] In this year 13 students were excluded from the university by order of the minister of public instruction.

[2] Besides 165 pharmaceutical and 6 foreign students.

During the scholastic year 1892–93 (including 99 pharmaceutical students).... 1,176
January 1, 1894 (including 57 pharmaceutical students)...................... 1,152

The students were distributed among the four faculties as follows:

	Students.	Per cent.
Historico-philological	29	2.67
Physico-mathematical	141	13.27
Law	351	32.35
Medical	561	51.70

According to religions they were distributed as follows:

	Students.	Per cent.
Orthodox Greek	192	17.70
Armenian Gregorian	2	.18
Roman Catholic	624	57.51
Lutheran and Reformed	51	4.70
Hebrew	216	19.91

According to birth there were—

	Students.	Per cent.
Sons of nobles and state officials	426	39.26
Sons of the clergy	47	4.33
Sons of merchants	22	2.03
Sons of urban classes (mioshtsban)	531	48.95
Sons of rural classes (krestjan)	38	3.50
Sons of foreign subjects	24	1.93

According to preliminary education there were—

	Students.	Per cent.
From gymnasia	1,048	96.13
From religious seminaries (Greek orthodox)	37	3.41
From other secondary schools	4	.46

These students came from the following educational circuits (okrugi):

	Students.	Per cent.
Warsaw	828	76.32
St. Petersburg	19	1.75
Moscow	16	1.45
Kazan	11	1.01
Orenburg	3	.27
Western and eastern Siberia	5	.46
Charkow	5	.46
Odessa	19	1.75
Wilno	56	5.16
Riga	36	3.32
Caucasus	11	1.01
Kieff	38	3.50
Religious seminaries	37	3.41
Foreign institutions	1	.001

In the scholastic year 1893-94 the university granted the following titles and degrees:

	As graduate students.	As candidates.
In the historico-philological faculty	3	1
In the physico-mathematical faculty	2	9
In the law faculty	38	27
In the medical faculty:		
Physicians		82
Pharmacists		121
Dentists		7

Report of the rector (1893-94).—The University of Warsaw is composed of four faculties, the historico-philological, the physico-mathematical, the law, and medical faculties, like the other Russian universities, excepting St. Petersburg and Odessa, which have no medical faculties; but the former has, beside the historico-philological, a most admirable oriental faculty.

The work done during the academic year 1893-94 shows that the University of Warsaw is a real universitas litterarum, not inferior to any European school of equal grade in the scope of instruction.

The historico-philological faculty.—This faculty consists of three great departments, the classical, Slavonic-Russian, and historical departments.

The principal studies are analogous to those of most of the other European universities here specially adapted to the needs of Polish students who are to be amalgamated to Russian professional, scientific, and literary life. The time to be devoted to study in this faculty embraces four years.

In philosophy there is at present only one chair, to which falls the instruction in psychology, logic, ancient and modern philosophy.

In the Greek language and literature, Greek dialectology, Euripides, Thucydides, as well as translation from Russian into Greek, is conducted by the head professor; the history of Greek literature, an introduction into Aristophanes, translation from Latin into Greek, interpretation of the orator Aischines is conducted by the associate professor of Greek.

The Latin department, conducted by 2 professors, embraces studies in literature, criticism, and hermeneutics in Tacitus, Juvenal, Martial, Cicero's philosophical works, and seminary practice.

Comparative studies of the Indo-European languages, their phonetics and morphology, and Sanscrit proper are taught by 1 professor ordinarius.

Russian and the other Slavonic tongues are taught by 2 professors and 1 lecturer, viz, Panslavic grammar, history of Russian literature in the eighteenth and nineteenth centuries, Russian grammar.

The history of Western-European literature is represented by 1 associate professor, who lectures on the epic poetry of western Europe and modern Greek literature.

Slavonic philology and antiquities are represented by 3 professors and 1 docent, embracing the history of Polish literature, Slavonic literature, and archæology at large, characteristics of the Slavonic races, ethnology, grammar of the Czech and Lusatian tongues.

Western European history, represented by 2 professors, who teach Greek history, German history in the nineteenth century, history of the Middle Ages, diplomatics and chronology, and practical exercises on the history of the Middle Ages.

Russian history, in the hands of 2 professors, treats of the reign of Alexander I and the modern period of Russian history, its ancient period, and the history of Western Russia.

The two principal Teutonic and the romance languages—German and English, French and Italian—are each represented by 1 poorly paid lecturer, generally a foreigner. In these departments lies the weakness not only of the University of Warsaw, but of all Russian universities, that of St. Petersburg not excluded. Instruction in modern languages amounts to mere "Sprachmeisterei." There is not even a beginning of modern philology and critical literature in a university sense, and the contrast with the other highly developed branches of learning is so much the more striking.

The physico-mathematical faculty.—This faculty is admirably fitted out with professors and apparatus. All the branches taught in the best universities are here well represented in 22 departments, embracing astronomy, geodesy, botany, mineralogy, and crystallography; general, special, and technical chemistry; experimental physics, zoology, geology, and paleontology; pure and applied mathematics, mathematical physics, physical geography, comparative anatomy, and histology; mechanics and heavenly mechanics.

The law faculty.—This consists of 14 principal departments, under 12 professors, beside the 2 departments of legal medicine and psychiatry. The students of law are obliged, for their general education, to attend during their first year the lectures in the historico-philological faculty on the Russian language, ancient Russian history, history of ancient philosophy and logic, history of the Middle Ages; during their second course, the lectures on modern Russian history, the history of modern philosophy and psychology, as well as the French or German language. This rule is exceedingly beneficial for the elevation of the juridic faculty and worthy of imitation with us, especially as no finished college education is required for entrance to most of our American law schools, as is required for entrance to the Russian juridical schools.

The principal departments in the Warsaw law faculty are the following: Encyclopædia of law and the history of Slavonic legislation, legal and political sciences; history of Russian law; Roman law and Byzantine law; political law, civil law, civil procedure, penal law, criminal procedure, police law, law on economics and finances, international law, statistics, commercial law.

The medical faculty.—As to completeness of studies, equipment of laboratories, clinics, and hospitals, this faculty ranks among the very best of Europe. It is older than the university, having been founded in 1857 as the Medico-Surgical Academy at Warsaw. It contains 29 full departments of medicine and its auxiliary sciences. The Russian language, its phonetics, morphology, and syntax, is continued with the students of medicine during their first professional course. The pharmaceutical students, too, are bound to take certain courses in Russian. There are 24 professors (professors ordinary), 2 associate professors (professor extraordinary), 3 demonstrators (prosectors), 4 docenten, 1 lecturer in Russian in the faculty. The studies, distributed over a curriculum of four years, are descriptive anatomy; histology, embryology, and comparative anatomy; physiology; medical chemistry; pharmacy and pharmacognocy; pharmacology and prescriptions; pathological anatomy; general pathology; materia medica and therapeutics; therapeutical clinic; theoretical surgery; hygiene and medical police; diseases of women and children; forensic medicine; toxicology; ophthalmology; clinic of surgery; venereal and skin diseases; surgical anatomy and operative surgery; chirurgical clinic; psychiatry; and the auxiliary studies, i. e., botany, mineralogy, chemistry, physics, zoology. All these branches, taught by excellent authorities, make the medical faculty of Warsaw very efficient and worthy of praise.

Institute of Veterinary Surgery.—Beside the medical faculty of the university, and outside of it, there is in Warsaw also an Institute of Veterinary Surgery, with 1 director, 1 vice-director, 3 docenten, 7 instructors in veterinary surgery, and 1 teacher of the German language. This institute is very important, there being only one other such school at Charkow.

The university library.—The library of the old University of Warsaw (founded in 1817) was formed out of the various public and private collections of the old Polish capital, and especially out of the treasures of many abolished cloisters. In 1830 it contained 130,000 volumes and 1,500 manuscripts. The cabinet of curiosities contained 20,000 objects. After the suppression of the university, in 1832, in consequence of the Polish revolution of 1830, most of the Polish volumes (excluding the historical and political books) were transferred to the principal library of the circuit (Lehrbezirk), the library being increased by the library of Turkula and some cloister libraries. In 1841 the principal library, together with the numismatic cabinet and the museum of antiquities, was given over to the new university. Its library is now very large and valuable, especially rich in works of Polish literature, Polish history, and law. Among the manuscripts are the diaries of the Polish Diets, letters of King Wladislaw (1635-1645), and many other documents important to Polish history. The library is well catalogued by J. Wierżbowski, Polonica, XV ac XVI ss. in bibl. Universitat. Varsov. 1, 1889.

The numismatic cabinet consisted on January 1, 1894, of 4,280 objects, the most precious being the silver and gold coins and medals of Polish mediæval history. There is besides connected with the university a museum of antiquities, a cabinet of plaster figures, an ethnographical museum, containing very valuable objects of ethnography from all parts of the Russian Empire, also many prehistoric antiquities. A physical cabinet and laboratory, with a mechanical and magnetic station, provide for the practical exercises of the physico-mathematical faculty.

The astronomical and meteorological observatory, with complete apparatus, provides for the needs of the respective departments.

The geodetic cabinet and the chemical laboratories, the mineralogical, geological-paleontalogic, botanical, zoological, zootomical, physiological, histological, and all the other medical cabinets, laboratories, clinics, and hospitals, render the complicated scholarly apparatus necessary for a university of the highest order well nigh complete.

The principal archives of the Polish kingdom.—These archives (Glawnij Archiv Tsarstva Polskago) are the most valuable source for the investigator of Polish history. The most important documents of these archives are those of the Metryka Koronna, i. e., the official records, conducted by the chancellor and the subchancellor of the kingdom, which contained all the documents provided with the royal seal—for instance, privileges, treaties, decrees. After the third partition (1795) the Polish and Lithuanian records were transferred to St. Petersburg, and only one part of the Polish registries was brought back to Warsaw. Another part of the Polish and Lithuanian matriculæ is now stored away in the archives of the Imperial Senate at St. Petersburg, a third part in the archives of the attorney-general at Moscow. A copy of the Lithuanian matriculæ (1386–1551) and some volumes of the original (1775–1792) are still in Warsaw. The archives contain, furthermore, the so-called "Sigillata" (regesta of royal documents from the year 1658 on), the chancellors' "Acta" (from 1742 on), the records of various old courts (for instance, of the crown tribunals of Piotrków and Ldnblin), of the state, and several provincial diets of King Stanislaus Augustus's commissions of education, finance, and military affairs. With the principal archives the secret archives of the Polish kingdom are combined. These were in Cracow till 1765; were then transferred to Warsaw; from there, in 1795, together with the above-mentioned matriculæ, to St. Petersburg, whence they were again brought to Warsaw. Those Polish documents which had been taken by the Prussians were also given back by that Government to the secret archives in Warsaw. The archives contain 1,462 documents, the oldest being a papal bull of 1215. These are documents of the highest value, not only to Polish history, but also to universal history, to the history of culture and civilization, and to a large extent to the unexplored history of the relations of the Poles with the Slavonic and Western European nations during the dark ages. There is, indeed, a mine for scientific and historical research in these archives, although treasures are yearly dug out and published by the Polish and Russian historians in Warsaw, Cracow, and Lemberg. The archives contain, furthermore, among other treasures, the documents of the last Polish king and of Kosciuszko, the diplomatic archives of the Polish crown and Lithuania (1579–1759), political documents from the time of the partitions; also documents from the Russian time (1826–1831). The archives are, according to their importance, excellently administered by the Polish professor of the university, Adolf Pawiński, well arranged and catalogued. They are under the control of the central government of the Tsarstvo of Poland and have about 80,000 volumes in folio.[1]

Archives of old records of the kingdom of Poland.—There are still other important archives in Warsaw (Archiv starych diel), which contain the remnant of the records, decrees, accounts, documents, contracts of the dissolved state council of the Polish king, the various commissions of the Polish government and other central magistrates. These archives form a part of the present chancellery of the Russian central government of the Polish Tsarstwo. By far the greater part of these old records had been destroyed or were sold at auction as waste paper after the last partition of the country; another part had been distributed among the various state ministries, provincial governments, and local magistracies.

Secondary education in Warsaw.—Of secondary schools Warsaw possesses 6 gymnasia, 1 real-gymnasium, 2 progymnasia (i. e., incomplete, the upper classes wanting), 1 (male) teachers' seminary, besides 4 (female) gymnasia, progymnasium, 1 school of drawing, 1 institute for the deaf and dumb and 1 for the blind, 1 Sunday business school for merchant clerks, 1 Sunday business school for tradesmen and mechanics. These are all Government schools. Outside of them there are, however, a large number of private schools of a higher order, which are all licensed and provided with teachers who have all finished their professional education and are provided with the respective diplomas.

Musical education in Warsaw.—A special feature of higher education are the musical institutes of Warsaw. In 1805 the Musical Society was organized. Its directors were Fr. Lessel and Count Fr. Krasicki. In 1812 it was changed to a "Musical Conservatory," under the directorship of Elsner. In 1823 the conservatory had already 164 pupils, among them Chopin and Dobrzynski, both pupils of Elsner. In 1858 Moniuszko was director of the conservatory and the leading spirit in Polish music. In 1861 Apolinary Kontski reorganized the conservatory, but the insurrection of 1863 greatly impaired the progress of that school, as well as of all the other institutions; yet the art of music developed to a high degree among the Poles, especially at the capital.

---

[1] There is an excellent description of this famous library by Bandtke and Herbart (lithogr.), 1840.

All these facilities for schools, from the lowest to the highest order, passing over the whole range of human knowledge—its unique libraries, its stupendous historical monuments, with their glorious reminiscences—make Warsaw the center of the intellectual life of the Polish people. Churches and cathedrals help to attain the highest standard of culture possible in a modern large city. Famous among them are the Catholic Cathedral of St. John, founded in 1360, connected with the old royal palace by corridors, containing the famous pictures and tombs of ancient celebrated Poles; the magnificent Greek Cathedral, finished in 1842; the Church of the Holy Cross, finished in 1695, with a splendid frontage and valuable images. The Capucin Church, built in 1681, contains the admirable marble statue of Jan III. (For a general description of the city, see the author's article "Warsaw," in Johnson's Universal Cyclopædia.)

Secondary education in the country at large.—As stated before, education has also been entirely reorganized since 1863 over the entire Polish country outside of Warsaw, and is steadily progressing, owing to the efforts of the Government to Russianize the nation by a thorough and extensive Russian education, and still more from the conviction of the Polish people that education alone can secure a high estimation and prestige of their nationality in the vast empire of which they are an integral part. In every Government town there is a gymnasium; the former district schools are rapidly changed into progymnasia. Although the official language in all the schools is Russian, as well as in the courts and all official affairs, yet the Polish language is generally known and used and even enriched and polished by the extensive printing of Polish books of all grades, while the pulpit is filled almost invariably by Polish priests for the Polish population, which is mostly Catholic. Especially difficult, if not impossible, is it to extirpate the Polish language in the primary schools which are being founded in almost all the villages that have an almost exclusive Polish population, unless it be mixed with numerous Jews and Germans. These schools, under the special supervision of Russian school inspectors, succeed, of course, in teaching the Russian language, but the latter is seldom used by the children at home and after the obligatory years of schooling are over.

The following secondary schools in the congressional Kingdom have certainly not yet lost their Polish character:

The city of Płock has 3 gymnasia, 1 teachers' seminary, 1 theological seminary.

The city of Połock (in White Russia) had a Jesuit academy up to 1820; from that time a high school, conducted by the order of "patres pii" (patres scholarum piarum). Połock has now only a county gymnasium. The cadet school was abolished in 1863.

The city of Sandomierz has a theological seminary and a gymnasium.

The city of Wloclawek has a theological seminary.
The city of Kielce has 1 theological and 1 teacher's seminary.
The city of Lublin has a theological seminary and a gymnasium.
The city of Lipno has a gymnasium.

Teachers' seminaries are also at Wymyślin, Tuchola, Lęczyca, Biata, Siedlce, Wajwery, an agricultural and forestry academy at Puławy, a business college at Lodz.

Outside of these there are about 50 public and private high schools in the congressional Kingdom.

Wilno.—We have briefly mentioned the history of the old and famous University of Wilno, the ancient capital of Lithuania, its foundation by Stephen Batory in 1570, its character as a Jesuit institute, its tendencies for good and for evil, its renewal by Alexander I in 1803, its prestige at that time, its suppression in 1833, and the removal of its library to St. Petersburg. A medico-surgical academy replaced it, but this was suppressed in 1842, and thus every trace of the university was blotted out.

But, although the University of Wilno is no longer in existence, yet the excellent libraries and archives of the renowned old capital of Lithuania make it still a unique center of learning, especially in Polono-Lithuanian history and diplomatics. Most valuable is the public library and museum (Publičnaja biblioteka i sostojaščij pri nej muzej). In 1856 Count Tyszkiewicz founded an antiquarian museum and an archæological commission with it. When the old museum was closed in 1865 the valuable manuscripts of the museum (538 manuscripts and 2,000 documents) were transferred to the newly established public library of Wilno. In connection with the scholarly expeditions and researches of the years 1860–1880, which dug up rich treasures of the literary past, a considerable collection of church-Slavonic manuscripts was accumulated. The rich archives of Prince Sapieha, of the court of lords at Grodno, containing Russian manuscripts of the sixteenth century and extensive correspondence of Polish magnates in Government service, were also transferred to this library. It contains, besides, some of the most important old Russian manuscripts (for instance, the Turov Evangelium of the eleventh century) and numerous literary productions from western Russia, partly in the western Russian dialects. For the older history of the country there is nowhere more documentary material than here. Russian and Polish documents of all descriptions abound.

The department of printed books has been enriched by the collections of the ancient Roman Catholic cloisters, by confiscations of the rich libraries of political criminals, mostly anti-Russian magnates, and from various donations and exchanges, mostly of Latin and Polish and theological books.

The antiquarian museum contains the rich collections of its founder, Count Tyszkiewicz. Enriched by further donations, it contained in

1858, among others, 2,900 historic objects and 3,200 coins. Some of these valuable objects were later on transferred to the Russian museum in Moscow. At present the Wilno museum contains prehistoric, ethnographical, and mythological objects, old weapons, Christian, old Greek, and Roman antiquities, medals and coins, seals, portraits, and works of sculpture; all the objects together numbered 11,700 in 1885.[1]

Wilno still possesses very numerous schools of a higher order—1 Roman Catholic theological seminary, 1 Greek Catholic seminary, 1 Christian and 1 Jewish teachers' seminary, 2 classical gymnasia, 1 progymnasium, 1 real school, 1 tradesmen's school, 2 girls' gymnasia, over 20 public and city schools.

The ruins of the old and historic castle of the Jagiellos still exist as a monument of Wilno's great past, when it was the capital of the Lithuanian princes from 1323 on. Among the 18 Roman and 12 Greek Catholic churches, the cathedral of St. Stanislaus especially excels with its magnificent marble chapel containing the silver coffin, weighing 3,000 pounds, with the remains of St. Casimir (died 1480), a place of pilgrimage for the Polish-Lithuanian people.[2]

Wilno has also the central archives of the ancient documents of the governments of Wilno, Grodno, Minsk, Ljublin, and Kowno (Centraluyj archiv drevnich aktovych knig).

As early as the fifteenth century provision had been made in the Lithuanian statute, and elsewhere, for the preservation of manuscript documents of the grand principality of Lithuania "in the stone houses and solid chests." Thus the materials of the Lithuanian supreme court of Wilno, as well as of other courts, various commissions, etc., i. e., state documents of the Lithuanian dukes, judiciary charters, local records, etc., were gradually collected so completely as to cover local history year for year. But the continuous wars and conflagrations proved very destructive to the archives, many things were purposely destroyed, many documents almost professionally falsified, so that great critical tests are necessary for the appreciation of these collections.

In 1852 the buildings of the suppressed University of Wilno (like those of Kief and Witebsk) were turned over to the storing of the central archives, and all the above-named documentary treasures, mostly Latin and White Russian and Polish, were deposited in that building and finally catalogued in 1863.

The oldest registers of these archives are the documents of the city council of Wilno from 1492 on. Among the most important documents, historically, are the letters and privileges of Jagiello [the bestowing of Magdeburg law (jus Magdeburgicum) upon the capital in 1387], of Sigismund Keistutowizs, Casimir, etc. The most recent additions are the

---

[1] Vide Systematischer Katalog der russ. Bücher, 2 Bände (mit Zusätzen), 1879-1888; and Katalog predmetov Muzeja (Catalogue of the objects of the museum), II. ed., 1885.

[2] See article Wilno, Johnson's Universal Cyclopedia.

archives of the Wilno Chapter, the archives of Ljublin, the archives of the Wilno Carmelites. In 1870 the Wilno archives numbered about 18,000 volumes and 1,700,000 documents.[1]

The searching, investigating, registering, and cataloguing of these documentary treasures, extending at present to 12 volumes of "Akty" with many single works, is being performed by the archæographic commission (Vilenskaja kommissija dla razbora i izdanija drevnych aktov), founded in 1864. In 1842, by the instrumentality and at the expense of Governor A. Semenov at Wilno, a temporary commission appointed for the investigation of the documents and their transfer to the archæographic commission at St. Petersburg was decreed.

Witebsk.—The central archives of Witebsk, situated in the ancient cloister of the Dominican monks and coming under the supervision of the ministry of the interior, was established in 1863 to store the judiciary and forensic documents of the old Polish governments of Witebsk and Mohylów (Mogilew) from the sixteenth century to 1800.

But, as in the Polish state the courts had administrative functions also, there are other valuable materials relating to the economic and political conditions, church history, and ethnography of those districts of the old Kingdom, amounting to 1,823 volumes.

Nevertheless, while there exists all the elements for the highest culture and education in this vast country, known for many centuries by the historical name of Lithuania, and called in the official Russian language the Country of the Northwest, it is at present perhaps the most inanimate country in Europe. According to Russian administrative division, Lithuania consists of the governments of Wilno, Grodno, Kowno, Mińsk, Mohylów, and Witebsk. It occupies a territory larger than the Kingdom of Italy, and has almost 9,000,000 inhabitants (that is about 40 per cent of the population of the Kingdom of Poland proper). The proportion of industrial wealth per inhabitant is 4 rubles annually against 23 rubles in Poland. Commerce is reduced to a minimum, and is mostly in the hands of Jews, who are more numerous in Lithuania than anywhere else in Poland.

Regarding public instruction, Lithuania occupies almost the lowest place among all the provinces of European Russia, only the district of Orenburg, with its Bashkir and Tartar population, ranks lower in this respect. There are but 20 secondary schools with 5,800 pupils (that is 40 per cent of what there were thirty years ago). Primary instruction is even more neglected. The most civilized province of the country, the government of Kowno, with 1,600,000 inhabitants, has but 12,500 children in the public schools.

Newspapers are almost entirely wanting. Beside the official Russian Wilenski Wiestnik (Messenger of Wilno) there is no journal in the

---

[1] Vide: Katalog drevnim aktovym knigam gub. Wilen, Grodn., Ljubl., Kovenskoj, 1872.

country, Polish publications being prohibited as well as the Polish language, since this country, though it was united with Poland for many centuries, is not considered as Polish territory.

HIGHER EDUCATION IN AUSTRIAN POLAND.

In Galicia (Polish Halicz), the Polish crown land of Austria, which comprises the old kingdoms of Galicia and Lodomeria, the duchies of Oswięcim (Auschwitz) and Zator, and the grand duchy of Cracow, the entire school system, with the exception of the universities and schools of technology and arts with university rank, is governed by the supreme council of schools at Lemberg. This supreme council of schools and the rectors of the universities of Cracow and Lemberg, who are also ex-officio members of the Galician Diet (Landtag), and the rector of the school of technology at Lemberg are directly responsible and subject to the minister of public worship and instruction in Vienna (Hungary has had her own minister of public instruction since 1867).

The primary schools in Galicia are steadily improving, but although the law enforces compulsory attendance at the national schools for children between 6 and 12 years, and although parents are subject to fines for neglecting to send them, the percentage of those children, who ought to attend the common schools is still very low.

The secondary schools are the gymnasia, real gymnasia, and real schools. A complete gymnasium provides for a course of eight years' study, divided into two parts of four years each. The lower course not only prepares for the higher, but is also complete in itself for those who are unable or unwilling to proceed further. In passing from one class to another the scholars undergo a very searching examination. The curriculum of an Austrian gymnasium does not differ greatly from that of the German gymnasia; only all the courses are conducted in Galician gymnasia and other secondary schools in the national language of the people, i. e., Polish and Ruthenian, the former being in the majority and greatly predominating in the west, the latter in the east.

Of the 11 universities of the Austro-Hungarian monarchy, Galicia alone has 2—Cracow and Lemberg. Of the 8 schools of technology, Galicia has 1 at Lemberg, admission to which generally is conditioned by a successful graduation from an upper real school, a gymnasium or a real gymnasium, which insures the possibility of imparting a high scientific education. The complete technical course extends over five years.

The standard of these institutions will be described somewhat in detail in the following pages.

The New University of Cracow.—The famous old Jagiellon University of Cracow (Universytet Jagielloński w Krakowie) has been illustrated in its most general characteristics in the foregoing pages of this study. We have noticed its respectable age, the papal bull of May 12, 1364, which permitted King Casimir the Great to establish a "studium generale in qualibet licita facultate," the many vicissitudes of its existence, its universal reputation and foremost rank at the end of the fifteenth century owing to the noble humanistic and astronomical studies at that stronghold of highest learning. For centuries the Uniwersytet Jagielloński formed the center of scientific life in Poland, was a strong advocate of religious toleration and of that noblest flower of the highest learning, freedom of thought and conscience. Roman Catholic, as the university always was, it sustained a long, protracted struggle with the Jesuit order, whose spirit it deemed harmful to the freedom of the Polish nation. But with the degeneration of the latter in its constant wars with Russia, the Cossacks, the Turks, the Swedes, the Brandenburgers, the Prussians, and in the eternal feuds among the magnates themselves, the university, too, degenerated and finally vanished entirely.

The university, completely reorganized, was reopened on October 18, 1817, and on October 5, 1826, was solemnly confirmed by the three protecting powers of the Republic of Cracow: Austria, Russia, and Prussia. In 1846 the Republic, and with it the university of the capital, became Austrian again, to increase the wealth of ten universities by a new brilliant star. But the attempt to introduce German as the official language into the philosophical, medical, and law faculties (the theological faculty being Catholic and Polish throughout could, of course, not be changed) by ministerial decree of October 29, 1853, failed. Between February 4, 1861, and April 30, 1870, the Polish language was gradually and completely restored to cultivate and to treasure up the valuable civilization of the first western Slavonic nation, a great and noble task which is being fulfilled with a peaceable and affectionate devotion.

The administration of the university in 1892 was conducted at an expense of about 339,550 florins, which included the establishment of the second course of the agricultural department in the philosophical faculty. The expenses of the fiscal year 1893 amounted to 393,794 florins, including 30,000 florins for the establishment of the third course of the agricultural department. The governmental contribution for covering the expenses was 379,151 florins. The budget of expenses for 1895 was 531,296 florins, of which 485,060 were paid by the Government.

The Imperial Academy of Sciences.—Closely connected with the university, if not actually a part of it, is the Imperial Academy of Sciences at Cracow which is composed of a body of the most eminent men in the mental and natural sciences. With the exception of the Academy of Sciences in Vienna, which had been proposed by Leibnitz, but was founded on May 30, 1846, and which publishes the great scholarly records of its sessions, the "Fontes rerum Austriacarum," the "Scriptores ecclesiastici latini," etc.; the former is the most important academy of sciences in the Austrian Monarchy. As for scholarship and brilliancy in Slavonic researches it surpasses even Vienna and accomplishes for the western Slavonic world what the South Slavonic Academy of Arts and Sciences at Agram (Croatia) (Jugoslavenska Akademija znanosti i umjetnosti) accomplishes for the south and that of Petersburg for the eastern Slavonic world. Both the latter academies are older, it is true, the Agram Academy having been founded in 1836 as "erudita societas," and as an academy in 1861, while that of St. Petersburg (Imperatorskaja Akademija nauk) began its activity in 1725 with foreign academicians throughout. The Academy of Sciences at Cracow was founded only in 1872, taking origin from the Society of Sciences which had existed since 1815.

The intellectual movement of the Bohemian nation has brought about the youngest but most active academy in the Austrian Monarchy. The imperial consent to the statute for the establishment of the Bohemian Emperor Francis Joseph Academy of Sciences, Literature, and Arts (Česká akademie cisaře Františka Josefa provedy, slovesnost a uměni) was granted on January 23, 1890; on October 18 the first general assembly took place. On May 18, 1891, the solemn opening of the academy was celebrated. This academy is divided into four classes: (1) Philosophy, state, law, and social sciences, history, and archæology; (2) mathematics, natural sciences, and medicine; (3) philology; (4) belles-lettres, fine arts, and music. The many publications of this academy are of the highest order and importance.

In fact among all the Slavonic peoples, not only in Austria and Russia, but also in the Danube Principalities, Bulgaria and Servia, this intellectual movement is going on and giving vent to its energy by the establishment of universities and academies of sciences.

The academy of Cracow has a fixed endowment of 16,000 florins from the Government; 20,000 florins in 1895. Its protector was Archduke Karl Ludwig (died a few weeks ago); the vice-protector is the Polish ex-minister of finance in Austria, the former professor of political economy at the University of Cracow, Julian Dunajewski; its president, Stanislaw Count Tarnowski, professor of Polish literature. The academy is divided into (1) the philological department, (2) the historico-philosophical department, and (3) the department of mathematics and natural sciences.

Since the greatest scholars of the Polish nation are members of the Academy of Sciences in Cracow (beside some eminent foreigners and the corresponding members), it may be appropriate to give the names of the actual members, to convey an idea of Poland's greatest scholars of the present time.

In the philological department [besides a few university professors of Cracow in the respective departments, Stefan Pawlicki, professor of dogmatics and religious philosophy; Fryderyk Zoll, professor of Roman law; Franciszek Kasparek, professor of international law and philosophy of law; Franciszek Piekosiński, professor of old Polish law; Ludwik Teichmann, professor of anatomy; Napoleon Cybulski, professor of physiology; Franciszek Michał Karliński, astronomy and higher mathematics; Szczęsny Kreutz, mineralogy; Józef Łepkowski, archæology; Wincentz Zakrzewski, general history; Stanisław Tarnowski, Polish literature; Stanisław Smolka, Polish history; Józef Rostafiński, botany; Lucyan Malinowski, Slavonic philology; Edward Janczewski, anatomy and physiology of plants; Kazimierz Morawski, classical philology; Maryan Sokołowski, history of art; Emil Godlewski, agricultural chemistry]: Baudouin de Courtenay, University of Dorpat; Alex. Brückner, University of Berlin; Jan Gebauer, Prague; Józef Hampel, Budapest; Vatrosl. Jagić, Vienna; Anton Kalina, Lemberg; Wład. Nehring, Breslau; Court Councillor Julian Claczko; author Wład. Lozinski, Lemberg; Wład. Łuszczkiewitz, professor of the school of arts, Cracow; Anton Malecki, University of Lemberg; Wład. Spasowitz, University of Petersburg; Anton Petruszewitz, custodian of the cathedral at Lemberg; Stojan Novakovič, prime minister, Belgrade; Sir Kasimierz Stronczyński, Piotrków; and 19 corresponding members. The director of this department is the classical philologist at the University of Cracow, Kazimierz Morawski.

These men represent the highest work that is being performed in the domain of Slavonic philology, language, and literature in general and Polish in special.

In the historico-philosophical department, Sir Alfred de Arneth and Leon Bilinski, directors of the House, Court, and State archives in Vienna; August Count Cieszkowski, replaced by Michal Bobrzynski, vice-president of the school council of Galicia, Lemberg; D. Mendelejew, Petersburg; Bishop William Fraknoi, Budapest; Udalrich Heyzmann, professor in Cracow; Wład. Tomek, University of Prague; Albert Kętrzyński, director of the Ossolinski Institute, Lemberg; Bishop Likowski, Posen; Edward Rittner, Vienna; Albert Sorel, secretary of the Senate, Paris; Józef Supinski, Lemberg; Jacob Caro, University of Breslau; Adolf Pawinski, University of Warsaw; Anton Randa, Prague; Isidor Szaraniewiczu and Thad. Woiciechowski, Lemberg; Heinrich von Zeissberg, Vienna; and 18 corresponding members. The director of this department is the professor of Roman law, Fryderyk Zoll. There has never been in Poland such a scientific movement, especially in the domain of Polish and Slavonic history, as at present. It is perhaps only surpassed by the revival of national learning in Bohemia, where the Czech University of Prague was absolutely severed from the old common university with its German preponderance, and opened in the academic year 1882-83. The Bohemian technical high school in Prague was erected in 1868, and has been administered as a State institution since 1875. Owing to this scientific movement the historical sciences have been marvelously revived, but, although it would be unjust to limit the many historical scholars of the Polish nation, still the above names fairly represent the leaders of thought in that science.

There is one great Polish historian in the garb of a novelist who has not yet attained the rank of an academician; it is Henryk Sienkiewitz, but he has attained the rank of the foremost Polish historical novelist, and may be well compared with the great German historical novelists Gustav Freytag, Felix Dahn, and Joseph Victor von Scheffel, who have been overwhelmed with academical honors in Germany. As these great historical novelists have illuminated German history and made it popular and accessible to the broad masses of the German people more than the tremendous volumes of the Monumenta Germaniæ Historica could ever do, so has Henryk Sienkiewitz in his three admirable historical novels, With Fire and Sword, The Deluge, and Rodzina Połonieckich, performed the most masterly work for the illustration of the downfall of the Commonwealth under King Jan Kazimierz.[1]

In the mathematical scientific department, Benedykt Dybowski, University of Lemberg; Heinr. Ferd. Hoyer, Warsaw; Franz Mertens, University of Graz; Julian Niedzwiedzki, Lemberg; Louis Pasteur (deceased), Paris; Bronislaw Radziszewski, Lemberg; Eduard Strassburger, Bonn; William Thomson, Glasgow; Rudolf Virchow, Berlin; Włąd. Zajaczkowski, Lemberg; Jan Franke, Lemberg; Marcell Nencki, University of Petersburg; Giov. Schiaparelli, director of the Astronomical Observatory, Milan; and 16 corresponding members.

This Imperial Academy of Sciences, in connection with the great Jagiellon University of Cracow, is undoubtedly the center of the highest learning in the Polish nation, and if Warsaw is still considered as the political capital, Cracow is surely to be considered as the intellectual seat of Polonism.

Cracow and Lemberg are the Polish universities par excellence; but as the latter has the strong Ruthenian element of Galicia to contend with, the former is the rallying point of the Polish students of the three adjoining countries, who wish to be educated in the Polish spirit and culture. The number of students in 1892 was 1,227, which increased in 1893 to 1,283, but fell off in 1894 to 1,242, and rose to 1,290 in 1895 (summer semester, 1,230). Of these, 1,137 were regular students who had fulfilled all the preceding conditions before matriculation—i. e., were provided with the certificate of maturity for university studies—and 105 were hearers who are not admitted to the State examinations without having subsequently fulfilled the conditions required. There were 66 (Catholic) theologians, 486 students in law, 517 in medicine, and 173 in philosophy. In 1895 there were in theology (Catholic) 69, in jurisprudence 608, in medicine 438, in philosophy 128, in agriculture 47, and in pharmacy 14. The present rector is Stanislaw Smolka.[2]

The university is in its four faculties well represented by the most

---

[1] Since this section was written I find in Minerva, Jahrbuch der Gelehrten Welt, 1895-96, that the celebrated Polish author has been elected to the full membership of this distinguished body.

[2] The rectorate of Professor Kreutz has just been announced for the ensuing year.

distinguished professors, mostly Poles. There are 7 full professors in the Catholic theological faculty who teach divinity in a four years' course, as follows: Pastoral theology, exegesis of the New Testament, church history, general dogmatics and religious philosophy, special dogmatics, exegesis of the Old Testament, Semitic languages, canon law.

The faculty of law and political sciences is represented by 8 full professors, 4 associate professors, and 4 privat-docenten, who prepare the students for the legal profession in a four years' course. Instruction is given in Roman law, philosophy of law and international law, Austrian civil law, Austrian political and administrative law and statistics, penal law and pleading, canon law, old Polish law (by 2 professors), political economy, commercial and banking law, Austrian law of finance and finance sciences, and German law. The Polish and local Galician legislative conditions, however, do not seem to be as well represented as in the same faculty of the Lemberg University. Two great seminaries—that of the legal sciences and that of the political sciences—provide for the practical education of the students.

The medical faculty is conducted by 12 full professors, 11 associate professors, and 7 privat-docenten. It is safe to say that no branch of the medical sciences is neglected, and it is only to be stated that the instruction in medicine, distributed over a course of five years, is as complete as possible. Practical education is given to the students in the medical clinic, in the surgical clinic, in the anatomical-surgical cabinet, in the ophthalmological clinic, in the gynecological clinic, in the aseptic-gynecological laboratory, in the pathological-chemical institute, the anatomical institute, the pharmacognostical institute, the physiological institute, the pathological-anatomical institute, the institute of veterinary surgery, the medico-forensic institute, the pediatric clinic, the clinic for skin and venereal diseases, and the institute for general and experimental pathology. All these medical institutions are carried on at an annual expense of 42,728 florins.

The philosophical faculty has 23 full professors, 5 associate professors, 11 privat-docenten, and 1 lector in French. Twelve members of this faculty belong also to the Academy of Sciences. The branches taught in this faculty are astronomy and higher mathematics (an astronomical observatory, founded in 1791, furnishes it with the scholarly apparatus for research); mineralogy (mineralogical institute); archæology (archæological institute); general history, Austrian history, and Polish history (historical seminary); Polish literature and Slavic philology (Slavonic seminary); botany, anatomy, and physiology of plants (botanical laboratory), to which department the botanical garden of Cracow, administered at an annual cost of 3,500 florins, is attached; mathematics with a mathematical seminary; geography; German philology, with a seminary; classical philology, with a philological seminary and proseminary; romance philology; physics, with a physical institute; history of art, with a corresponding institute; geology and paleontology, with a geological institute; chemistry and agricultural chemistry, with two chemical institutes and laboratories and an institute for agricultural chemistry; zoology and zootomy, with the two respective institutes; farming and agriculture, cattle raising, with institute; comparative anatomy; philosophy, pedagogics and didactics, and Sanscrit, represented only by 1 privat-docent, respectively. The laboratories and institutes are conducted at an expense of at least 12,100 florins a year.

The university library.—The library attached to the university is one of the oldest and richest in the Austrian Monarchy. At the end of 1892 it contained 213,779 works, in 283,858 volumes; 5,150 MSS., in 6,485 volumes; 1,702 maps, 7,693 engravings and pictures, 3,057 musical works, and 9,476 coins and medals. At the beginning of 1895, 224,774 works, in 300,029 volumes; 5,321 MSS., in 6,755 volumes; 1,751 maps, 7,730 engravings, 3,222 musical works, and 9,481 coins and medals. The library has a most interesting history, which has been excellently narrated by G. S. Bandtke, Historya biblioteki Uniwersytetu Jagiellońskiego w Krakowie. Krak. 1821.[1]

When King Władisław Jagiello reorganized the University of Cracow, in 1400, and granted to it rich endowments and revenues, a library was also founded and was continually improved. Endowment was left to it from time to time by public-spirited citizens. Andreas Olszowski, archbishop of Gnesen, left in 1671 the sum of 10,000 florins for the opening of a reading hall. In 1775 the newly established commission of education arranged the library, and attached to it and catalogued all the distracted collections of the bursæ and collegia of the university. After the third partition the library fell a share to Austria, to which State it has belonged ever since, except during the time of the independent republic of Cracow (1809–1846).

The manuscripts of the library are catalogued by Wład., Wisłocki Catalogus Codicum manuscriptorum bibliothecæ universitatis Jag. Cracoviensis, Cracov. 1877–1881, 2 vols. The other treasures are described by Karol Estreicher. Biblioteka Jagiellońska. Kraków 1881, and Przechadzka (guide) po bibliotekie Jagiellońskiej. Kraków 1882.

The library is maintained at an annual cost of 20,570 florins (21,470 florins in 1895) in addition to the regular fees, and was used by 2,356 readers and 2,383 guests; 6,000 works, in 15,000 volumes, were loaned out in the year 1894.

The State archives.—The archives of the town and rural forensic affairs of the palatinate of Cracow (Archivum actorum castrensium et terrestrium palatinatus Cracoviensis) were founded at the end of the eighteenth century by the unification of various smaller archives. They contain Acta judicii capitanealis Cracoviensis 1428–1792, Acta judicii terrestris Cracov. colloquiorum generalium, judiciorum in curia regis

---

[1] Cf. also Matejko, Geschichte der Univ.-Bibliothek zu Krakau, 1864, 8°, vide Minerva, p. 381.

et in conventione regni 1338–1642, 1767–1797, Acta juris supremi theutonici castri Crac. 1380–1794, Acta magnæ procurationis in arce Cracov. 1549–1794, Acta consularia et scabinalia civitatis Cracov. 1392–1797, Acta castra Biecensis 1436–1793, Acta terrestria Czechoviensia 1401–1783. These archives are endowed with 6,000 florins.

As to secondary schools, Cracow has three gymnasia—that of St. Anne, founded in 1588, with 560 pupils; that of St. Hyacinthe, founded in 1858, with 458 pupils, and the Third Imperial Gymnasium, founded in 1883, with 497 pupils. There are several real schools, besides two theological seminaries. The following institutions supply instruction in all the other pursuits not covered by the university and the polytechnic school: The Polish State Commercial College, with 86 pupils and 2,000 florins state, subvention; the Agricultural College, the Tradesmen College, the Czartoryski Museum,[1] and the Academy of Fine Arts. The great painter Jan Matejko, who died in 1893, was the director of the last-named institution. Two State teachers' seminaries—one for males and one for females—both founded in 1871, have 183 and 240 candidates, respectively. The official language is Polish.

The Polish State Industrial School, with an architectural, mechanical engineering, and chemical department, and workshops for decorative drawing and designing, has 158 pupils and 135 in the trade school attached to it.

The University of Lemberg (Lwów).—An admirable history of the University of Lemberg, of 442 large octavo pages, was published at the end of the year 1894 by the two professors of the university, Drs. Ludwik Finkel and Stanisław Starzyński, under the title Historya Universytetu Lwowskiego, Lwów, Nakładem Senatu Akademickiego, 1894. The older history up to the year 1869 was written by Professor Finkel, the last twenty-five years of its development by Professor Starzyński. For the first time, all the archives were opened and searched by the authors to give an authentic account of the history of Galicia and Lodomeria as related to the university.

After an introduction of 9 pages by the rector of 1894, Ludwik Cwikliński, a list of the rectors of the university is given from 1784 to 1894.

The academical schools before the foundation of the university are treated at length. In the same year in which the Jagiellońska Akademia was founded, two months after the issue of the letter patent erecting the studium generale at Cracow which was "to attract the dwellers of distant lands" (longinquarum incolas regionum ad eius allicere accessum),

---

[1] This museum was originally founded, in 1813, by Prince Adam Czartoryski, at Puławy, on the Vistula, and taken to Petersberg in 1830, but a part of it was rescued and carried to Galicia and Paris. In 1876 the whole collection was carried to Cracow. The museum contains 100,000 volumes, 5,070 MSS., and 1,202 documents. Catalogus manuscriptorum musei principum Czartoryski Cracoviensis, edid. Jos. Korzeniowski. Fasc. I–III, Crac. 1887–1891; see Minerva, p. 383; 1895–96.

according to the Codex diplomaticus univ. studii generalis Cracoviensis, ed. 1870, King Jagiello ordered a high school ("szkoła metropolitalna") to be erected at Lemberg and to be governed by the commune itself (ut ipsi cives scholas construant edificent et reforment rectoremque scholarum eligant valentem et plebano presentent.)[1] For two centuries this metropolitan school was in a flourishing condition. Its pupils were divided in three classes—primani, secundani, et tertiani. Instruction was given not only in the seven arts, but also in Latin, and with the dawn of the renaissance, in Greek, too. The graduates of this school study philosophy in Cracow, and in the foreign universities of Padua, Bologna, Rome, and Paris, whence they bring home their doctorates. Among its many distinguished scholars the three greatest names of the early epoch of Polish humanism—Bursius, Ursyn, and Simonides—are grouped around this school in the last quarter of the sixteenth century until they are drawn to the famous new academy founded by Jan Zamoyski.[2] "Whatever there is of brilliant scholarship in our city," write the aldermen of Lemberg as late as 1662 to the rector of the University of Cracow, "is derived from the Metropolitan Academy. Our Senate, our Government, is composed in its majority of pupils of this academy."

When about the middle of the sixteenth century, during the storms of the Reformation, not only the Academy of Cracow, but all the other schools of renown began to become disintegrated, there sprang up Protestant, Calvinist, and Dissenting schools, and against them Catholic schools, ready and prepared to war for the old faith. All the other schools fell, as it were, into lethargy waiting for better times. With especial zeal the Society of Jesus undertook to spread education among the Catholic youths to make them strong for the impending battle. The Jesuit schools, called collegia, sprang up in all the Catholic countries. Introduced into Poland in the year 1564 by the famous Cardinal Hosius, the founder of the still flourishing Lyceum Hosianum in Braunsberg (Prussia), they established colleges in all the larger towns of Poland. In 1584 Jacób Wujek, S. J., a famous Bible scholar, and Benedykt Herbest, S. J., some time professor in the Metropolitan Academy, came to Lemberg and began scholastic work. In the next year a rebellion arose against the Jesuit fathers, but Aquaviva, the then general of the order and the author of the celebrated Ratio-studiorum of the Jesuit schools, succeeded in establishing a permanent settlement in 1591, the first prefect (superior) of which was Martin Laterna, a scholar of the Braunsberg school and of the Academy of Wilno, the adviser of King Stephen Batory, and the author of the Spiritual Harp. In 1596 there were already in the Lemberg college 6 professors and 1 superior. In 1608 it was raised in rank, had 32 professors, among whom were 16

---

[1] Cf. also H. Denifle, Die Entstehung der Universitäten des Mittelalters bis 1400, Berlin, 1885, p. 9.
[2] Cf. J. Kallenbach, Les humanistes polonais Fribourg, 1891, pp. 19-45; also my article "Zamoyski," Johnson's Universal Cyclopedia.

priests, and 200 students. The humanities were taught by 3 professors, moral theology by 2, controversial theology by 1. In 1612 a philosophical, in 1613 a mathematical course, were added. In 1633 the number of students reached 550 and the college became more flourishing; but the frightful wars that swept over Poland, the Cossack and Tartar invasions, the Russian, the Swedish, the Brandenburg wars, so graphically described in Henryk Sienkiewicz's masterly historical novel, The Deluge, gradually ruined the college. In 1649 there were only 26 students; in 1653 only 4 theological hearers; in 1656 the theological course was entirely closed.[1]

When the waters of the deluge that had swept over Poland began to subside, King Jan Kazimiersz turned his attention to the city of Cracow, which almost lay in ruins. In January, 1661, was issued from the royal chancery the order for the foundation of the academy or university of Lemberg, which was to be placed on the same footing with the universities of Cracow and Wilno. The very interesting Latin document is reprinted on pages 21, 22, and shows the pride of the King in the Polish institutions of learning and his desire to emulate his great predecessors. The university was to be founded under the auspices of the Jesuits:

* * * faciliter ac libenter in animum induximus, ut Collegio Leopoliensi Societatis Jesu Academicæ dignitatis accessio Nobis annuentibus fiat, titulusque Universitatis deferatur. Damus igitur potestatem in eodem Leopoliensi Societatis Jesu Collegio Generalo Studium in omni licita facultate constituendi: Theologiae nimirum tam Scholasticae quam Moralis, Philosophiae, Matheseos; Juris utriusque, Medicinae Liberaliumque Artium et Disciplinarum ac Scientiarum omnino omnium, quascunque prædicti patres Societatis Jesu tractandas ibidem per se vel per alios censuerint, pro ipsorum arbitrio ac instituto, consuetoque Academiarum atque Universitatum more et praxi. * * *

But there was an outcry all over the Kingdom against this foundation. The Jagiello university especially resented "the interference of the Jesuits with its own rights and privileges." The Academy of Zamojski, too, opposed it. Even the commune of Lemberg—senatus populusque Leopoliensis—arose against the foundation. And, indeed, the school was never successful; in 1672 only one class was opened; in the humanities and philosophy there were only a few students. Even when, in 1677, the number rose to 500, among whom were the sons of the most distinguished families, and, though physics and anatomy were taught, for which no privilege existed, as appears from an edict of Augustus II (May 13, 1706), "that only the one university of Cracow shall have the right of the four faculties," the academy could not stand against the public opinion of the whole country. In spite of a royal

---

[1] The principal source for the history of this college is a MSS. in the Imperial Library of Vienna: "Historia collegii Leopoliensis Societatis Jesu manu propria Matthiae Wielewicz pro tunc (1664) rectoris diligentissime collecta, etc., descripta ad annum 1665, quo anno obdormivit in Domino." The best account on the Jesuit colleges in Austria is given by J. Kolle, Die Jesuiten-Gymnasien in Oesterreich, Prague, 1873.

edict of 1763, however, to close the academy, and a papal renunciation of the bull granting its establishment, instruction was carried on till the dissolution of the order by papal decree. (Bull of Clemens XIV of 1773.) Meanwhile the political upheaval of the first partition of Poland entirely changed the constellation of the affairs of Lemberg as well as those of the whole realm.

Under Austrian rule Galicia had the advantages of the school reform carried on by Empress Maria Theresa in all her dominions.[1] Count J. A. Pergen, the director of the Oriental Academy in Vienna, who had elaborated a masterly plan of public education, but a rash and radical man who would "with one stroke of the pen revolutionize everything," was appointed the first administrator and governor of the newly acquired province of Galicia with almost sovereign powers. The edict of appointment[2] reads as follows: "Cum plena facultate, ut nomine Nostro (i. e., Mariæ Theresiæ (occupatas provincias administret et quidquid ad ordinandam iustæ administrationis normam spectare visum fuerit, in opus redigat." First of all the bad sanitary condition of the country and the great mortality made the establishment of a medical college indispensable; physicians, surgeons, and midwives were wanting; the other higher schools could be gradually founded. Thus a number of eminent medical men were dispatched from Vienna to establish the school and to organize medical service over the new province.

The public schools, being in a wretched condition, had to be reorganized and put under proper inspection. The Jesuit college and the academy were transformed into an Austrian lyceum, professors for the German language were appointed, chairs for logic, metaphysics, and ethics as well as for all the branches of jurisprudence were established, even mechanics and technology, cartography, and geodesy for the surveying of the new territory were taught. In 1776 the Collegium nobilium or Collegium Theresianum (Ritterakademie) was established for the sons of the noble families of Galicia. All these new schools were administered by a special commission in Lemberg established by the Empress for the Galician schools (in Studiensachen aufgestellte k. k. Commission in den Königreichen Galicien und Lodomerien).

The Empress conceived the idea of founding a university in Lemberg as early as 1774. In 1776 the imperial chancery wrote to the Lemberg government on the question, "whether the city would be suitable for a university rather than Zamość," where an academy already existed, or Przemyśl which lay in the center of the country and was the seat of a bishop. But the plan did not mature during her life. An edict of 1777 speaks only of "several trunks (corpora) of higher schools;" there was not one large body which could be called a university. The war of the

---

[1] Cf. J. A. Helfert, Die Gründung der österreichischen Volksschule durch Maria Theresia, Prague, 1860; Adolf Beer und Franz Hochegger, Die Fortschritte des Unterrichtswesens in den Kulturstaaten Europas, Vienna, 1867.

[2] Cf. Edicta et Mandata universalia Galiciæ, Lwów, 1773.

Bavarian succession, the difficulties with Prussia, and the death of the great Empress in 1780 prevented the establishment of a great university in Lemberg. Her noble son, Joseph II, finished in 1784 what his great mother had begun,[1] and the present Emperor laid the last corner stone by the establishment of the medical faculty in September, 1894.

Emperor Joseph II, the most enlightened ruler of Austria in the last century, wanted the university to be built anew, not handicapped by any old privileges and duties, as a monument of modern times. Roman Catholic and Greek orthodox theology were to be treated side by side. The German and Roman law (ius publicum für Reichsgeschichte und Staatenkunde), heretofore the only branches taught in the faculties of law, were to be enlarged for the special needs of the Polish population (Wolf, p. 6: "Da diese Kanzeln sich meistens nur mit dem deutschen Staatsrechte und der deutschen Staatsgeschichte beschäftigen, diese aber für die galizischen Einwohner nie von einem besonderen Nutzen sein kann"). Never was a university founded with such a high spirit of liberty, generosity, and toleration for the individuality of a conquered nation, never were the good wishes for the divided nation more sincerely expressed than in Emperor Joseph's diploma of October 21, 1784:

* * * Die landesväterliche Sorgfalt, welche unser vorzügliches Augenmerk jederzeit auf die Bildung der Jugend lenket, hat uns bewogen für unsere Königreiche Galizien und Lodomerien, dann die Herzogthümer Oswięcim und Zator eine hohe Schule oder vollständige Universität in der Hauptstadt Lemberg zu errichten. * * *

From such beginnings the university arose and through many vicissitudes reached its present high standard, in numbers the fourth university of the Austrian Crown (after Vienna, Budapest, Prague). As to the Austrian possessions of the old Kingdom of Poland the University of Lemberg is the second great center of Polish learning of the highest order, though in numbers it surpasses even the University of Cracow by 141 students (cf. Minerva, 1895-96). Lemberg (Lwów), being the principal city in the old palatinate of Little Russia (Ruska) in the Polish and restricted sense of the term, has a strong Mało-Russian or Ruthenian population with their own language, to which large concessions must be made in the university and higher and lower schools. The Staropigiiski Institute is devoted to the encouragement of the study of the Mało-Russian language, and has issued some important works, such as editions of old South Russian chronicles. A good library is attached to the institute.

King Augustus III intended to establish a university in Lemberg, and even obtained the sanction of Pope Clemens XIII in 1759; but the disturbances of the Seven Years' war did not allow this plan to mature. Only in 1784 was the old plan realized by the great and noble reformer,

---

[1] G. Wolf, Geschichte der Lemberger Universität. Kleine historische Schriften, Vienna, 1892.

Emperor Joseph II; the university later on, bearing the name "K. K. Franzens-Universität in Lemberg (Cesarska Krolewska Universytet imienia Cesarsza Franciszka I we Lwowie)," was founded at this time without the sanction of the Pope. On the 3d of November, 1784, the solemn inauguration took place; but it was not prosperous at first, and in 1803 the university was changed into a simple lyceum. On the 21st of November, 1817, it was reestablished and reorganized as a university, without a medical faculty, however, which was established only in September, 1894. During the Polish Revolution, in 1848, the bombardment of the city also damaged the university building, but the most irreparable loss was the burning of about 40,000 volumes of books.

The old policy of the Austrian Government having been the Germanization of its Polish domain, the language for instruction and affairs was German throughout until the 22d of March, 1862. The necessity of allowing perfect freedom in the use of the native Polish and Ruthenian languages was then acknowledged. Since July 4, 1871, the Polish language has been generally used. In the theological faculty, however, the lectures and seminary instruction are given in the Latin language, with the exception of pastoral theology, catechetics, and methodology as well as pedagogics which are given in the Polish and Ruthenian (Russian) languages. In the law faculty all lectures are delivered in Polish excepting the courses on the Austrian penal laws and penal process by 1 professor and 1 privat-docent which are delivered in Ruthenian. Of course, Ruthenian philology and literature and German philology and literature are taught in their respective languages. With the establishment of the medical faculty in the academic year 1893-94, the university is now complete.

The financial management of the university, which, of course, is a State institution, was in 1892 conducted with an appropriation of 106,800 florins, which rose to 245,356 florins during the fiscal year 1895, the Government contributing 213,674 florins. An extraordinary appropriation of 14,100 florins served for the purchase of the scientific apparatus in the chemical laboratory (1,000 florins), changes in the university building (4,100 florins), last installment for the erection of the chemical institute (4,000 florins), second installment for the scientific equipment of the latter institute (1892).

In 1893 the university expenses amounted to 169,805 florins, toward which sum the Government had to contribute 158,578 florins.

The university, like all the other Austrian universities, is divided into four faculties—the theological, the law, the medical (about which no data have yet been given out), and the philosophical faculties, the latter embracing both the historico-philological and the physico-mathematical faculties of Warsaw and most of the other Russian universities.

At the head of the University of Lemberg stands the Imperial Royal Academic Senate (Cesarski Krolewski Senat Academicki), composed of the rector magnificus,[1] at the same time the president of the academic council, the prorector, i. e., the rector of the preceding year, the deans (dziekani) of the faculties, and the deans of the preceding year (prodziekani), 1 delegate from each faculty, respectively, and the secretary and notary, 12 members in all.

The academic senate takes care of the general affairs of the university, its property, the discipline of the collegium of instructors, and decides all disputes that may arise between the faculties. Disputes between the senate itself and the faculties are decided by the ministry for cultus and education.

The matriculation of students as regular hearers can take place only after they have passed the examination of maturity in a gymnasium. At the beginning of the academic year (October) 1892-93, there were 1,283 matriculated hearers in the University of Lemberg. In October, 1893, there were 950 regular and 124 special hearers, distributed as follows: 322 in theology, 585 in law, 167 in philosophy. In the summer semester, 1894, there were 1,413 students. In 1895 the number of matriculated hearers was 1,445.

The Catholic theological faculty of Lemberg is composed of 8 professors, 1 privat docent, 2 instructors (nauczyciele) for Polish and Ruthenian catechetics and methodology, respectively, and 2 adjuncts, all of them being priests and doctors of theology.

The study of theology, like that of law and philosophy, is distributed over four years. The curriculum in the summer semester 1893-94 will give a fair example of what is being done in theology at the University of Lemberg:

First year.—General dogmatics, five hours a week. Sacred history (historia sacra) from the beginning of the world to Christ's birth, including biblical geography and archæology and a special introduction to the Holy Scriptures, four hours a week. Exegesis to Jesaias from the Latin Vulgate, two hours a week. Exegesis to First Book of Samuel from the original Hebrew text, three hours a week. Grammar of the Arabic language with practical exercises, two hours a week. Philosophico-theological propædeutics, four hours a week.

Second year.—Special dogmatics, five hours. Introduction to the New Testament (second part), three hours. Exegesis of the New Testament from the text of the Vulgate, three hours. Exegesis of the New Testament from the original Greek text (Epistle of St. Paul to the Romans), three hours. Higher exegesis (exegesis sublimior) from the original Greek text of the Second Epistle of St. Paul to the Corinthians, one hour.

Third year.—Moral theology, five hours. Church history, five hours. Pedagogics, two hours (Polish and Russian).

Fourth year.—Pastoral (practical) theology, five hours (Polish and Russian). Institutions of canon law, five hours. Catechetics and methodology, five hours (Polish and Russian).

---

[1] The rector magnificus in the Austrian, as in the German universities—in opposition to the Russian universities, where he is appointed for an indefinite time, and like the American university president—is elected from the number of the professores ordinarii or emeriti for one year from each faculty alternately by a body of the professors (4 from each faculty) under the parting rector as chairman.

The distribution of students was as follows:

	Theology.	Law.	Philosophy.	Total.
Hearers	338	813	186	1,337
Regular matriculates	296	786	113	1,195
Hospitants	42	27	73	142
Austrians	320	787	173	1,280
Foreigners	9	26	13	48
Poles	90	672	146	908
Russians (Ruthenians)	248	137	40	425
Germans		3		3
Italians		1		1
Roman Catholics	89	447	102	638
Greek Catholics	248	149	40	437
Greek Orientals		1	1	2
Armenian Catholics	1	4	3	8
Protestants		5	1	6
Hebrew		206	39	245

Among the 73 hospitants (students not having the gymnasial certificate of maturity) there are 40 students of pharmacy.

The law faculty of the university is composed of 15 professors and 5 privat-docenten. The circle of studies contains the various aspects of the Pandects (Roman law) taught by 3 professors, German law, Catholic church law, philosophy of law, international law, encyclopedia of law and the political sciences, Austrian private law, Austrian penal law and equity pleading (in Polish and Ruthenian), political economy by 2 professors, Austrian civil law, Austrian banking law, Austrian statistics with a reference to the neighboring European States, commercial law, economic administration of Galicia, Polish private law and pleading, Austrian political law, science of political accounts in the Austro-Slavonic countries.

One of the most remarkable and beneficial features of the Lemberg law faculty are the numerous juridical seminaries, conducted by the most eminent professors: The seminary of administrative and political sciences, the seminaries of German international law, of Polish law, of canon law, of penology, of Roman law, and the seminary of political economy.

The philosophical faculty consists of 21 professors, 11 privat-docenten, 3 docenten, and 3 instructors in modern languages (analogous to the lectores of the German and Russian universities).

In the philosophical department proper the following branches were taught in the last summer semester: Logic with regard to the needs of the candidates for the middle or secondary schools (szkół średnich); elucidation of John Stuart Mill's Utilitarianism; methodology of the mathematical and cognate sciences; on the task and method of academic studies; introduction to the history of philosophy.

In the department of history and its auxiliary sciences, extensive studies in Austrian, Polish, classical, and universal history were conducted: The history of the Austrian State from the beginning of the Thirty Years' war to the close of the Karlowitz peace (1618–1699); history of the Slavonic peoples and states within the Austro-Hungarian

Monarchy; history of Poland and Lithuania in the fifteenth and sixteenth centuries; Polish diplomatics; survey of the history from the downfall of the Roman Empire to the thirteenth century; Italy at the time of the Renaissance; modern history; history of the pragmatic sanction; Raphael's life and works; history of Polish art in the nineteenth century. Two historic seminaries supply practical exercises for historical investigations. A full chair for the study of geography is provided.

The department of philology and literature has a classical and a modern division. The curriculum of studies is excellent and complete. The classics have had such an old citizenship in Poland that the standard of classical studies in the University of Lemberg can be stated as simply the highest possible. A philological seminary and proseminary aids in the very best training of the students in classics.

In the modern division, Polish and Slavonic literature are naturally the foremost. But the German language is also excellently represented; the history of German literature was studied last summer, and in the middle high German division of the Germanic Seminary Gudrun was treated. Unfortunately there is no scientific treatment (in the university sense) of English philology and the Romance languages, the former being represented only by one instructor (nauczyciel) twice a week, the latter by one instructor five times a week. Polish and German stenography are also taught.

The Slavonic studies are so much the better represented in the following courses: History of Polish literature from the second half of the tenth to the end of the fifteenth century, seminary exercises in the history of Polish literature, scientific Polish grammar, an elementary course in Old Slavonian, reading and interpretation of Servian poets. There are courses also in the history of Russian literature from 1709 to 1848, Old Slavonian and Russian language, seminary practice in Russian philology, which are conducted in Ruthenian.

Equally good and complete is the department of the mathematical and cognate sciences, with the following courses: Optics, thermodynamics, physics, electricity, magnetism, all branches of higher mathematics (with two mathematical seminaries), mineralogy, geology, geology of the Carpathian Mountains, botany, chemistry, pharmacognostics, etc. All these various scientific studies are properly aided by corresponding laboratories and museums: The physical museum, the meteorological observatory, the chemical laboratory (with a complete scientific apparatus), the mineralogical museum, the botanical museum and laboratory (with herbaria and collections), a botanical garden, a zoological museum, a pharmacognostic collection, an anatomical and physiological collection. More than 7,000 florins are spent on these laboratories every year. The course in pharmacy is usually completed in two years in scientific education and laboratory work in the botanical, chemical, and pharmaceutal laboratories.

The university library was founded at the same time as the university. The Garelli library, containing about 11,000 volumes, which was combined with various libraries of abolished Jesuit colleges after the suppression of the Theresian Academy in Vienna, formed the original stock of the Lemberg University library. It contained at the end of 1892, 120,900 volumes, 396 manuscripts, 241 documents, and 10,657 coins and medals. The financial support of the library amounts to 18,073 florins a year for salaries and purchase of new books.

This valuable library is fully described in Karl Reifenkugel's work, Biblioteka uniwersitecka we Lwowie, in the magazine Przewodnik naukowy i literacki. Lemberg 1873.

Count Ossoliński Library.—Besides the university library and as a supplement for the documentary study of Polish history, there is in Lemberg another great library of paramount importance, which is exceedingly rich in manuscripts and early printed Slavonic books; it is the Count Ossoliński National Institute (Zakład narodowy imienia Ossolińskich). It was founded in 1817 by Joseph Maximilian Count of Tenczyn and opened to the public in 1826. The aim of this beneficial institute is the collection of printed works, manuscripts, pictures, engravings, etc., and of antiquities of Polish origin, the publication of manuscripts and important works in its own printing office, aid to poor deserving Polish students, and the maintenance of a public reading hall.

There are in the library 91,400 printed volumes (besides 8,640 duplicates), 3,496 manuscripts, 1,168 documents, 2,810 autographs, 25,240 engravings, 856 pictures, 2,200 museum objects, 670 weapons, 1,880 maps and charts, 18,100 coins, and 4,237 medals. The report of 1895 gives 93,550 books (besides 8,740 duplicates), 3,601 MSS., 1,174 documents, 2,851 autographs, 25,511 engravings, 866 pictures, 2,237 museum objects, 670 weapons, 1,892 maps, 18,100 coins, and 4,237 medals.

Among the many publications on the treasures of the Ossoliński Library perhaps the most important are: Biblioteka Ossolińskich, Zbiór materiałow do historyi polskiej (collection of material for Polish history), Lwow, 1874 ff.; Catalogus codicum manuscriptorum Bibliothecæ Ossolinianæ Leopoliensis, Tom. I, II, III (still appearing). The institute had, in 1893, a fortune of 545,000 florins. The expenses were 17,780 florins. The Polish magnate, Prince Andreas Lubomirski, is the present curator of the institute.

Archives for the Grod and Terrestral Court Documents of Poland.— These archives, founded in 1878 as a State institute, afford an indispensable mine of information to the student on the old Polish town and country court institutions and the forensic conditions of Galicia in general. It contains the documents of the ancient grod and terrestral courts of the palatinates of Reussen, Cracow-Sandomir, and Belz and the starostaships of Oswięcin (Auschwitz) and Zator for the years 1409–1785.

The appropriation for the archives in 1894 was 6,000 florins.

The documents have been edited in 11 volumes. "Akta grodzkie i ziemskie," Lemberg, 1868–1886. (First volume edited by a commission; second to eleventh volumes by H. Liske); vide Minerva, p. 410.

The Imperial Royal School of Technology in Lemberg.—In the same year that the University of Lemberg was reorganized (1817) the first real school (Realschule) of Galicia was erected and thus a new stimulus given to the technical sciences. The school developed so that in 1835 a separation of the technical and commercial branches could take place. In 1843 this real and commercial academy was extended by a technical course, out of which gradually an academy of technology grew up. In 1846, when the Republic of Cracow was conquered by Austria, the institute of technology of that city soon outreached that of Lemberg, which lost in importance.

In 1871 the Polish language was introduced officially and the academy was built up as a school of technology (with the rank of a university) by the founding of new chairs. The regulations of 1872 put it on an equal footing with the other Technische Hochschulen in Austria, like Graz, Brünn, Vienna, Budapest, Prague (German and Czech).

The technical high school of Lemberg, like all the other Austrian high schools, consists of four professional schools—i. e., the school of engineering, of architecture, of mechanical engineering, and the chemico-technological school. The course in the schools of engineering and architecture requires five years, that in the other two schools four years. Regular students must have the certificate of maturity from a secondary (middle) school or a gymnasium, in which latter case they have to give sufficient proof of efficiency in geometry and free-hand drawing. Hospitants must be 18 years of age and give sufficient proof of their ability to follow the courses.

The administration of the institute in 1892 was carried on at an expense of 101,900 florins; in 1893, 105,648 florins, toward which the State had to contribute 100,975 florins; in 1895, 113,264 florins (107,445 florins Government contribution). In the same year there were 188 regular students and 12 hospitants in the school, and in 1895 227 students and 34 hospitants.

The instruction in these four branches is given by most eminent professors in all the technical branches usually taught in such schools, besides studies specially adapted to an Austrian school of technology, as, for instance, a course in taxation of whisky, beer, sugar, and mineral oils, encyclopedia of the science of forestry, Austrian political economy, and commercial and banking law. There are in the institution 19 professors, 9 honorary docenten, 11 privat-docenten, 1 lector in German philology, and 3 teachers in French, English, and water-color painting, respectively.

The school has a laboratory for general chemistry (yearly appropriation, 900 florins; extra allowance, 200 florins), a laboratory for chemical technology (yearly appropriation, 900 florins; extra allowance, 200 florins), a physical cabinet (600 florins), a technological cabinet (600 florins), an electro-technical institute (500 florins), a mineralogico-geological collection (400 florins), a collection of natural historic objects (210 florins), an observatory for higher geodesy and spheric astronomy (200 florins), collections of apparatus for mechanical engineering (700 florins), practical geometry (600 florins), architecture (Hochbau) (500 florins), engineering sciences (500 florins), mechanics (315 florins), street and water works, hydraulics (250 florins), ornamental drawing (120 florins), descriptive geometry (100 florins), knowledge of articles of merchandise (100 florins). A good technical library under the supervision of a full professor, and with an allowed expenditure of 4,960 florins, exclusive of fees (245 florins in 1891-92; respectively, 5,360 and 420 florins, in 1895), is attached to the Lemberg technical high school.

Five gymnasia, 1 real school, 1 Roman Catholic, and 1 Ruthenian-Catholic seminary in Lemberg (Lwów), complete the educational facilities of the present capital of Austrian Poland. According to the Jahrbuch des höheren Unterrichtswesens in Oesterreich of 1893, the status of the Lemberg secondary schools was as follows:

The imperial academic state gymnasium, with the Ruthenian language, dates back to the fourteenth century. It obtained its name "gymnasium academicum" in the first half of the eighteenth century; theological and philosophical courses were given at the school, but after the foundation of the Lemberg University (1784 and again in 1817) were transferred to the latter institution. By imperial order of May 31, 1873, Ruthenian was introduced as the official language. Five hundred and eight pupils were in attendance in 1893 in 8 classes. The second State gymnasium, with 467 pupils, founded in 1818, is German. The Francis Joseph state gymnasium, the fourth and fifth state gymnasia, founded in 1858, 1879, and 1892, with 624, 736, and 573 pupils, respectively, are thoroughly Polish, and show the growth of the Polish population and its educational proclivities.

The imperial state real school of Lemberg, founded in 1857, enlarged in 1872, has 430 pupils.

There is in Lemberg a State teachers' seminary with 150 male candidates and 62 male pupils in its preparatory class, and a similar institution for females with 204 candidates, and 30 pupils in the department for kindergarten education. Both Polish and Ruthenian are official languages.

One industrial school with Polish as the official language, and with the departments of architecture and industrial art, with trade schools in cabinetmaking, turning, artistic embroidery, decorative designing and drawing in an open drawing-room for women, and an industrial workshop help to complete the round of useful studies.

Secondary schools in Galicia.—Secondary schools are freely spread over the whole country to serve as feeders for the two Polish universities and the school of technology. Most of them are governmental schools, and the few which are not, are under the supervision of the provincial school authorities and the minister of public instruction in Vienna, so as to insure the same high standard of scholarship which has to be reached in the imperial or state gymnasia and real gymnasia. The curriculum of all is, mutatis mutandis, equal to that of the other schools of equal grade in the monarchy, only all branches are taught in the Polish language by national teachers, thus propagating and increasing a specifically Polish culture, which makes this great province one of the most precious jewels in the crown of Austria-Hungary.

The following secondary schools in Galicia with Polish as the official language [1] may be mentioned:

The state gymnasium at Bochnia, with 365 pupils; founded in 1817. The administration and instruction is conducted by 1 director, 12 professors, and 6 associates (supplenten), about the usual number of the teaching force of such schools. All these officers are regular graduates of Austrian universities provided with their special facultas docendi.

The state gymnasium at Brzeżany, with 382 pupils; founded in 1805; completed in 1863.

The under gymnasium of Buczacz under the Basilian Brothers; founded in 1754 by the starosta, Count Nicolaus Potocki, with 346 pupils.

The private gymnasium of the Jesuits at Bąkowice, near Chyrów, originated from the old convict school of the Jesuit Society at Tarnopol. The school, with its 8 classes and 306 pupils, has, under the ministerial decree of December 28, 1891, all the rights and privileges of a state gymnasium.

The Francis Joseph state gymnasium at Drohobycz, founded in 1858 as a communal school, taken under state control in 1874, the community granting it annually 18,000 florins, has 347 pupils.

The state gymnasium at Jaroslau, opened in 1868 as communal school, taken under state control by imperial decree in 1872, has 401 pupils.

The state gymnasium at Jasło, founded in 1868 as communal school, since 1875 administered by the state. The community takes charge of the building, heating material, and service, and pays an annual contribution of 500 florins. It has 496 pupils.

The state gymnasium at Kołomea, founded in 1861 as a communal under gymnasium. Since 1878 it has been a full gymnasium, with obligatory drawing in the lower classes. In 1892 the first parallel class with Ruthenian as official language was opened. It has 569 pupils.

The state gymnasium at Podgórze, opened on September 5, 1892, with 2 classes and 113 pupils.

The state gymnasium at Przemyśl originated in the Jesuit college founded in 1617. After the suppression of the order it received secular

---

[1] Jahrbuch des höheren Unterrichtswesens in Oesterreich. Bearbeitet von Joh. Neubauer und Dr. Josef Diviš. 6. Jahrgang, 1893. Wien. F. Tempsky.

teachers in 1773. The philosophical institute, opened in 1820, was combined with the gymnasium in 1849. With the scholastic year 1888-89 the first parallel class with Ruthenian was opened by imperial decree of July 29, 1887. There are 564 pupils in the Polish and 218 in the 5 Ruthenian parallel classes; together, 782.

The state gymnasium at Rzessów, completed in 1858, has 605 pupils.

The Archduchess Elizabeth state gymnasium at Sambor existed as a Jesuit gymnasium from 1680 to the suppression of the order; was supported by the community from 1792 to 1815; since 1815 has been a state gymnasium; has had its complete 8 classes since 1853; 469 pupils.

The state gymnasium at Novy-Sandec, founded in 1818 with 6 classes, was transferred to the Jesuits in 1839, provided with secular teachers in 1849, completed in 1866. The community pays annually 1,680 florins toward its support. It has 279 pupils.

The state gymnasium at Sanok was opened in 1881 with 2 classes; supported entirely by the community; it has 291 pupils.

The state gymnasium at Stanislau, founded as Jesuit gymnasium in the eighteenth century; it has 627 pupils.

The state gymnasium at Stryj, subventioned by the city with 5,000 florins; it has 342 pupils.

The state gymnasium at Tarnopol, established as a Jesuit gymnasium in 1820; with a philosophical institute in 1821; organized in 1850 as a full gymnasium with secular teachers; has 472 pupils.

The state gymnasium at Tarnów, established in 1784; complete since 1849; has 551 pupils.

The state gymnasium at Wadowice, complete since 1878, with obligatory drawing in the lower classes; has 269 pupils.

The state gymnasium at Złoczów, completed in 1881; subventioned by the city with 4,000 florins and all the necessary material; it has 296 pupils.

Two real schools (Realschulen) at Stanislau and Tarnopol, and the teachers' seminaries (normal schools) at Rzeszów (202 candidates), Sambor (Polish and Ruthenian, with 142 candidates), Stanislau (Polish and Ruthenian, with 195 candidates), Tarnopol (Polish and Ruthenian, with 197 candidates), Tarnów (165 candidates), and Przemyśl (with 115 female candidates) contribute to furnish the country with good primary teachers.

Higher female schools have not yet obtained full and due appreciation, yet good private and convent schools contribute largely to a high intellectual and moral education of women in Galicia.

EDUCATION IN THE ANCIENT POLISH PROVINCES OF PRUSSIA.

In the official Jahresberichte über das höhere Schulwesen in Preussen, by Conrad Rethwisch, Berlin, 1893, no instruction or education in the Polish language is mentioned, at least so far as the secondary schools in Prussia are concerned. But the solution of the Polish linguistic and educational problem is not yet entirely accomplished. It still exists in three provinces of the Kingdom of Prussia, in the province of Prussia (proper), Posen, and Silesia.

Ever since Adalbert, Bishop of Prague, went to preach the gospel to Prussia, about the year 997, Pruzzia, as called by his companion Gaudentius, because it was inhabited by the Bor-Russians (Bordering-on-Russia), a fierce, warlike tribe closely related with the Letts and Lithuanians, this country was the Eris apple of the surrounding German and Slavonic powers. King Knut of Denmark and the Polish dukes, the Grand Masters of the Teutonic Order and the Polish kings, the Hohenzollern dukes, and later the Electors stamped their character and nationality upon the country, as St. Adalbert—according to Carlyle—"has stamped his life upon it, in the form of a crucifix." Thus its inhabitants are, according to their descent and language, Lithuanians or Letts, Masurs, Kures, Kassubes, but mostly Poles and Germans, the latter strongly mixed with Swiss and Palatine emigrants and colonists, French Huguenot refugees, so liberally received by the Great Elector, and Salzburg exiles, driven out by their archbishop. The Massurs live in the southern part of the government districts of Gumbinnen, Königsberg, and Marienwerder, and are unmixed Slavs as well as the Kassubes.

But this whole population, so long under the superior, leveling influence of Prussia, has been welded together, with the exception of the two Slavonic constituents, into one pseudo-German element, of course the purely German majority itself excepted. But the province of West Prussia, formed in 1878 for administrative reasons, contains still a Polish population, amounting to one-third of the entire population, among whom the Polish language is still cultivated and has a secondary place beside German in the schools. But a glance at the network of the most excellent German schools of all descriptions proves that this province is in Germanism equal to any other Prussian province beyond the Elbe.

"This acquisition [i. e., the share taken by Prussia in 1772]," says Frederick the Great somewhere in his memoirs, "was one of the most important we could make, because it joined Pommerania to East Prussia (ours for ages past), and, since it rendered us masters of the Weichsel River, we gained the double advantage of being able to defend that Kingdom (Ost-Preussen), and to draw considerable tolls from the Weichsel, as all the trade of Poland goes by that river."

Carlyle puts the adequate question, What became of West Preussen under Friedrich? and Gustav Freytag responds, not an impartial witness toward Poland, but in this case history corroborates his statement:[1]

Acquisition of Polish Prussia.—Frederick was the first conqueror who once more pushed forward the German frontier toward the East, reminding the Germans

---

[1] G. Freytag, Neue Bilder aus dem Leben des deutschen Volkes, Leipzig.

again that it was their task to carry law, culture, liberty, and industry into the east of Europe. All Frederick's lands, with the exception only of some Old Saxon territory, had, by force and colonization, been painfully gained from the Slav. At no time since the migrations of the middle ages had this struggle for possession of the wide plains to the east of the Oder ceased. When arms were at rest, politicians carried on the struggle.

In what state Frederick found the Polish Provinces.—Some few only of the larger German towns, which were secured by walls, and some protected districts inhabited exclusively by Germans, as the Niederung, near Dantzig, the villages under the mild rule of the Cistercians of Oliva, and the opulent German towns of Catholic Ermeland, were in tolerable circumstances. The other towns lay in ruins, so also most of the hamlets (Höfe) of the open country. Bromberg, the city of German colonists (founded by the Teutonic Order, but entirely Polonized), the Prussians found in heaps and ruins. No historian, no document, tells of the destruction and slaughter that had been going on in the whole district of the Netze there during the last ten years before the arrival of the Prussians. * * * The country people hardly knew such a thing as bread; many had never in their lives tasted such a delicacy; few villages possessed an oven. * * *

The peasant noble (unvoting, inferior kind) was hardly different from the common peasant; he himself guided his hook plow (hackcu-pflug), and clattered with his wooden slippers upon the plankless floor of his hut. It was a desolate land, without discipline, without law, without a master. On 9,000 English square miles lived 500,000 souls, not 55 to the square mile.

Gustav Freytag is doubtless right about the then condition of that section of Poland. Mr. W. A. Day, in his above-mentioned Russian Government in Poland, pages 134–135, corroborates the statement. But Freytag is wrong when he puts all the blame upon the Polish government, administration, and necessary national character. The counter picture of what Germany, and Brandenburg in particular, was after the thirty-years war, and the fact that the Great Elector preceded the Great King in raising her people from absolute brutality, might have enabled the great novelist-historian to seek for the causes of desolation somewhere else.

Frederick sets to work.—The very rottenness of the country became an attraction for Frederick; and henceforth West Prussia was, what hitherto Silesia had been, his favorite child, which, with infinite care, like that of an anxious, loving mother, he washed, brushed, new dressed, and forced to go to school and into orderly habits, and kept ever in his eye. The diplomatic squabbles about this "acquisition" were still going on when he had sent a body of his best officials into this waste, howling scene to set about organizing it. The *Landschaften* (counties) were divided into small circles (Kreise); *   * new parishes, each with its church and parson, were called into existence as by miracle; a company of 187 schoolmasters, partly selected and trained by the excellent Semler, were sent into the country; multitudes of German mechanics, too, from brick makers up to machine builders. Everywhere there began a digging, a hammering, a building; cities were peopled anew, street after street rose out of the heaps of ruins, new villages of colonists were laid out, new modes of agriculture ordered. The great canal was dug which connects, by the Netze River, the Weichsel with the Oder and the Elbe. * * * And when Goethe, himself now become an old man, finished his Faust, the figure of the old King again rose on him and stepped into his poem, and his Faust became transformed into an unresting, creating, pitilessly exacting master, forcing on his salutiferous drains and fruitful canals through the morasses of the Vistula.

So far Freytag's description of the fact is essentially true and correct. Education, which was raised and increased by degrees from that time on, is materially a Prussian, i. e., a German, creation in those regions.

It was not, therefore, simply as a conqueror that Prussia came. Frederick believed that his "share" was necessary for her security, but it must be humanized and strengthened; its people must be educated— it was but natural with him and his successors that they must be educated in German. In villages the most remote, schools were introduced and churches rebuilt and endowed; Polish-speaking teachers were sent to the western provinces, where they could make no use of the Polish language and would even forget it; German teachers who knew no Polish whatever were sent to the east to teach in German exclusively, which they did frequently not to much advantage. Yet the "noiseless Germanization" of the old Polish provinces ever went on.

Meanwhile the originally Polish population became more conscious of its nationality, owing to its better educational equipment. A Polish nobility of the highest order of education and culture arose to cultivate the treasures of their old civilization. It can be safely stated that there is no Prussian subject of Polish nationality who objects to learning and mastering the German language. Only when there was coercion to unlearn Polish did a strong reaction take place against it from all strata of Polish society. Everybody knows and values German, but wants to be free to speak the language of his fathers at home, in the church, and in the school, at least for religious instruction. Although the point how far to concede the latter privilege is still a matter of controversy, forbearance and toleration is the present principle of the Prussian policy, and in consequence the representatives of the Polish population in Prussia are faithful supporters of the Government, loyal adherents to the monarchy and its enlightened dynasty. In the army, in the civil service, in all professional and practical pursuits, there are thousands of Poles in distinguished, frequently the most elevated, positions. A difference or discrimination exists no longer.

The primary-school controversy, how much Polish shall be taught in the elementary schools of the Polish-Prussian provinces, whether in religion alone, which can be felt and understood by the child only in the mother language, or also in other branches of instruction, has not subsided yet. Some sharp contrasts of opinion are yet existing, but the conciliatory, natural, tolerant opinion prevails, counting among its supporters men like Professor Delbrück, of the University of Berlin, editor of the influential Preussische Jahrbücher. Although Polish is still an important element in the eastern social life of Prussia, owing to a highly cultured nobility and an excellently educated "bourgeoisie," still it has no longer a preponderating influence.

But so much may be safely maintained: that the Polish language in Prussia will not die out and its literature will not be forgotten, since the unique German universities develop it into an integral constituent of their Slavonic departments, and since more and more young men are taking up Slavonic studies in order to investigate, search, and complete the round of the Indo-European languages, literatures, and histories.

Polish origin of the University of Koenigsberg.—The University of Koenigsberg, which to-day is so absolutely German that the Polish seminary under H. Pelka and the Lithuanian seminary under M. Lackner are the only traces of its past, is more closely related with the history of Polish culture than is generally assumed. It was established in 1544 as Collegium Albertinum by Albert, Duke of Prussia, first cousin to King Sigismund Augustus, with the object of promoting religious, literary, and scientific culture among the German, Polish, and Lithuanian populations which inhabited the dominions of Prussia. Indeed, the university contributed much to the spread of Scriptural knowledge in Poland. The first Polish gospel and the first Protestant works in that language appeared under the auspices of this institution. More than that, the university obtained its consecration and baptism from Poland.

At a time when the privilege of the Pope, or his worldly representative, the Emperor, seemed indispensable to the foundation of a university, the first rector of Koenigsberg, Sabinus, applied to Cardinal Bembo to obtain, by his instrumentality, from the Pope, a charter for a university established with the avowed purpose of opposing his authority. Of course this request was declined by Bembo, and likewise by the Emperor. But Sigismund Augustus, King of Poland, although a Catholic monarch, granted to the Protestant university of Koenigsberg a charter, proprio motu datum, Wilno, March 28, 1561. He expresses by the above-mentioned charter that he was founding by it the said university (universitatem condidimus et ereximus), to which he gave equal rights with that of Cracow. This charter for the erection of a Protestant university was—in honor of Polish toleration be it mentioned—countersigned by Padniewski, vice-chancellor of Poland and Roman Catholic bishop of Przemysl. When the privileges of that university were confirmed by Wladislaw IV, King of Poland, the act of confirmation was likewise countersigned by the vice-chancellor, Gembicki, also a Catholic prelate. The Polish monarch had an opportunity of exercising his supremacy as liege lord of Prussia in a manner beneficial to the privileges of the University of Koenigsberg in 1617. The Duke of Prussia, having appropriated to himself the right of nominating professors, which was vested in the university by its charter, the affair was referred to the King of Poland, whose commissaries decided in favor of the university.

The prime object of the theological faculty of the university was to train ministers fit to expound the word of God to the Polish and Lithuanian populations of Prussia in their national languages. Heretofore a translator was always standing near the pulpit, who translated to the congregation the German sermon, unintelligible to most of the Poles and Lithuanians. The theological seminary established at the university contained 24 students, 14 of whom were for the Polish and Lithuanian languages. In 1425 a separate seminary was established for the Poles and Lithuanians of Prussia, besides a foundation made by the Princes Radziwill for Protestant scholars from Poland and Lithuania.[1]

The Lyceum Hosianum; secondary schools in Prussia.—The Lyceum Hosianum at Braunsberg, so called after the celebrated Cardinal Stanislaus Hosius, which at present is absolutely Germanized, is of thoroughly Polish origin. An adversary of the Reformation, Hosius, as bishop of Warmia, founded in 1568 the Jesuit college at Braunsberg, as a means for the suppression of the reformatory movement in Poland. The school became an episcopal seminary for the training of priests. After its destruction by the French in 1807 it was rebuilt, and by royal decree of May 19, 1818, was raised to a Catholic theological and philosophical faculty, and endowed by the secularized estates of the monastery of Neuzelle, near Frankfort on the Oder. At present, however, not a trace of its Polish origin is left.

The great number of excellent schools in the province shows that the Prussian Government neglects nothing to raise the standard of culture in the two provinces to a height never reached before.

There is a royal academy of fine arts at Koenigsberg, 16 gymnasia, 2 progymnasia, 6 real schools, 2 real progymnasia, 1 higher Bürgerschule (high school), 12 public high schools for girls, 8 middle schools for boys, 8 teachers' seminaries (male), 2 royal and 10 private preparatory schools for the latter, 2 schools of navigation, 2 schools of midwifery, 1 trade and 1 architectural school, the agricultural institute connected with the university, 2 (secondary) agricultural schools, and 7 lower agricultural schools, beside 4 schools for the deaf and dumb and 1 for the blind. Only here and there a little Polish is taught as a facultative branch, but otherwise the Germanization has been absolute and complete.

Libraries: Two cities in West Prussia are especially notable for their libraries—Danzig and Elbing.

The city library of Danzig was founded in 1591 by the donation of Giovanni Bonifacio Marchese d'Oria and increased by later purchases, donations, and legacies. It is especially rich in local, Polish, and German history, geography, literature, art history, and political economy. It contains about 70,000 volumes, among which there are 440 incunabula and 1,182 manuscripts. The library is especially rich in Polonica, relating to the history of Poland and her relation with Prussia. The first volume of a catalogue of the library relating to the manuscripts concerning Dantsic was published by A. Bertling, 1892.

The Danzig city archives, besides those of Lübeck, the richest city

---

[1] Vide Arnold's Geschichte der Universität Königsberg.

archives in North Germany, were arranged anew in 1850, by order of the Danzig city magistracy, for the public service and scientific use. They contain four chief departments: (1) The archive library, containing mostly manuscripts and chronicles, but few printed works; (2) the library of maps and plans, containing the oldest maps and views of the city and its territory; (3) the great collection of historical records and documents, most of them of the greatest historical value—the books of the national delegates, sent to diets and other missions, from 1420, the acta internunciorum from 1515 on, the records of the Hansa and the Prussian States; (4) the collection of documents, containing more than 50,000 numbers, the oldest from 1253.

The city library of Elbing, founded in 1601, increased in 1710 by manuscripts and incunabula from the Dominican monastery at Elbing after its suppression, contains about 27,000 volumes, 121 incunabula, 205 manuscripts, and 770 maps and engravings. The library is well catalogued.

The Province of Posen.—The Grand Duchy or Province of Posen has a population which is mostly Polish by descent and language, especially preponderating in the southeast of the province; but the German element is strongly represented, especially in the cities and towns, and is steadily progressing. Education is almost exclusively in German hands, though Polish is studied almost everywhere in the primary and secondary schools and from the pulpit.

There is no university in this province, owing to the close neighborhood of Kœnigsberg, Berlin, and Breslau, but a network of excellent secondary schools is spread over the country.

There are 14 gymnasia, 2 progymnasia, 4 real schools, 13 middle schools, various high schools for girls, 5 teachers' seminaries (male), 4 royal preparatory schools for the latter, 1 (female) teachers' seminary, 2,187 public primary schools, 3 institutes for the deaf and dumb, 1 for the blind. Nevertheless public education stands lower in Posen than in any other Prussian province, sending the highest percentage of analphabets to the army, 8.55 per cent in 1884–85.

At the head of the Polish Roman Catholic clergy stands the Archbishop of Posen-Gnesen, now himself a Pole, under whom are the metropolitan chapters at Gnesen and Posen, the archpriesthoods, the collegiate abbeys and cloisters.

Among the finest buildings of the city of Posen, dating back to Polish times, are the city hall, built in 1580, Slavonic-Roman style, with a beautiful tower, built in 1730, and a rich collection of books; the palace, decorated with a magnificent frontage, with 24 Corinthian pillars, donated by Count Raczynski; the Dzyalinski palace, with a rich collection of Polish documents; and the palace of the archbishop, with a large gallery of precious pictures and works of art, partly referring to Polish history. The city of Posen has 24 Catholic and 3 Protestant churches, among which the cathedral, built in Gothic style in 1775, is the most significant. It contains valuable fresco paintings, numerous monuments and tombs, and the so-called golden chapel, which Count Raczynski, with some other Polish nobles, built in 1842 in Byzantine style and adorned with many works of art, especially the gilded brass monuments of the first Polish kings, Mieczyslaw and Boleslaw, executed by Rauch, the famous sculptor of the tomb of Queen Louise of Prussia.

The city is amply provided with excellent schools, namely, 1 real gymnasium, the building of which is an architectural ornament of the city; 2 gymnasia, partly with Polish instruction; 1 (female) teachers' seminary, 1 girls' high school, several boys' high schools, and a school of midwifery.

Posen, besides Gnesen, is one of the oldest Polish cities, and is still a center of Polish culture, education, and the seat of the Polish book trade in Prussia. After his conversion to Christianity, King Mieczyslaw founded here a bishopric in 996. By its trade with Germany the city became very flourishing and the seat of a "woiewó dstwo" (military governorship). The work of Lukaszewicz, Obraz historiczno-statystytczny miasta Poznania, Posen, 1838 (German translation in 1881), gives a fair picture of such an old boundary town between the Germanic and Slavonic domain, its culture, struggles, aspirations, influence, life, and thought. No German author has from a German standpoint so finely defined the contrast between Slavonic and Teutonic life as Gustav Freytag, to repeat an earlier statement, has done in his Credit and Debit, and especially in his classical historical novels, Die Ahnen and Bilder aus der Deutschen Vergangenheit.

Libraries: The capital of the Grand Duchy of Posen has two important libraries, with a large stock of books and documents relating to Polish history, literature, education, and political conditions.

The family library of the counts of Raczynski was bequeathed as an eternal, particular property to the city of Posen on February 22, 1829, together with the newly built library building and an endowment of 189,500 marks. It contains 50,000 volumes (189 incunabula), 360 manuscripts, and 230 documents. The allowance for yearly expenditures is 4,600 marks. The library is well catalogued in 4 volumes by M. E. Sosnowski and L. Kurtzmann.

Besides the Raczynski library, the royal State archives in Posen have a large stock of Polish historical and court documents; about 3,000 documents from 1153-1793, Acta from 1793 on, grod books from 1386-1793; collections from the western and south Prussian times; also the very important and unique city archives of Posen, Gnesen, and Fraustadt, which do now and will for a long time furnish rich sources for the investigation of Poland and her relations to the surrounding neighbors, as well as for her standard of culture and civilization.

(Sonder-Abdruck aus dem Pädagogischen Archiv XXXVII. Jahrgang Heft 11 und 12.)

Verlag von A. W. Zickfeldt, Osterwieck/Harz.

Das Comité der Fünfzehn,

Bericht des Subcomités über die Wechselbeziehung der Lehrzweige im Elementar-Unterricht.

William T. Harris, Vorsitzender,

Vereinigte Staaten Kommissär des Erziehungswesens, Washington D. C.

Übersetzt von Professor Hermann Schönfeld, Washington.

Vorrede.

Seit mehreren Jahren hat eine mächtige Bewegung in den führenden Kreisen, denen das Erziehungswesen der Vereinigten Staaten von Amerika obliegt, Platz gegriffen, mit Zuhilfenahme der Erfahrung aller civilisierten Länder und beständiger Beachtung der vorliegenden Verhältnisse alle Stufen des Unterrichts von dem Kindergarten bis zur Universität zu verbessern und - wenn nötig — zu reformieren. Um eine gewisse Einheitlichkeit dieser Verbesserungen und Reformen zu sichern, hat die Nationale Gesellschaft des Erziehungswesens („National Educational Association"), die bei der Souveränität der einzelnen Staaten ja sogar der einzelnen Gemeinden in Erziehungsangelegenheiten nicht anders als unoffiziell sein kann, die aber die besten und fähigsten Erzieher des Landes umfaßt und einen durchaus maßgebenden Einfluß auf das Schulwesen des ganzen Landes ausübt, nach langjährigen Untersuchungen, Debatten und Vereinbarungen in der erzieherischen Landespresse und in Versammlungen endlich im Jahre 1892 auf dem Kongreß zu Saratoga Beschlüsse gefaßt und die Reformen angebahnt.

Ein Comité von zehn Personen wurde zunächst ernannt, um die Unterrichtsgegenstände und Lehrmethoden in den Mittelschulen in Erwägung zu ziehen und über dieselben zu berichten. Präsident Eliot von der Harvard Universität war der Vorsitzende dieser Kommission, und neun andere hervorragende Schulmänner von im Rang sehr verschiedenen Schulanstalten bildeten die hier unter dem Namen „Comité der Zehn" berühmt gewordene Körperschaft. Diese ernannte wiederum neun Konferenzen von je zehn Mitgliedern, welche mit möglichst gerechter Verteilung einerseits die höheren Schulen (Colleges), andererseits die zu ihnen führenden Vorbereitungsschulen und Mittelschulen vertraten. Die zur Beratung vorliegenden Lehrgegenstände waren Latein, Griechisch, Englisch, andere neuere Sprachen, Mathematik, Naturphilosophie (einschl. Physik, Astronomie, Chemie), Naturgeschichte und Biologie (einschl. Botanik,

Zoologie, Physiologie), Geschichte (einschl. Regierungs- und Verfassungskunde und Nationalökonomie), Geographie (einschl. physische Geographie, Geologie, Meteorologie).

Dieser Bericht wurde im Frühjahr 1894 vollendet und veröffentlicht. Dreißigtausend Kopien wurden von dem vereinigten Staaten-Bureau des Erziehungswesens über das Land verteilt, und seitdem wurde von der Nationalen Gesellschaft des Erziehungswesens eine Auflage nach der andern gedruckt und vertrieben. Kein erzieherisches Dokument hat je in diesem Lande mehr Staub aufgewirbelt und dem Mittelschulunterricht, welcher in dem ganzen Lehrsystem für den schwächsten Teil galt, mehr Anregung gegeben, die Lehrgegenstände in besseres Gleichgewicht gebracht.

Der Erfolg des „Berichtes der Zehn" hat ein lebhaftes Interesse für eine ähnliche Untersuchung der in den Elementarschulen geleisteten Arbeit erweckt. Bereits im Februar 1893 war von dem Departement der Superintendenten (einer Körperschaft, bestehend aus den Aufsichtsbehörden des öffentlichen Unterrichtswesens in den Staaten und wichtigen Städten der Union)*) in der Nationalen Gesellschaft des Erziehungswesens ein Comité ernannt worden, welches aus fünfzehn Mitgliedern bestehen sollte und seitdem als das „Comité der Fünfzehn" zu hohem Ansehen gelangt ist. Vorsitzender dieses Comités wurde Herr W. H. Maxwell, Superintendent der öffentlichen Schulen in Brooklyn, N. Y., welcher dasselbe wiederum in drei Subcomités organisierte: 1) Über die Erziehung der Elementarlehrer; 2) über die Wechselbeziehung der Unterrichtsgegenstände im Elementarunterricht; 3) über die Organisation der Stadtschulsysteme.

Der Bericht des „Comités der Fünfzehn" wurde dem Departement der Superintendenten in seiner jüngsten Versammlung (Februar 1895) in Cleveland, Ohio, vorgelegt und liegt nun im Drucke vor (Educational Review," New-York, Verl. von Henry Holt & Co., März). Der erste und dritte Bericht des Subcomités beschäftigt sich mit den unendlich wichtigen Maßnahmen zur Vervollkommnung unserer Normalschulen (Schullehrerseminare) und der Anstellung tüchtiger Superintendenten oder Inspektoren unserer Stadtschulsysteme, sowie mit den Mitteln und Wegen, parteipolitische Einflüsse aus der Oberaufsicht der letzteren zu entfernen.

---

*) Die fünfzig Staaten der Union haben je einen Staatssuperintendenten, der in den meisten Fällen die Lehrer in den Landdistrikten licensiert. Über 800 der wichtigeren Städte haben erfahrene Stadtsuperintendenten an der Spitze ihrer öffentlichen Schulen.

Die wahre und bleibende Bedeutung des „Berichtes der Fünfzehn" aber scheint mir in dem Spezialbericht des zweiten Subcomités „Über die Wechselbeziehung der Unterrichtsgegenstände im Elementarunterricht" zu liegen, dessen Vorsitzender Dr. William T. Harris, der Vereinigten Staaten Kommissär des Unterrichtswesens, ist, zwar nicht in seiner offiziellen Kapacität, aber als der angesehenste Schulmann und Philosoph dieses Landes und vielleicht der bedeutendste Hegelforscher der Gegenwart. Die vier anderen Glieder dieser Kommission sind die Herren J. M. Greenwood, C. B. Gilbert, L. H. Jones, W. H. Maxwell, die hochangesehenen Superintendenten der Stadtschulsysteme von Kansas City, St. Paul, Cleveland und Brooklyn, welche sich mit den Hauptzügen des Gedankenganges des von Dr. Harris verfaßten Berichtes einverstanden erklären und nur in einigen kleineren Nebenpunkten abweichen.

In Anbetracht der Bedeutung des Berichtes habe ich die Übertragung desselben ins Deutsche übernommen in der Hoffnung, daß derselbe auch in deutschen pädagogischen Kreisen Interesse und Anregung bieten wird.

Hermann Schönfeld,
Professor der deutschen Sprache und Litteratur an der
Columbian Universität, Washington, D. C.

Das Comité der Fünfzehn.
Bericht des Subcomités über die Wechselbeziehung der Studien*) im Elementarunterricht.

Das endesunterzeichnete Comité stimmt hinsichtlich des folgenden Berichtes überein, wobei jedoch jedes Mitglied sich den Ausdruck seiner individuellen Abweichung von der Meinung der Mehrzahl vorbehält durch eine mit Namensunterschrift versehene Feststellung, welche die Punkte der Meinungsverschiedenheit und ihre Begründung anführt.

I. Wechselbeziehung der Lehrgegenstände.

Ihr Comité versteht unter Wechselbeziehung der Lehrgegenstände:

1) **Die logische Anordnung der Lehrfächer und Lehrzweige.**

Erstens die Anordnung der Fächer in richtiger Reihenfolge im Lehrkursus, so daß jeder Zweig sich in einer dem natürlichen und leichten

---

*) Der Übersetzer behält das Wort „Studien" für das englische „studies" bei, obwohl der deutsche Begriff einen etwas verschiedenen und höheren Sinn hat. Wir würden sagen: „Fächer".

Fortschritt des Kindes angemessenen Ordnung entwickel, und daß jeder Schritt zur richtigen Zeit gemacht wird, um sein Aufsteigen zu dem nächsten Schritte in demselben Zweige oder zu den nächsten Schritten in anderen Zweigen des Studienganges zu unterstützen.

2) Die harmonische Gesamtheit in der Welt des menschlichen Wissens.

Zweitens die Anpassung der Lehrzweige derart, daß der ganze Lehrkursus zu jeder Zeit alle großen Abteilungen des menschlichen Wissens darstellt, soweit dies bei dem jedesmaligen Reifezustande, den der Schüler erreicht hat, überhaupt möglich ist, und daß jede verwandte Gruppe von Lehrgegenständen durch irgend einen ihrer für das besagte Lebensalter geeignetsten Lehrzweige dargestellt wird. Es wird dabei vorausgesetzt, daß innerhalb jeder Gruppe eine mehr oder minder thatsächliche Gleichberechtigung der Lehrgegenstände bestehe, und daß jeder Zweig des menschlichen Wissens durch ein gleichwertiges Lehrfach vertreten werde, so daß, während keine Gruppe unvertreten bleibt, doch auch wieder keine Gruppe überflüssige Vertretung findet und dadurch andere Gruppen an einer angemessenen Vertretung hindert.

3) Psychologische Harmonie — der gesamte Geist

Drittens die Auswahl und Anordnung der Zweige und Fächer innerhalb jeden Zweiges psychologisch betrachtet im Hinblick darauf, den Anlagen des Geistes die beste Übung zu gewähren und die Entfaltung jener Fähigkeiten in ihrer natürlichen Ordnung zu sichern, so daß keine Anlage derart überbildet oder vernachlässigt wird, daß abnorme oder einseitige geistige Entwickelung erzeugt wird.

4) Wechselbeziehung des Lehrganges des Schülers zu der Welt, in welcher er lebt — seine geistige und natürliche Umgebung.

Viertens und vor allem versteht Ihr Comité unter Wechselbeziehung der Lehrfächer die Auswahl und logische Reihenfolge in der Anordnung solcher Lehrgegenstände, welche dem Kinde einen Einblick in die Welt, in welcher es lebt, gewähren und ein Bemeistern der Hilfsquellen der Welt ermöglichen, wie es durch ein hilfreiches Zusammenwirken mit unseren Mitmenschen erzielt wird. Mit einem Worte, die Haupterwägung der nach der Meinung Ihres Comités alle anderen untergeordnet werden müssen, ist dieses Erfordernis der Civilisation, in welche das Kind geboren wird, welches denn auch bestimmt, nicht nur was es in der Schule lernen soll, sondern auch die Sitten und Gewohnheiten, die ihm in der Familie beigebracht werden sollen, bevor es das Schulalter erreicht;

ferner wie dasselbe sich mit einem Handwerk, Beruf oder einer Thätigkeit aus einer bestimmten Reihe derselben in den Jahren, die der Schule folgen, tüchtig bekannt machen soll; und zuletzt, daß diese Frage der Beziehung des Schülers zu seiner Civilisation bestimmt, welche politischen Pflichten es übernehmen und welchen Religionsglauben oder welches geistige Streben er für seine Lebensführung annehmen soll.

Um die Gründe klarzulegen, weshalb Ihr Comité die objektive und praktische Grundlage der für den Lehrgang auszuwählenden Gegenstände der von erzieherischen Schriftstellern so lange begünstigten subjektiven Grundlage vorzieht, möchte dasselbe die bereits erwähnte psychologische Basis als bloß formal in ihrem Charakter darstellen, als sich nur auf die Ausübung der sogenannten geistigen Fähigkeiten beziehend.

Eine solche Grundlage würde eine der gymnastischen Ausbildung der Körpermuskeln analoge Ausbildung der geistigen Kräfte zu Wege bringen. Die Turnkunst kann Kraft und Behendigkeit entwickeln, ohne doch zu einer Geschicklichkeit in Handwerken oder zu einem nützlichen Beruf zu führen. So kann auch eine abstrakte psychologische Erziehung den Willen, den Verstand, die Phantasie oder das Gedächtnis entwickeln ohne aber zu einer Ausübung der erworbenen Kräfte im Interesse der Civilisation zu führen. Das Schachspiel würde eine gute Schule für die Ausbildung der Kräfte der Aufmerksamkeit und Berechnung abstrakter Kombinationen liefern, aber es würde dem Meister in demselben wenig oder gar keine Kenntnis vom Menschen oder der Natur geben. Das psychologische Ideal, das in reichem Maße in der Erziehung vorherrschend ist, hat in der alten Phrenologie und in den neueren Studien in physiologischer Psychologie zuweilen einem biologischen Ideal Platz gemacht. Anstatt des Gesichtspunktes des Geistes, welcher von Kräften, wie Wille, Verstand, Phantasie, und Stimmung, gebildet ist, welche alle als für die Seele notwendig gedacht werden, wenn sie in Einklang mit einander entwickelt sind, wird hier der Begriff von Nerven und Gehirncentren als das letzte regulierende Prinzip in Anwendung gebracht, um die Auswahl und Anordnung der Lehrgegenstände zu bestimmen. Jeder Teil des Gehirns hat nach dieser Voraussetzung seinen Anspruch auf die Aufmerksamkeit des Erziehers, und das Studium wird für das wertvollste gehalten, das in normaler Weise die größere Anzahl von Gehirncentren beschäftigt. Diese Ansicht erreicht ein Extrem, wenn man sich durch formale im Gegensatze zu objektiven oder praktischen Gründen zur Auswahl eines Studienkursus bestimmen läßt. Während die alte Psychologie mit ihren geistigen Fähigkeiten ihre Aufmerksamkeit auf die geistigen Vorgänge richtete und die Welt der bestehenden Gegenstände und Beziehungen vernachläſſigte, auf welche dieſe Vorgänge gerichtet waren, hat dagegen die phyſiologiſche Pſychologie die Tendenz, ihre Aufmerkſamkeit auf den phyſiſchen Teil des Vorganges, die organiſchen Veränderungen in den Gehirnzellen und ihre Funktionen zu beſchränken.

Ihr Comité iſt der Meinung, daß die Pſychologie beider Arten, die phyſiologiſche ſowohl, wie die rein geiſtige, bei der Löſung der Fragen, die auf die Wechſelbeziehung der Studien gerichtet ſind, nur eine untergeordnete Stellung behaupten kann. Die zu lernenden Zweige und das Maß, in welchem ſie gelernt werden ſollen, werden hauptſächlich durch die Forderungen unſerer Civiliſation beſtimmt. Dieſe werden vorſchreiben, was am nützlichſten iſt, das Individuum mit der phyſiſchen und der menſchlichen Natur vertraut zu machen, ſo daß der Schüler als Individuum in den Stand geſetzt wird, ſeine ſpäteren Pflichten in den verſchiedenen Inſtitutionen — der Familie, bürgerlichen Geſellſchaft, Staat und Kirche — zu erfüllen. Aber in zweiter Reihe wird dann die Pſychologie wichtige Erwägungen liefern, welche die Methoden des Unterrichts, die Studienordnung der verſchiedenen Gegenſtände (in der Weiſe, daß die Schularbeit ſich dem Wachstum der Fähigkeit des Schülers anpaßt), und das Maß der Arbeit, (ſo daß ſeine Fähigkeiten nicht durch zu Viel überladen oder die Entwickelung ſeiner Kraft durch zu Wenig zum Stillſtand gebracht werde), in hohem Maße beſtimmen werden. Eine große Zahl untergeordneter Einzelheiten, die in das Gebiet der Unterrichtspathologie gehören, wie die hygieniſchen Züge der Schularchitektur und inneren Ausſtattung, die Programme, die Länge der Schulſtunden und Klaſſenübungen, die Erholung und die körperliche Reaktion gegen geiſtige Anſtrengung, wird ſchließlich durch wiſſenſchaftliche Empirie auf dem Gebiete der phyſiologiſchen Pſychologie beſtimmt werden.

Inſofern Ihr Comité auf die Betrachtung der Wechſelbeziehung der Studien in der Elementarſchule beſchränkt iſt, hat dasſelbe die Frage des Lehrganges im allgemeinen nur ſoweit in Betracht gezogen, als es notwendig erſchien, die Gründe für die Auswahl der Studien, für den Zeitraum der Schulerziehung zu erörtern, d. h. die acht Jahre vom ſechſten bis zum vierzehnten Lebensjahre oder die Schulperiode zwiſchen dem Kindergarten einerſeits und der Mittelſchule andererſeits. Es iſt nicht möglich geweſen, einige Unterſuchung des wahren Unterſchiedes zwiſchen Mittelſchul- und Elementarſtudien zu vermeiden, da eine der wichtigſten Fragen, die ſich der Aufmerkſamkeit Ihres Comités aufdrängt die Abkürzung des Elementarlehrkursus von acht oder mehr Jahren auf sieben oder sogar sechs Jahre ist und die entsprechende Vermehrung der Zeit, die gewöhnlich den Mittelschulfächern zugewiesen wird und aus inneren Gründen dem Mittelschulunterricht zuzukommen scheint.

Studiengang — Werte der Erziehung.

Ihr Comité berichtet, daß dasselbe im einzelnen die verschiedenen Lehrzweige erörtert hat, die in dem Curriculum der Elementarschule Raum gefunden haben, im Hinblick auf die Thatsache, ihren erziehlichen Wert für die Ausbildung und Entwickelung der Geistesfähigkeiten und insbesondere für die Verbindung des Schülers mit seiner geistigen und natürlichen Umgebung in der Welt, in welcher er lebt, zu entdecken.

A. Sprachlehre.

Zuerst ist die hervorragende Stellung des Sprachstudiums ins Auge zu fassen, welches bei der Arbeit der ersten acht Schuljahre in Lesen, Rechtschreiben und Grammatik besteht. Man behauptet, daß die Parteilichkeit, die man diesen Studien erweist, durch die Thatsache gerechtfertigt ist, daß die Sprache das Werkzeug ist, welches die soziale Organisation der Menschen möglich macht. Sie befähigt jeden Menschen, seine individuelle Erfahrung seinen Mitmenschen mitzuteilen, und gestattet demnach jedem, von der Erfahrung aller Nutzen zu ziehen. Die geschriebenen und gedruckten Sprachformen erhalten die menschliche Kenntnis und machen den Fortschritt in der Civilisation möglich. Man kommt zu dem Schlusse, daß Lesen- und Schreibenlernen das vornehmlichste Studium des Schülers in seinen ersten vier Schuljahren sein sollte. Lesen und Schreiben sind nicht so sehr Zwecke an sich als Mittel zur Aneignung aller anderen menschlichen Kenntnisse. Diese Erwägung allein würde genügen, ihre gegenwärtige Stellung in der Arbeit der Elementarschule zu rechtfertigen. Aber außerdem erfordern diese Zweige von dem Lernenden einen schwierigen Gedankenprozeß der Analyse. Der Schüler muß die getrennten Worte in dem Satze, den er behandelt, identificieren und muß nächstdem die getrennten Laute in jedem Worte erkennen. Es erfordert für das Kind oder den Wilden eine beträchtliche Anstrengung, seinen Satz in die Worte, aus denen er besteht, zu zerlegen, und eine noch größere Anstrengung, seine elementaren Laute zu unterscheiden. Lesen, Schreiben und Buchstabieren in ihrer elementarischen Form bilden daher für das Kind von 6—10 Jahren eine ernstliche Ausbildung in geistiger Analyse. Man sagt, daß es für den Geist bei weitem bildender ist als irgend eine Art der Beobachtung der Unterschiede bei materiellen Dingen, weil das Wort einen doppelten Charakter hat — an den äußeren Sinn gerichtet als gesprochener Laut für das Ohr oder als geschriebene und gedruckte Worte für das Auge —, aber auch eine Meinung oder einen Sinn enthält, der sich an den Verstand richtet und nur durch Einsicht erfaßt werden kann. Der Schüler muß die entsprechende Idee durch Gedanken, Gedächtnis und Phantasie ins Leben rufen, oder im andern Falle wird das Wort aufhören, ein Wort zu sein, und nur ein Schall oder ein Zeichen bleiben.

Andererseits umfaßt Beobachtung der Dinge und Bewegungen nicht notwendig diesen zweifachen Akt der Analyse, nämlich der intuitiven und objektiven Analyse, sondern nur die letztere. Zugestanden muß werden, daß wir alle häufig Gelegenheit haben, schlechte Methoden des Unterrichts zu verurteilen, die viel mehr Worte als Dinge lehren; aber wir geben doch zu, daß wir viel mehr leere Worte oder Zeichen meinen als wirkliche Worte. Unsere Anregungen für eine richtige Lehrmethode beziehen sich in diesem Falle einfach darauf, die Bedeutung des Wortes zu betonen und den Lehrvorgang vielmehr auf den Weg der Inhalts- als der Formanalyse zu führen. Bei Worten, die man anwendet, um äußere Beobachtung sich zu eigen zu machen, soll der Lehrer den Akt der Beobachtung wiederholen und wieder lebendig machen, durch den das Wort seine ursprüngliche Bedeutung erhielt. Bei einem Worte, das eine Beziehung zwischen Thatsachen oder Ereignissen ausdrückt, soll der Schüler Schritt für Schritt durch den Vorgang der Reflexion geführt werden, mittelst dessen die Idee aufgebaut wurde. Da das gesprochene und geschriebene Wort das einzige Werkzeug ist, durch welches die Vernunft sowohl die sinnlichen Ergebnisse als auch die zwischen ihnen durch Reflexion entdeckten Beziehungen zu fixieren, zu erhalten und mitzuteilen im stande ist, so hat keine Methode in der Erziehung vermocht, die Zweige Lesen und Schreiben in der Schule zu ersetzen. Aber die wirklichen Verbesserungen in der Methode haben die Lehrer veranlaßt, den inneren Faktor des Wortes, seine Bedeutung mehr und mehr zu betonen, und haben in mannigfaltiger Weise gezeigt, wie die ursprünglichen Erfahrungen, die den konkreten Worten ihre Bedeutung gegeben haben, und die ursprünglichen Vergleichungen und logischen Deduktionen zu wiederholen seien, durch welche die Ideen der Beziehungen und die kausalen Vorgänge in dem Geiste entstanden und abstrakte Worte nötig machten, um sie zu erhalten und mitzuteilen.

Man hat behauptet, daß es besser wäre, erst eine Grundlage der

Kenntnis der Dinge und dann in zweiter Reihe eine Kenntnis der Worte zu haben. Aber darauf hat man geantwortet, daß der Fortschritt des Kindes beim Sprechenlernen sein Aufsteigen von bloßen Eindrücken zum Besitz wahrer Kenntnis erweist; denn es benennt die Gegenstände erst, nachdem es seine Eindrücke in einer gewissen Synthese zusammengefaßt und allgemeine Ideen gebildet hat. Es erkennt denselben Gegenstand unter verschiedenen Umständen von Zeit und Raum und erkennt andere Gegenstände, die zu derselben Klasse gehören, durch ihre Namen und mit denselben. Demnach erweist der Gebrauch des Wortes einen höheren Grad der Selbstthätigkeit, während das Stadium der bloßen Eindrücke ohne Worte oder Zeichen ein verhältnismäßig passiver Zustand des Geistes ist. Was wir erst unter Dingen, dann Worten verstehen, ist darum nicht so sehr das Begreifen der Gegenstände durch passive Eindrücke als die aktive Erforschung und die Empirie, welche erfolgt, nachdem Worte angewendet und die höheren Formen der Analyse ins Leben gerufen worden sind durch jene Erfindung des Verstandes, die als Sprache bekannt ist, welche letztere, wie oben gesagt, eine Synthese von Ding und Denken, von äußerem Zeichen und innerer Bedeutung ist.

Vernünftige Erforschung kann der Erfindung der Sprache ebensowenig vorausgehen, wie das Schmiedehandwerk der Erfindung von Hammer, Amboß und Zange vorausgehen kann. Denn die Sprache ist das notwendige Werkzeug des Denkens und wird in der Handhabung der Synthese und Analyse in der Erforschung gebraucht.

Ihr Comité möchte diese Erwägungen zusammenfassen in der Behauptung, daß die Sprache mit Recht den Mittelpunkt des Unterrichts in der Elementarschule bildet, daß aber der Fortschritt in den Lehrmethoden wie bisher hauptsächlich dadurch erzielt werden muß, daß man die innere Seite des Wortes, seine Bedeutung, stärker betont, indem man sich besser abgestufter Schritte bedient zum Aufbau der Kette der Erfahrung oder des Gedankenganges, welchen das Wort ausdrückt.

Die ersten drei Jahre der Schularbeit des Kindes sind hauptsächlich von der Beherrschung der gedruckten und geschriebenen Formen der Worte seines mündlichen Wortvorrats in Anspruch genommen, Worte, mit denen es bereits zur Genüge vertraut ist, soweit sie an das Ohr gerichtete Laute sind. Es muß mit den neuen an das Auge gerichteten Formen vertraut werden, und es wäre eine unweise Methode, von demselben zu verlangen, viele neue Worte zu gleicher Zeit zu lernen, während es seine alten Worte in ihrer neuen Gestalt erkennen lernt. Aber sobald das Kind einige Leichtigkeit im Lesen desjenigen erlangt hat, das in dem mündlichen Stil gedruckt ist, kann es zur Auswahl von Lesestücken aus den klassischen Schriftstellern schreiten. . Die ausgewählten litterarischen Stücke sollten abgestuft sein und sind auch in fast allen in den Elementarschulen gebrauchten Lesebüchern in der Weise gestuft, daß sie die Stücke, welche die wenigsten Worte, die außer dem Bereich des mündlichen Wortschatzes liegen, enthalten, in die unteren Stufen der Lesebücher bringen und die Schwierigkeiten Schritt für Schritt erhöhen, je nachdem der Schüler an Reife zunimmt. Die ausgewählten Stücke sind litterarische Kunstwerke, welche die erforderliche Einheit und eine geeignete Reflexion dieser Einheit im einzelnen haben, wie sie gute Kunstwerke haben müssen. Aber sie malen Seelenvorgänge oder Lebensbilder oder komplizierte Reflexionen, die das Kind durch seine Fähigkeit, zu fühlen und zu denken, einigermaßen auffassen kann, obwohl sie an Inhalt und Umfang seinen Gesichtskreis weit überschreiten. Sie sind deshalb geeignet, das Kind aus sich selbst und über sich selbst hinaus als geistige Leitsterne zu führen.

Der litterarische Stil verwendet außer solchen Worten, die dem mündlichen Wortschatze gemeinsam sind, Worte, welche, in einem halbtechnischen Sinne gebraucht, feine Gedankenschattierungen und Seelenstimmungen ausdrücken. Das litterarische Kunstwerk liefert einen treffenden Ausdruck für einen Seelenzustand oder Gedankengang, der bisher in geeigneter Weise unaussprechlich war. Wenn der Schüler dieses litterarische Erzeugnis lernt, findet er sich mächtig unterstützt in dem Verständnis seiner selbst und seiner Mitmenschen. Die praktischste Kenntnis von allen ist zugestandenermaßen eine Kenntnis, die den Menschen befähigt, sich mit seinen Mitmenschen zu verbinden und mit ihnen den physischen und geistigen Reichtum seiner Nation zu teilen. Von diesem hohen humanisierenden oder civilisierenden Charakter sind die beliebten Litteraturwerke, die man in den Schullesebüchern findet, zu deren Material ungefähr hundert und fünfzig englische und amerikanische Schriftsteller herangezogen werden. Solche sind Shakespeare's Reden des Brutus und Antonius, Hamlet's und Macbeth's Monologe, Milton's L'Allegro und Il Penseroso, Gray's Elegie, Tennyson's Angriff der Leichten Brigade und Ode auf den Tod des Herzogs von Wellington, Byron's Waterloo, Irwing's Rip Van Winkle, Webster's Erwiderung an Hayne, Knapp's Prozeß für Mord und Bunker Hill Rede, Scott's Lochinvar, Marmion und Roderick Dhu, Bryant's Thanatopsis, Longfellow's Lebenspsalm, Paul Revere und Die Brücke, O'Hara's Totenbivouac, Campbell's Hohenlinden, Collin's Wie die Braven schlafen, Wolfe's

Bestattung des Sir John Moore und andere schöne Prosastücke und Poesien von Addison, Emerson, Franklin, Die Bibel, Hawthorne, Walter Scott, Goldsmith, Wordsworth, Swift, Milton, Cooper, Whittier, Lowell und andere. Das Lesen und Studieren schöner ausgewählter Stücke in Poesie und Prosa liefert das vorzüglichste ästhetische Bildungsmaterial der Elementarschule. Aber dieses sollte noch verstärkt werden durch einiges Studium photographischer oder anderer Darstellungen der großen Meisterwerke in der Architektur, Skulptur und Malerei der Welt. Der wiederholte Anblick dieser Darstellungen ist gut; der Versuch, sie mit dem Bleistift zu kopieren oder einen Abriß davon zu machen, ist noch besser; am besten ist eine ästhetische Lektion über ihre Zusammensetzung, ein Versuch, die Idee des Ganzen in Worten zu beschreiben, welches dem Kunstwerk seine organische Einheit verleiht, und die Pläne zu enthüllen, die der Künstler verfolgt hat, um diese Idee im einzelnen wiederzuspiegeln und ihre Kraft zu verstärken. Der ästhetische Geschmack des Lehrers und Schülers kann durch solche Übungen gepflegt werden, und wenn er einmal auf dem richtigen Weg der Entwicklung ist, kann er sich durch das Leben weiter entwickeln.

Eine dritte Phase des Sprachstudiums in der Elementarschule ist die formale Grammatik. Die litterarischen Kunstwerke in den Lesebüchern durch ergänzende Lektüre (zu Hause) der ganzen Werke, von denen die Auswahl für die Bücher getroffen worden ist, vervollkommnet, werden das Kind in dem Gebrauch eines höheren und besseren englischen Stiles ausbilden. Technische Grammatik kann dies nie leisten. Nur Vertrautheit mit schönen englischen Werken wird einen guten und korrekten Stil sichern. Aber die Grammatik ist die Wissenschaft der Sprache und hat als die erste der sieben freien Künste, als das erziehliche Studium par excellence, in der Schule lange das Scepter geführt. Ein Überblick über ihren subjektiv und objektiv erziehlichen Wert befestigt gewöhnlich die Überzeugung, daß sie auch in der Zukunft den ersten Platz behaupten muß. Ihr hauptsächlicher objektiver Vorzug ist der, daß sie den Bau der Sprache und die logischen Formen des Subjekts, Prädikats und Bestimmungswortes zeigt, so das Wesen des Denkens selbst enthüllend, das wichtigste aller Objekte, weil es Selbst-Objekt ist. In subjektiver oder psychologischer Hinsicht begründet die Grammatik ihren Anspruch auf den ersten Platz durch ihre Verwendung als Disciplin in feiner Analyse, in logischer Einteilung und Klassifikation, in der Kunst des Fragens und in der geistigen Vervollkommnung, genaue Definitionen zu machen. Noch ist die Grammatik eine leere, formale Disciplin, denn ihr Gegenstand, die Sprache, ist ein Erzeugnis der Vernunft eines Volkes nicht als Individuen, sondern als eines sozialen Ganzen, und das Vokabularium enthält in seinem Wortschatze die verallgemeinerte Erfahrung jenes Volkes, einschließlich sinnlicher Wahrnehmung und Reflexion, Gefühls und Stimmung, Instinkts und Willens.

Keine formale Arbeit auf einem großen objektiven Gebiet kann je ganz verloren sein, da sie zum mindesten das Verdienst hat, den Schüler mit dem Inhalt eines ausgedehnten Grenzgebietes seines Lebens, mit dem er in Beziehung treten muß, vertraut zu machen; aber leicht kann irgend eine besondere formale Disciplin, wenn zu lange fortgesetzt, das Wachstum in jenem Stadium der Entwickelung paralysieren oder zum Stillstand bringen. Die Übersättigung des Wortgedächtnisses hat die Tendenz, das Wachstum der kritischen Aufmerksamkeit und des Nachdenkens zu hemmen. Auch das Gedächtnis der nebensächlichen Einzelheiten, das in der Schule so geschätzt wird, wird ebenfalls oft auf Kosten der Einsicht in das organisierende Prinzip des Ganzen und den Kausalnexus, der die Teile verbindet, gepflegt. Desgleichen kann das Studium der Quantität, wenn im Übermaß getrieben, den Geist zu einer Gewohnheit der Vernachlässigung der Qualität in seiner Beobachtung und Reflexion verdrehen. Da es in dem quantitativen Urteil kein Subsummieren, sondern nur tote Gleichheit oder Ungleichheit giebt (A ist gleich oder größer oder kleiner als B), so ist eine Tendenz zur Atrophie in der Fähigkeit des konkreten syllogistischen Denkens bei einer sich ausschließlich mit Mathematik beschäftigenden Person vorhanden. Denn der normale Syllogismus macht von Urteilen Gebrauch, worin das Subjekt dem Prädikat subsummiert wird (Dieses ist eine Rose — die individuelle Rose wird unter die Klasse Rose subsummiert; Sokrates ist ein Mann, ꝛc.). Solches Denken betrifft Individuen nach zwei Gesichtspunkten, erstens als konkrete Ganze und zweitens als Mitglied höherer Totalitäten oder Klassen, Spezies und Genera. So ist auch die Grammatik, reich wie sie in ihrem Inhalt ist, nur eine formale Disciplin in Bezug auf den wissenschaftlichen, historischen oder litterarischen Inhalt der Sprache und verhält sich ihnen gleichgiltig gegenüber. Ein vier- oder fünfjähriges Drillen in Auflösung und grammatischer Analyse an litterarischen Kunstwerken (Milton, Shakespeare, Tennyson, Scott) geübt, ist eine Erziehung des Schülers zu Gewohnheiten der Gleichgiltigkeit und Vernachlässigung des Genius, der in dem litterarischen Kunstwerk offenbart ist, und zu Gewohnheiten einer ungehörigen und kleinlichen Aufmerksamkeit, die den Elementen der bloßen Materie und äußeren Hülle gewidmet ist, während sie in demselben Maße die aufbauende Form, welche allein das Werk des Künstlers ist, vernachlässigt. Eine Parallele hierfür wäre die Gewohnheit des Maurers, seine Aufmerksamkeit nur den Ziegeln und dem Mörtel, dem Stein und Cement bei der Besichtigung der Architektur, z. B. des Sir Christopher Wren, zuzuwenden. Ein Kind, das in der Analyse und Klassifikation von Farbenschattierungen überbildet worden ist — und derartige Beispiele findet man gelegentlich in einer Elementarschule, deren Specialität „Anschauungsunterricht" ist —, dürfte im späteren Leben eine Kunstgallerie besuchen und ein Inventar der Farben machen, ohne auch nur einen Blick von einem Bilde als Kunstwerk zu gewinnen. Solche Überbildung und Mißbrauch der Grammatik, wie man sie in der Elementarschule findet, besteht — wie zu fürchten ist — in gewissem Maße auch in den Mittel = (Sekundär=) Schulen und selbst in den Universitäten bei der Arbeit, die klassischen Autoren beherrschen zu lernen.

Ihr Comité ist einmütig in der Überzeugung, daß formale Grammatik die Stelle des Studiums des litterarischen Kunstwerkes nach litterarischer Methode nicht widerrechtlich einnehmen dürfe. Das Kind kann allmählich dazu herangebildet werden, die technischen „Motive" eines Gedichtes oder Kunstwerkes in Prosa zu sehen und die ästhetischen Erfindungen des Künstlers zu genießen. Die Analyse eines Kunstwerkes sollte die Idee entdecken, die ihm die organische Einheit verleiht; den entstehenden Konflikt und die Verwickelung; die Lösung und das dénouement. Natürlich müssen diese Dinge in der Elementarschule erreicht werden, ohne daß man auch nur ihre technischen Ausdrücke erwähnt. Der Gegenstand des Stückes wird ausgeführt; Erwägungen über die Bedingungen von Zeit und Raum werden daran geknüpft, um das Interesse zu erhöhen, dadurch daß man seine Bedeutung zeigt; seine zweiten und stärkeren Erwägungen über die verschiedenen Einzelheiten eines Konfliktes und Kampfes; seine Erwägungen über die Entwickelung (dénouement), worin sein Kampf in Sieg oder Niederlage endet und die ethischen oder Vernunftsinteressen gerechtfertigt werden, — und die Resultate schreiten vorwärts, immer wieder in immer weiteren Kreisen zu der Umgebung zurückkehrend, — etwas Derartiges ist in jedem Kunstwerke zu finden, und es giebt springende Punkte darin, die in vertraulicher Sprache selbst mit den jüngsten Schülern kurz, aber nutzbar besprochen werden können. Es giebt einen ethischen und einen ästhetischen Inhalt in jedem Kunstwerke. Es ist nützlich, diese beiden zum Vorteil der wachsenden Einsicht des Kindes in die menschliche Natur klarzulegen.

Das Ethische sollte indes dem Ästhetischen gegenüber in Unterordnung gehalten werden, aber nur darum, damit das Ethische selbst zu seinem Rechte des höchsten Interesses kommt. Sonst artet das Studium eines Kunstwerkes zu einer schöngeistigen Schauspielerei aus, und seine Wirkungen auf das Kind verursachen eine Reaktion gegen das Sittliche. Das Kind schützt seine innere Individualität gegen die Verwischung durch äußere Autorität dadurch, daß es eine widerspenstige Haltung gegen Geschichten mit einer angehängten Moral annimmt. Hierin ist die Überlegenheit des Ästhetischen in der litterarischen Kunst zu sehen. Denn das ethische Motiv hat der Dichter verborgen, und der Held ist mit all seinem gebrechlichen Individualismus und Selbststreben dargestellt. Seine Leidenschaften und seine Selbstsucht, mit schönen Zügen von Tapferkeit und edlen Sitten vergoldet, interessiert die Jugend, interessiert uns alle. Die Einrichtung der sozialen und moralischen Ordnung scheint dem ehrgeizigen Helden ein Hindernis in der Entfaltung der Reize seiner Individualität. Die Gewaltthat wird vollbracht, und die Nemesis ist erregt. Nun fällt die That auf den individuellen Thäter zurück, unsere Sympathie wendet sich gegen ihn, und wir fühlen Befriedigung über seinen Fall. So enthält die ästhetische Einheit die ethische Einheit in sich. Die Lehre des großen Dichters oder Novellisten nimmt man sich zu Herzen, während die ethische Ankündigung an sich vielleicht erfolglos geblieben wäre, besonders bei den selbstthätigsten und strebsamsten Schülern. Aristoteles betonte in seiner Poetik diesen Vorteil der ästhetischen Einheit, den Plato in seiner Republik verfehlt zu haben scheint. Die Tragödie reinigt uns von unseren Leidenschaften, um Aristoteles' Ausdruck zu gebrauchen, weil wir unsere eigenen schlechten Neigungen mit denen des Helden identifizieren, und aus Sympathie leiden wir mit ihm und sehen unsere beabsichtigte That mit tragischer Wirkung auf uns zurückfallen, und wir werden dadurch gebessert.

Ihr Comité hat in so ausführlicher Weise bei der ästhetischen Seite der Litteratur verweilt, weil es glaubt, daß es die allgemeine Tendenz in den Elementarschulen ist, die litterarische Kunst um der litterarischen Formalitäten willen zu vernachlässigen, welche letztere vielmehr das mechanische Material als die geistige Form angehen. Jene formalen Studien sollten nie aufhören, wohl aber dem höheren Studium der Litteratur untergeordnet werden.

Ihr Comité behält sich den Gegenstand: Sprachaufgaben, Aufsatzschreiben, und was sich auf den schriftlichen Ideenausdruck des Kindes bezieht, unter Teil 3 dieses Berichtes, der vom Programm handelt, zur Erwägung vor.

B. Arithmetik.

Neben dem Sprachstudium steht in den Schulen das Studium der Rechenkunst und nimmt den zweitwichtigsten Platz unter allen Lehrgegenständen in Anspruch. Es ist dargethan worden, daß die Mathematik die Gesetze von Zeit und Raum — sozusagen ihre aufbauende Form — betrifft, und daß sie folglich die logischen Bedingungen aller Materie sowohl in Ruhe als auch in Bewegung bestimmt. Wie dem auch sein mag, die hohe Stellung der Mathematik als der Wissenschaft aller Quantität ist allgemein anerkannt. Der Elementarzweig der Mathematik*) ist das Zahlenrechnen, und dieses wird in den öffentlichen Schulen sechs bis acht Jahre und sogar länger getrieben. Die Beziehung der Arithmetik zu dem gesamten Gebiet der Mathematik ist von Comte, Howison und anderen als der letzte Schritt in einem Prozeß der Berechnung dargestellt worden, in welchem die Resultate zahlenmäßig gegeben werden. Es giebt Zweige, die quantitative Funktionen entwickeln oder ableiten: so ist die Geometrie da für räumliche Formen und die Mechanik für Bewegung und Ruhe und die Kräfte, die sie hervorbringen. Andere Zweige verwandeln diese quantitativen Funktionen in solche Formen, wie sie in wirklichen Zahlen berechnet werden können, nämlich die Algebra in ihrer gewöhnlichen oder niederen Form und in ihrer höheren Form als Differential- und Integralrechnung und Variationsrechnung. Die Arithmetik findet den zahlenmäßigen Wert für die so angeleiteten und verwandelten Funktionen. Der erzieherische Wert der Arithmetik wird demnach sowohl in Bezug auf die psychologische Seite als auch in Bezug auf ihre objektive, praktische Anwendung, nämlich den Menschen mit der Naturwelt in Wechselbeziehung zu bringen, angedeutet. In letzterer Hinsicht ist die Arithmetik, insofern sie den Schlüssel zu der äußeren Welt liefert, soweit diese Sache unmittelbarer Aufzählung ist, d. h. fähig ist, gezählt zu werden, — der erste große Schritt in der Eroberung der Natur. Sie ist das erste Werkzeug des Geistes, das der Mensch bei der Bemühung erfindet, sich von der sklavischen Abhängigkeit von äußeren Kräften zu befreien; denn durch die Beherrschung der Zahlen lernt er trennen und erobern. Er kann eine Kraft zu einer anderen Kraft ins

---

*) Die englischen Ausdrücke „mathematics" und „arithmetic" decken sich nicht nur mit den analogen deutschen Wörtern, sondern schließen auch die niedere und niedrigste Rechenkunst der Elementarschulen ein.   D. Übers.

Verhältnis setzen und gegen ein Hindernis genau dasjenige, was erforderlich ist, um es zu überwinden, konzentrieren. Die Zahl macht auch die anderen Naturwissenschaften möglich, welche auf genauem Messen und genauem Aufzeichnen der Erscheinungen in Bezug auf die folgenden Punkte beruhen: Ordnung der Reihenfolge, Datum, Zeitdauer, Örtlichkeit, Umgebung, Bereich der Einflußsphäre, Zahl der Erscheinungen, Zahl der Wechselfälle. Alle diese können nur mittelst der Zahl genau bestimmt werden. Der erzieherische Wert eines Lehrzweiges, welcher den unentbehrlichen ersten Schritt zu aller Naturwissenschaft liefert, liegt auf der Hand. Psychologisch erscheint seine Wichtigkeit ferner darin, daß er mit einem wichtigen Schritt in der Analyse beginnt, nämlich der Trennung der Idee der Quantität von dem konkreten Ganzen, welches sowohl Qualität wie Quantität in sich schließt. Beim Rechnen läßt man den qualitativen Gesichtspunkt fallen und betrachtet nur den quantitativen. So lange die individuellen Unterschiede (welche insofern qualitative sind, als sie einen Gegenstand von dem anderen unterscheiden) betrachtet werden, können die Gegenstände nicht zusammen gezählt werden. Beim Zählen verliert man die Unterschiede als gleichgiltig aus dem Auge. Da Zählen der fundamentale Vorgang der Arithmetik ist und alle anderen arithmetischen Operationen einfach Mittel zum Schnellrechnen sind, indem man auswendig gelernte Rechnungen anwendet, anstatt jedesmal wieder die Entwickelung der Formel zu wiederholen, so ist damit für den Lehrer der Hinweis auf die ersten Lektionen in der Arithmetik gegeben. Dieser Wink ist denn auch im allgemeinen befolgt worden, und man hat dem Kinde zunächst das Zählen so ähnlicher Gegenstände aufgegeben, daß der qualitative Unterschied ihm gar nicht in den Sinn kommt. Es baut Schritt für Schritt seine Additions-, Subtraktions- und Multiplikationstabellen auf und prägt sie seinem Gedächtnis ein. Dann macht es einen Schritt vorwärts zum Verständnis des Bruches. Dieser ist ein ausgedrücktes Verhältnis zweier Zahlen und deshalb ein komplizierterer Gedanke als irgend einer, dem der Schüler bei der Behandlung einfacher Zahlen begegnet ist. Bei der Idee fünf Sechstel denkt er zuerst fünf und dann sechs, und diese beiden im Gedächtnis behaltend, denkt er das Resultat des ersteren durch das zweite modifiziert. Hier sind drei Schritte anstatt eines, und das Resultat ist nicht eine einfache Zahl, sondern eine Folgerung, die auf einer unvollendeten Operation beruht. Diese psychologische Analyse zeigt den Grund für die Verlegenheit des Kindes bei seinem Eintritt in das Studium der Brüche und der anderen Operationen, die Überlegung voraussetzen. Der Lehrer findet, daß alle seine Hilfs=

quellen in Bezug auf Methode zur Verwendung kommen, um Schritte und Halbschritte zu erfinden, um dem Schüler zu einem ununterbrochenen Fortschritt an dieser Stelle behilflich zu sein. Alle diese Mittel der Methode bestehen in Stufen, mittelst deren der Schüler zu der einfachen Zahl herabsteigt und zu der komplizierten Zahl zurückkehrt. Er verwandelt den einen der Ausdrücke in eine qualitative Einheit und wird so befähigt, den anderen als einfache Zahl zu gebrauchen. Der Schüler nimmt z. B. den Nenner und erklärt seinen Begriff ein Sechstel als seine qualitative Einheit, dann ist ihm fünf Sechstel so klar als fünf Ochsen. Aber er hat diese Rückkehr von dem Verhältnis zu einfachen Zahlen in jeder der elementaren Operationen zu wiederholen — im Addieren, Subtrahieren, Multiplizieren, Dividieren und im Reduzieren der Brüche — und findet im besten Falle den Weg lang und schwierig. Bei den Dezimalbrüchen ist der psychologische Vorgang noch komplizierter; denn der Schüler muß hier von dem ihm gegebenen Zähler den Nenner aus der Stellung des Dezimalzeichens selbst ableiten. Dies verdoppelt die Arbeit des Lesens und das Erkennen der Bruchzahl. Aber es macht Addition und Subtraktion der Brüche beinah so leicht wie das der einfachen Zahlen und unterstützt auch bei der Multiplikation der Brüche. Aber die Division der Dezimalbrüche ist ein viel komplizierterer Prozeß als der der gewöhnlichen Brüche.

Der Mangel einer psychologischen Analyse dieser Vorgänge hat viele gute Lehrer dahin geführt, Dezimalbrüche mit ihren Schülern zu versuchen, ehe sie die gewöhnlichen Brüche aufgenommen haben. Am Ende haben sie sich gezwungen gesehen, zur Unterstützung des Schülers einleitende Schritte zu machen und dabei die Theorie des gewöhnlichen Bruches einzuführen. Sie haben dadurch ihre eigene Theorie widerlegt.

Außer (a) einfachen Zahlen und den vier Species ihrer Berechnung, (b) den gewöhnlichen und Dezimalbrüchen giebt es einen dritten Zahlenvorgang, nämlich (c) die Potenz- und Wurzeltheorie. Es ist dies ein weiterer Schritt im Denkvorgang, nämlich die Beziehung der einfachen Zahl zu sich selbst als Potenz und Wurzel. Die Materialmasse, welche die in der Elementarschule gebrauchte Arithmetik ausmacht, besteht aus zwei Arten von Beispielen, erstens denjenigen, in welchen eine direkte Anwendung einfacher Zahlen, Brüche und Potenzen stattfindet, und zweitens der Klasse von Beispielen, die Berechnungen involvieren, um zahlenmäßige Lösungen durch indirekt gegebene Faktoren zu finden, welche letztere demnach mehr oder minder Veränderung der Funktionen mit sich bringen. Dazu gehören der größte Teil der sogenannten höheren Arith=

metik und solche Aufgaben in den Schulrechenbüchern, die nicht mit Unrecht von dem Direktor der technischen Hochschule in Boston, Dr. Francis A. Walker, in seiner Kritik der Elementarschularithmetik numerische „Rätselspiele" genannt worden sind. Ihre Schwierigkeit ist nicht in dem streng arithmetischen Teile des Lösungsprozesses (der oben beschriebenen dritten Phase) zu finden, sondern vielmehr in der Verwandlung der gegebenen quantitativen Funktion in diejenige Funktion, die leicht numerisch berechnet werden kann. Die Verwandlung von Funktionen gehört streng der Algebra an. Lehrer, welche für die Arithmetik Vorliebe haben, und die selbst erfolgreich die sogenannten numerischen Rätsel ausarbeiten, verteidigen mit großem Ernste die landläufige Praxis, welche so viel Zeit auf die Arithmetik verwendet. Sie sehen darin eine wertvolle Erziehung zur Originalität und logischen Analyse und glauben, daß der Fleiß, der arithmetische Mittel entdeckt, die gegebenen Funktionen bei solchen Aufgaben in einfache numerische Rechnungen der Addition, Subtraktion, Multiplikation und Division zu verwandeln, gut angewendet ist. Andererseits behaupten die Gegner dieser Methode, daß es in der Schule nicht bloß formalen Drill um seiner selbst willen geben und daß immer ein wesentlicher Inhalt gewonnen werden sollte. Sie behaupten, daß die Arbeit des Schülers bei der Umwandlung quantitativer Funktionen durch arithmetische Methoden verloren ist, weil der Schüler einen angemesseneren Ausdruck als Zahl zu diesem Zwecke braucht, und daß dies in der Algebra entdeckt worden ist, die ihn befähigt, mit Leichtigkeit solche quantitativen Umwandlungen vorzunehmen, welche den Schüler in der Arithmetik in Verlegenheit bringen. Sie behaupten deshalb, daß die reine und einfache Arithmetik abgekürzt und die elementare Algebra gleich, nachdem die zahlenmäßigen Rechnungen mit Potenzen, Brüchen und einfachen Zahlen zugleich mit ihren Anwendungen auf Gewichts- und Maßtabellen, Prozente und Zinsen gelernt worden sind, eingeführt werden solle. Im siebenten Jahre des Elementarkursus würde man Gleichungen ersten Grades und die Lösung arithmetischer Aufgaben, die unter die Verhältnisrechnung oder die sogenannte Regel de Tri fallen, zugleich mit anderen Aufgaben, welche komplizierte Bedingungen enthalten, lehren. Im achten Jahre könnten quadratische Gleichungen und andere Beispiele höherer Arithmetik gelernt werden, die in einer befriedigenderen Weise als durch zahlenmäßige Methoden gelöst werden. Man behauptet, daß diese frühere Einführung der Algebra nebst einer sparsamen Anwendung von Buchstaben für bekannte Größen einen bei weitem höheren mathematischen Fortschritt sichern würde, als er gegenwärtig bei allen Schülern erreicht wird, und daß dieselbe viele Schüler befähigen würde, zum mittleren und höheren Unterricht fortzuschreiten, die jetzt unter dem Vorgeben einer mangelhaften Vorbereitung in der Arithmetik zurückgehalten werden, während die wirkliche Schwierigkeit in vielen Fällen eine mangelhafte Fähigkeit ist, algebraische Aufgaben durch eine niedere Methode zu lösen.

Ihr Comité berichtet, daß der Gebrauch, im Rechnen zwei Lektionen täglich zu erteilen, von denen die eine „Kopfrechnen" und die andere „schriftliches Rechnen" genannt wird (weil die Übungen des letzteren mit Bleistift oder Feder geschrieben werden), in vielen Schulen noch fortbesteht. Auf Grund dieser Praxis muß der Schüler dem Rechnen zweimal so viel Zeit opfern als irgend einem anderen Lehrzweige. Die Gegner dieser Praxis behaupten mit einigem Grunde, daß zwei Lektionen täglich in dem Studium der Quantität eine Tendenz haben, dem Geiste eine Neigung in der Richtung quantitativen Denkens zu geben mit einer entsprechenden Vernachlässigung der Kraft der Beobachtung und der Reflexion über qualitative und kausale Gesichtspunkte. Denn die Mathematik giebt keine Rechenschaft über Ursachen, sondern nur über Gleichheit und Verschiedenheit in Größe. Man wirft ferner ein, daß der Versuch, in den in der Elementarschule gelehrten Zweigen sogenannte Gründlichkeit zu erzielen, oft zu weit getrieben wird; in der That so weit, daß in den mechanischen und formalen Stadien des Wachstums ein Stillstand in der Entwickelung (eine Art geistiger Paralyse) hervorgebracht wird. Der Geist verliert in diesem Falle das Streben nach höheren Methoden und weiteren Verallgemeinerungen. Das Apperzeptionsgesetz, sagt man uns, beweist, daß vorläufige (temporäre) Methoden, Aufgaben zu lösen, nicht so vollkommen beherrscht werden sollten, daß sie unwillkürlich oder aus unbewußter Gewohnheit angewendet werden, weil man in diesem Falle eine höhere und angemessenere Lösungsmethode nur mit größerer Schwierigkeit sich wird zu eigen machen können. Je gründlicher eine Methode gelernt wird, um so mehr wird sie ein Teil des Geistes, und um so größer wird der Widerwillen des Geistes gegen eine neue Methode. Aus diesem Grunde raten Eltern und Lehrer jungen Kindern die Gewohnheit, an den Fingern zu zählen, ab, in dem Glauben, daß es schwer halten wird, später diese häßliche Gewohnheit zu beseitigen und sie durch rein geistige Vorgänge zu ersetzen. Die Lehrer sollten besonders bei frühreifen Kindern vorsichtig sein, nicht zu lange bei einem Verfahren zu beharren, welches mechanisch wird, denn dann wird es bereits zur zweiten Natur und zu einem Teile des unbewußten Auffassungsvorganges, infolge dessen der Geist gegen die Umgebung reagiert, ihre Anwesenheit erkennt und sich dieselbe erklärt. Das Kind, welches mit Arithmetik übersättigt worden ist, reagiert in seinem Auffassungsvermögen gegen seine Umgebung hauptsächlich dadurch, daß es ihre zahlenmäßigen Beziehungen bemerkt — es zählt und addiert; da seine anderen begrifflichen Reaktionen schwach sind, vernachlässigt es Eigenschaften und kausale Beziehungen. Ein anderes Kind, das im Erkennen von Farben dressiert worden ist, bemerkt die Farbenschattierungen und vernachlässigt alles Andere. Ein drittes Kind, das durch die beständige Anwendung geometrischer Körper und viele Übung in der Betrachtung geometrischer Grundformen, welche den vielfachen in der Welt existierenden Dingen zu Grunde liegen, in Formstudien übermäßig ausgebildet worden ist, wird natürlicherweise geometrische Formen begreifen und auffassen, dagegen die anderen Phasen der Gegenstände nicht bemerken.

Es ist wirklich ein Fortschritt gegenüber unmittelbaren Sinneswahrnehmungen, den konkreten ganzen Eindruck trennen oder analysieren und die Quantität getrennt für sich betrachten zu können. Aber wenn ein Stillstand in dem geistigen Wachstum hier eintritt, so ist das Endergebnis beklagenswert. Daß solcher Stillstand durch zu ausschließliche Erziehung im Erkennen zahlenmäßiger Beziehungen verursacht werden kann, steht außer allem Zweifel.

Ihr Comité glaubt, daß bei richtigen Methoden und weiser Benutzung der Zeit bei der Vorbereitung der Rechenaufgabe in und außer der Schule fünf Jahre für das Studium der bloßen Arithmetik genügen, — die fünf Jahre sollten mit dem zweiten Schuljahre beginnen und mit beendetem sechsten Schuljahre schließen. Das siebente und achte Jahr sollte der algebraischen Methode gewidmet werden, welche sich mit den Aufgaben beschäftigt, die bei der Verwandlung quantitativer indirekter Funktionen in zahlenmäßige oder direkte quantitative Daten Schwierigkeiten enthalten.

Ihr Comité wünscht indessen nicht dahin verstanden zu werden, daß es empfiehlt, die Algebra, wie sie in den meisten Mittelschulen gelehrt wird, in das siebente oder sogar das achte Jahr der Elementarschule zu übertragen. Der Algebrakursus in den Mittelschulen, in dem Schüler von fünfzehn Jahren unterwiesen werden, beginnt sehr richtig mit schweren Übungen im Hinblick darauf, den Schüler im Analysieren komplizierter Buchstabenausdrücke zu erziehen und ihn zu befähigen, sofort die Faktoren zu erkennen, die in solchen Kombinationen der Quantitäten enthalten sind. Die vorgeschlagene Algebra in der siebenten Stufe muß Buchstaben für die unbekannten Größen gebrauchen und die zahlenmäßige

Form der bekannten Größen beibehalten, selten Buchstaben für diese letzteren verwendend, ausgenommen wo man die allgemeine Lösungsformel oder die sogenannte „Regel" in der Arithmetik darstellen will. Diese Art Algebra hat den Charakter einer Einführung oder eines Überganges zur eigentlichen Algebra. Die letztere sollte in der Mittelschule gründlich gelehrt werden. Früher war es eine gewöhnliche Praxis, Elementaralgebra dieser Art in der Vorbereitungsschule zu lehren und das Studium der eigentlichen Algebra für die höhere Schule vorzubehalten. Aber in diesem Falle wurde eine genügende Übung im Bestimmen von Buchstabengrößen oft vernachlässigt, und infolge dessen war der Schüler oft in seiner vorgeschritteneren Mathematik, z. B. der analytischen Geometrie, der Differentialrechnung und Mechanik in Verlegenheit. Der Vorschlag Ihres Comités beabsichtigt den zwei bereits erwähnten Übeln abzuhelfen: erstens die Schüler in der Elementarschule zu unterstützen, durch eine höhere Methode die schwierigen Probleme zu lösen, welche jetzt in der vorgeschrittenen Arithmetik Platz finden, und zweitens den Schüler für einen gründlichen Kursus der reinen Algebra in der Mittelschule vorzubereiten.

Ihr Comité empfiehlt, daß das sogenannte Kopfrechnen mit der schriftlichen Arithmetik zwei Jahre lang abwechseln sollte, und daß zwei Lektionen täglich in diesem Lehrgegenstande nicht gegeben werden sollten.

C. Geographie.

Der führende Zweig der sieben freien Künste war die Grammatik, die erste im Trivium (Grammatik, Rhetorik, Logik). Die Arithmetik aber stand an der Spitze der zweiten Abteilung, des Quadriviums (Arithmetik, Geometrie, Musik und Astronomie). Wir haben die Gründe betrachtet sowohl für die führende Stellung der Grammatik unter den humanistischen Studien als auch für die führende Stellung der Arithmetik unter den Naturstudien. Das zweitwichtigste Studium nach der Arithmetik unter den Zweigen, die den Menschen mit der Natur in Wechselbeziehung bringen, ist die Geographie. Es ist interessant zu bemerken, daß das alte Quadrivium des Mittelalters die Geographie unter dem Titel Geometrie als den der Arithmetik folgenden Zweig bei der Aufzählung einschloß; der Inhalt und Gegenstand der mittelalterlichen sogenannten „Geometrie" war hauptsächlich eine Abkürzung von Plinius' Geographie, welcher einige wenige Bestimmungen geometrischer Formen beigefügt waren, etwa gleich dem Elementarkursus in der Kunde geometrischer Körper in unseren Elementarschulen. So lange es Elementarunterricht gegeben hat, ist etwas Geographie eingeschlossen worden. Die griechische Erziehung legte auf den Unterricht rücksichtlich des zweiten Buches von Homer's Ilias Gewicht, da dieses den Katalog der Schiffe und eine kurze Erwähnung der Geographie und Geschichte aller griechischen Stämme, die an dem trojanischen Kriege teilnahmen, enthielt. Die Geschichte bleibt im Mittelalter von der Geographie und Geometrie ungetrennt. Die Geographie hat diese umfassende Bedeutung als einen Lehrzweig in den Elementarschulen bis zum heutigen Tage beibehalten. Nach der Arithmetik, die von den abstrakten oder allgemeinen Bedingungen der materiellen Existenz handelt, kommt die Geographie mit dem praktischen Studium des materiellen Wohnsitzes des Menschen und dessen Beziehung zu ihm. Es ist nicht eine einfache Wissenschaft für sich, wie Botanik oder Geologie oder Astronomie, sondern eine Sammlung von Wissenschaften, die in Kontribution gesetzt werden, um die Erde als den Wohnsitz des Menschen zu beschreiben und einigermaßen ihre hervorragenderen Züge zu erklären. Ungefähr ein Viertel des Stoffes gehört streng zur Geographie, ungefähr ein halb zu den Bewohnern, ihren Sitten, Gewohnheiten, Einrichtungen, Industrien, Erzeugnissen, und das übrigbleibende Viertel zu Elementen, die den Wissenschaften der Mineralogie, Meteorologie, Botanik, Zoologie und Astronomie entlehnt sind. Dieses Vorherrschen menschlicher Züge in einem Studium, das sich ersichtlich auf die physische Natur bezieht, betrachtet Ihr Comité als notwendig und gänzlich gerechtfertigt. Das Kind beginnt mit dem, was seinen Interessen am nächsten liegt, und schreitet allmählich zu dem fort, das entfernt liegt und um seiner selbst willen gelernt werden muß. Es ist deshalb ein Fehler, vorauszusetzen, daß die erste Phase der Geographie, die dem Kinde vorgeführt wird, der Vorgang der Landformation sein sollte. Es muß mit den natürlichen Unterschieden von Klima und Land und Wasser und den Hindernissen, welche die Völker trennen, anfangen, die Mittel und Wege studieren, durch welche der Mensch diese Unterschiede durch Gewerbfleiß und Handel auszugleichen oder zu überwinden strebt, alle Orte und alle Völker zu verbinden und es jedem möglich zu machen bemüht ist, sich in die Erzeugnisse aller zu teilen. Die industrielle und kommerzielle Idee ist darum die erste Idee und der Mittelpunkt in dem Studium der Geographie in den Elementarschulen. Sie führt unmittelbar zu den natürlichen Elementen des Unterschiedes in Klima, Boden und Erzeugnissen und auch zu denen in Rasse, Religion, politischem Zustand und Beschäftigungen der Bewohner, unter dem Gesichtspunkt, die Gründe und Ursachen für diesen Gegenprozeß der Civilisation zu erklären, der die Unterschiede zu überwinden strebt. Dann kommt die tiefere Erforschung des Vorganges der Landformation, des physischen Kampfes zwischen dem Zerstörungs- oder Aufbauprozesse der Kontinente und demjenigen ihrer Vernichtung durch Luft und Wasser, endlich die Erklärung der Berge, Thäler und Ebenen, der Inseln, der vulkanischen Gewalten, der Winde, der Regenverteilung. Aber das Studium der Städte, ihrer Lage, der Zwecke, denen sie als sammelnde und verteilende Fabrikcentren dienen, führt auf dem geradesten Wege zu dem unmittelbaren Zwecke der Geographie in den Elementarschulen. Von diesem Anfang und daran als einem bleibenden Interesse festhaltend, schreitet die Erforschung der Ursachen und Bedingungen in konzentrischen Kreisen zu den Quellen des Rohmaterials, den Methoden ihrer Produktion und den klimatischen, geologischen und anderen Ursachen vor, die ihre Lage und ihr Wachstum erklären.

In jüngster Zeit sind, besonders durch das wissenschaftliche Studium der physischen Geographie die Vorgänge, die zur Bildung des Klimas, Bodens und der allgemeinen Gestaltung der Landmassen führen, so genau bestimmt und die Lehrmethoden so vereinfacht worden, daß es möglich ist, ganz früh in dem Lehrkursus von der erwähnten Centralidee zu den physischen Erklärungen der Elemente geographischen Unterschiedes weiterzuführen. Von der Idee des Gebrauches ausgehend, den die Civilisation von der Erde gemacht hat, kann der Schüler in dem fünften und sechsten Jahre seines Schulbesuches (im Alter von elf oder zwölf Jahren) seine Untersuchungen ganz ungezwungen bis zu den physischen Erklärungen der Landgestaltungen und des Klimas ausdehnen. Im siebenten und achten Jahre des Schulbesuches kann noch viel mehr in dieser Richtung geleistet werden. Aber wir glauben, daß das rein menschliche Interesse, das in den ersten Jahren seines Studiums mit der Geographie verbunden ist, nicht dem rein wissenschaftlichen Interesse der physischen Vorgänge weichen sollte, bis der Schüler das Studium der Geschichte aufgenommen hat.

Der erzieherische Wert der Geographie, wie sie in den Elementarschulen ist und gewesen ist, ist ersichtlicherweise sehr groß. Sie ermöglicht eine gewisse Genauigkeit in der geistigen Vorstellung von entfernten Orten und Ereignissen und entfernt ein großes Gebiet bloßen Aberglaubens aus dem Geiste. In unserer Epoche der Zeitungen ist unser Schatz geographischen Wissens fortwährend in Anspruch genommen. Ein Krieg auf der entgegengesetzten Seite der Erdkugel wird in diesem Jahre mit größerem Interesse verfolgt als ein Krieg in der Nähe unserer Grenzen vor der

Aera der Telegraphen. Eine allgemeine Kenntnis der Lokalitäten und Grenzen der Nationen, ihres Standes der Civilisation und ihrer natürlichen Vorteile, zum Weltmarkte beizutragen, ist dem Bürger von großem Nutzen, wenn er sich bei seinem täglichen Lesen eine richtige Ideebil den soll.

Der erzieherische Wert der Geographie erscheint sogar noch deutlicher, wenn wir die Behauptung derjenigen zugestehen, die da versichern, daß die gegenwärtige Epoche der Anfang einer Aera ist, in welcher die öffentliche Meinung durch den Einfluß der periodischen Schriften und Bücher sich zu einer herrschenden Macht ausgebildet hat. Sicherlich kann weder die Zeitung noch das Buch ein ungebildetes Volk beeinflussen: sie können kaum Meinungen bilden, wenn die Leser keine Kenntnis der Geographie haben.

Was den psychologischen Wert der Geographie betrifft, darüber braucht man wenig zu sagen. Sie übt in mannigfaltiger Weise das Formengedächtnis und die Phantasie, sie bringt die Denkkraft in Aktion, indem sie die verschiedenen Reihen der Ursachen zur Einheit zurückführt. Was es an erzieherischem Werte in der Geologie, Meteorologie, Zoologie, Ethnologie, Nationalökonomie, Geschichte und Politik giebt, das ist auch in dem tieferen Studium der Geographie zu finden und in verhältnis= mäßigem Umfang in dem Studium ihrer bloßen Elemente.

Ihr Comité ist der Meinung, daß in jüngsten Jahren in den Unterrichtsmethoden in diesem Zweige eine große Besserung eingetreten ist, die in reichem Maße den geographischen Gesellschaften dieses und anderer Länder zu verdanken ist. Zuerst herrschte eine Art Geographie vor, die man mit dem Namen Seemannsgeographie bezeichnen konnte. Der Schüler mußte alle Kaps und Vorgebirge, Busen und Häfen, Fluß= mündungen, Inseln, Golfe und Landengen in der Welt auswendig lernen. Er belebte dies einigermaßen durch eine kurze Erwähnung von Kuriositäten und sonderbaren Eigentümlichkeiten, als da sind Katarakte, Wasserfälle, Höhlen, merkwürdige Tiere, öffentliche Gebäude, malerische Trachten, nationale Übertreibungen und solche Dinge, die guten Stoff für Matrosen= geschichten liefern würden. Wenig oder nichts wurde gelehrt, den in endloser Anzahl aufgehäuften, unvermittelten Einzelheiten Einheit zu verleihen. Es war ein Fortschritt, als die Methode, Hauptstädte und politische Grenzen auswendig zu lernen, folgte. Damit kam die Aera des Kartenzeichnens. Das Studium der Wasserscheiden und Handels= wege, der Gewerbefleißprodukte und Manufaktur= und Handelsmittel= punkte wurde in den besseren Schulen aufgenommen. Der Unterricht in der Geographie bessert sich beständig durch die unausgesetzte Ein=

führung neuer Mittel, den bestimmenden Einfluß physischer Ursachen in der Vorführung der Elemente des Unterschiedes und des Gegenprozesses des Gewerbefleißes und des Handels klar und verständlich zu machen, durch welchen jeder Unterschied für die ganze Welt nutzbar und jeder Ort zum Teilnehmer der Erzeugnisse aller gemacht wird.

D. Geschichte.

Der nächste Gegenstand, nach der Wertordnung klassifiziert, ist für die Elementarschule die Geschichte. Aber, wie man sehen wird, ist sowohl der praktische wie der psychologische Wert der Geschichte am Anfange geringer und am Ende größer als derjenige der Geographie. Denn die erstere bezieht sich auf die Einrichtungen der Menschen und besonders auf den politischen Staat und seine Entwickelung. Während die Biographie die Laufbahn des Individuums erzählt, berichtet die staatliche Geschichte die Laufbahn der Nationen. Die Nation ist von Leuten, die sich für den erzieherischen Wert der Geschichte interessierten, mit dem Individuum verglichen worden. Der Mensch hat zwei Ichs, sagen diese Leute, das individuelle Ich und das kollektive Ich des organischen Staates oder der Nation. Das Studium der Geschichte ist danach das Studium dieses größeren, zusammengeschlossenen, sozialen und bürgerlichen Ichs. Die Wichtigkeit dieses Gedankens ist in der Weise in seiner erzieherischen Bedeutung klarer dargelegt. Denn dieses bürgerliche Ich lernen heißt den bedeutsamen Zustand lernen, der die Existenz des zivilisierten Menschen in allen seinen anderen sozialen Verbindungen möglich macht — der Familie, der Kirche und den mannigfachen verbundenen Thätigkeiten der bürgerlichen Gesellschaft. Denn der Staat schützt diese Verbindungen gegen gewaltsame Zerstörung. Er bestimmt die Grenzen der individuellen und der verbundenen Thätigkeit, innerhalb deren die einzelne Bemühung die Bemühungen aller verstärkt, und er verwendet die Macht der ganzen Nation, solche Handlungen zu verhindern, die diese sicheren Grenzen überschreiten und einem Konflikt mit der normalen Thätigkeit der anderen Individuen und sozialen Einheiten zustreben. Hobbes nannte den Staat einen Leviathan, um seine erstaunliche Individualität und organisierte Selbstthätigkeit zu betonen. Ohne diesen, sagt er, lebt der Mensch in einem Zustande „beständigen Krieges, Furcht, Armut, Schmutz, Unwissenheit und Elend; innerhalb des Staates wohnen Frieden, Sicherheit, Reichtum, Wissenschaft und Glück." Der Staat ist der Mensch in seiner Gesamtheit, der „die vernünftige Entwickelung des individuellen Menschen, gleichwie eines sterblichen Gottes möglich macht, indem er seine Laune und Leidenschaft unterwirft und dem Gesetze Gehorsam erzwingt, die Ideen der Gerechtigkeit, Tugend und Religion entwickelt, Besitztum und Eigentum, Nahrung und Erziehung erschafft." Die Erziehung des Kindes zu einer Kenntnis dieses höheren Ichs beginnt früh im Schoße der Familie. Das Kind sieht einen Polizisten oder irgend einen städtischen Beamten, irgend ein öffentliches Gebäude, ein Gericht oder ein Gefängnis; es sieht oder hört von einer Gewaltthat, einem Raub oder Mord, dem die Verhaftung des Schuldigen folgt. Das allgegenwärtige, bisher unsichtbare höhere Ich wird nun in seinen Symbolen und noch mehr in seinen Handlungen für dasselbe sichtbar.

Es wird behauptet, daß die Geschichte in der Schule der besondere Lehrzweig für die Erziehung in den Pflichten des Staatsbürgertums sein sollte. Eine solche Behauptung ist wohlberechtigt. Die Geschichte verleiht ein Gefühl der Zugehörigkeit zu einer höheren sozialen Einheit, welche im Interesse der Sicherheit des Ganzen das Recht absoluter Kontrolle über Person und Eigentum besitzt. Dieses ist natürlich die Grundlage des Bürgertums; das Individuum muß dies fühlen oder diese Solidarität des Staates sehen und seine höchste Autorität erkennen. Aber die Geschichte zeigt auch den Konflikt von Nationen und den Sieg eines politischen Ideals von der Niederlage eines anderen begleitet. Die Geschichte enthüllt eine Entwicklung der Regierungsformen, welche immer mehr geeignet sind, individuelle Freiheit und die Teilnahme aller Bürger an der Verwaltung der Regierung selbst zu gestatten.

Völker, welche ihre eigene Regierung erschaffen, haben ein besonderes Interesse an dem Schauspiel politischer Entwicklung, wie sie sich in der Geschichte darstellt. Aber es muß zugestanden werden, daß diese Entwicklung von populären Geschichtsschreibern nicht wohl dargestellt worden ist. Man nehme z. B. das bekannte Beispiel der veralteten Pädagogik, in welcher die römische Republik als eine freiere Regierung aufgefaßt wurde denn das römische Kaisertum, das auf dieselbe folgte; Leute, die sie so auffaßten, wurden scheinbar von den Ideen repräsentativer Selbstverwaltung, die mit dem Worte Republik verbunden scheint, irre geführt. Es war der Anfang einer neuen Epoche, als dieser Irrtum zerstreut und der Student der Hochschulen mit der wahren römischen Bedeutung der Republik bekannt wurde, nämlich dem herrschenden Übergewicht einer Oligarchie an der Tiber, welche entfernte Provinzen in Spanien, Gallien, Klein=Asien, Germanien und Afrika zu ihren eigenen selbstsüchtigen Zwecken mit immer steigendem Übermute regierte. Da das Volk daheim in Rom an den Feldzügen in den Grenzlanden keinen Anteil hatte, wußte es die Eigenschaften der großen Führer nicht zu schätzen, welche wie Cäsar die Nationen durch Geduld, Großmut, Vertrauen und die Anerkennung einer Freiheitssphäre sich unterthan machten. Diese wurde dann den Unterworfenen von den römischen bürgerlichen Gesetzen gesichert, und der Eroberer verschaffte ihr sogar mit Waffengewalt Nachdruck. Der Übergang von der Republik zum Kaisertum bedeutete die endliche Unterordnung dieser tyrannischen Oligarchie und die Anerkennung der Rechte der Provinzen zu römischer Freiheit. Diese Illustration zeigt, wie leicht schlechter Geschichtsunterricht seinen guten Einfluß oder Zweck in einen schlechten verkehren kann. Denn die römische Monarchie unter dem Kaiserreich verschaffte trotz der Wahl solcher Tyrannen wie Nero und Caligula zu dem kaiserlichen Purpur dennoch einen Grad von Freiheit, wie er nie zuvor unter der Republik erreicht worden war. Der Civildienst ging wie gewöhnlich vor sich, indem durch denselben die Angelegenheiten entfernter Länder verwaltet, deren Bewohner in römischem Recht erzogen und mit Liebe zum Anhäufen von Privatbesitz erfüllt wurden. Diese Länder hatten zuvor kommunistisch gelebt nach Art des Stammes oder im besten Falle nach Art der Dorfgemeinde. Der römische Privatbesitz an Land gab der Entwickelung der freien Individualität einen solchen Impuls, wie er unter der sozialen Entwickelungsstufe, die als Dorfgemeinde bekannt ist, stets unmöglich gewesen war.

Geschichte in richtiger Weise lehren, heißt diese hohle Illusion zerstreuen, die dem Individualismus schmeichelt, und die Augen des Schülers für die wahre Natur der Freiheit öffnen, nämlich die Freiheit durch Gehorsam, die man gerechten Gesetzen zollt, welchen ihrerseits von einer starken Regierung Nachdruck verliehen wird.

Ihr Comité hat diese Abschweifung gemacht, um seine Überzeugung von der Wichtigkeit des Geschichtsunterrichts in einem verschiedenen Geiste als dem einer abstrakten Freiheit, welche zuweilen Anarchie bedeutet, ausdrücklich festzustellen, obgleich es auch die Möglichkeit eines entgegengesetzten Extrems zuläßt, nämlich der Gefahr, daß das fortschrittliche Element in dem Wachstum der Nationen und dessen Offenbarung in neuen und besseren politischen Mitteln, welche allen Bürgern politische Vertretung verleihen, ohne die Centralgewalt zu schwächen, zu wenig betont sind. Daß die Geschichte der eigenen Nation in der Elementarschule gelehrt werden soll, scheint durch allgemeine Zustimmung festgestellt zu sein. Die Geschichte der Vereinigten Staaten schließt erst einen Abriß des Zeitalters der Entdeckungen ein, dann das Zeitalter der

Kolonisation. Dies paßt glücklicherweise für die pädagogischen Erfordernisse. Denn das Kind tritt gern an die ernste Wirklichkeit einer festbegründeten Civilisation durch die Stadien ihres Wachstums mittelst individuellen Unternehmungsgeistes heran. Hier kann man von der Biographie als Einleitung in die Geschichte Gebrauch machen. Sie handelt von ausnahmsweisen Charakteren, deren Leben sie in einer oder der anderen Weise zu nationalen oder selbst welthistorischen Beziehungen führt. Diese Individuen werfen auf die Natur und Notwendigkeit der Regierungen Licht und werden ihrerseits durch das Licht, das von ihren Institutionen, welche sie fordern oder hindern, auf sie fällt, beleuchtet. Das Zeitalter des halbprivaten Abenteuerzuges, mit welchem amerikanische Geschichte beginnt, ist für das Studium des Schülers auf der Elementarstufe seiner Erziehung wunderbar geeignet. So auch das nächste Zeitalter, das der Kolonisation. Der Pionier ist der Civilisation einen Schritt näher als der Forscher und Entdecker. In der Kolonialgeschichte interessiert sich der Schüler für die Unternehmung strebsamer Individualitäten, für ihre Überwindung von Hindernissen des Klimas und Bodens, ihre Kämpfe mit der Urbevölkerung, ihre Auswahl von Land für die Niederlassung, das Wachstum ihrer Städte, vor allem für ihre verschiedenen Versuche und den schließlichen Erfolg in der Bildung einer Verfassung, welche lokale Selbstregierung sichert. Eine Epoche wachsender wechselseitiger Beziehung der Kolonien folgt, ein Streben nach Einheit in großem Maßstabe, eine Folge der großen europäischen Kriege, in die England, Frankreich und andere Länder verwickelt wurden, und welche auch die Beziehungen ihrer Kolonien in Amerika tief berührten. Diese Epoche ist auch reich an heroischen Persönlichkeiten, wie Wolfe, Montcalm und Washington, und an gefährlichen Abenteuern besonders in der indianischen Kriegsführung.

Die vierte Epoche ist die Revolution, durch welche die Colonien mit vereinten Kräften ihre Unabhängigkeit und nachher ihre Einigung zu einer Nation sicherten. Der Gegenstand wird schnell mehr kompliziert und stellt an die Geisteskräfte des Schülers im achten Lebensjahre in der Elementarschule schwere Anforderungen. Die Bildung der Verfassung und ein kurzes Studium der wesentlichsten Züge der Verfassung selbst beschließen das Studium des Teiles der Geschichte der Vereinigten Staaten, welcher genügend entfernt ist, um nach Art eines erzieherischen Klassikers behandelt zu werden. Alles ragt bis zu diesem Punkte in starken individuellen Zügen hervor und ist für jenen elementaren Studienkursus wunderbar geeignet. Über diesen Punkt hinaus ist der Krieg mit

England im Jahre 1812 und der Rebellionskrieg nebst den politischen Ereignissen, die dazu führten, bei der gegenwärtigen Generation noch im Gedächtnis von Eltern und Großeltern und ist deshalb zu einem eindringlichen Studium in der Schule nicht so wohl geeignet wie die schon klassisch gewordene Periode unserer Geschichte. Aber diese späteren und spätesten Perioden können und werden zu Hause nicht allein in dem Textbuch der Geschichte, wie man es in der Schule braucht, gelesen werden, sondern auch in den zahlreichen Abrissen, die in Zeitungen, Monatsschriften und in anspruchsvollerer Form erscheinen. In dem eindringlichen Studium, das in Bezug auf die klassische Periode unserer Geschichte unternommen werden sollte, möge der Schüler in der für die historische Forschung angemessenen Methode unterwiesen werden, ebenso in den vielen Gesichtspunkten, von denen jedes Ereignis betrachtet werden sollte. Er sollte zwischen der theatralischen Ansicht der Ereignisse und den wesentlichen Einflüssen unterscheiden lernen, welche als ethische Ursachen von innen wirken. Obgleich er für sehr weitreichende Reflexionen zu unreif ist, muß man ihm doch helfen, die ursächlichen Vorgänge der Geschichte zu sehen. Mit dieser Zucht in historischer Methode ausgerüstet, wird der Schüler all sein verschiedenartiges Lesen und Denken auf diesem Gebiete mit einer mehr angemessenen intellektuellen Reaktion betreiben, als vor dem eindringlichen Studium in der Schule möglich war.

Das Studium der großen Züge der Verfassung zehn oder fünfzehn Wochen lang in dem Schlußjahre der Elementarschule ist von großem erzieherischen Werte befunden worden. Wenn richtig gelehrt, begründet es die Idee der wesentlichen Dreifaltigkeit der Verfassung einer freien Regierung und die notwendige Unabhängigkeit jeder verfassungsmäßigen Gewalt, sei sie gesetzgebend, richterlich oder ausführend. Dies und einiger Einblick in die Art und Weise, in diesen drei Abteilungen die Ämter zu besetzen, und in dem Charakter der Pflichten, mit denen jede Abteilung beauftragt ist, legen die Grundlagen zu einem intelligenten Bürgertum.

Außer diesem eindringlichen Studium der Geschichte der Vereinigten Staaten in dem siebenten und achten Schuljahre möchte Ihr Comité mündliche Aufgaben über die hervorstechenden Züge der allgemeinen Geschichte empfehlen, und zwar eine volle Stunde von sechzig Minuten wöchentlich, am liebsten auf einmal, wegen der systematischeren Behandlung des Gegenstandes der Aufgabe und wegen des tieferen Eindrucks, den derselbe dadurch auf den Geist des Schülers macht.

E. Andere Zweige.

Ihr Comité hat die Hauptzweige des elementaren Studienkursus im Lichte ihres erzieherischen Inhalts und ihrer Bedeutung vorgeführt: Grammatik, Litteratur, Arithmetik, Geographie und Geschichte sind die fünf Zweige, auf welche die erzieherische Thätigkeit der Elementarschule sich vereinigt. Insofern Lesen die erste der Schulkünste ist, ist es interessant zu bemerken, daß der gesamte Elementarkursus als eine Ausdehnung des Lernprozesses der Lesekunst bezeichnet werden kann. Zuerst kommt die Beherrschung des mündlichen Wortvorrats in gedruckten und geschriebenen Zeichen., daran schließt sich das fünffache Eindringen in die besonderen Vokabularien, die a) in der Litteratur erforderlich sind, um die feinen Schattierungen der Seelenstimmung und die feineren Gedankenunterschiede, b) die Technik der Arithmetik, c) der Geographie, d) der Grammatik, e) der Geschichte auszudrücken.

Bei der ernsten Arbeit, diese verschiedenen technischen Wortschätze zu bemeistern, werden dem Schüler tägliche Aufgaben angewiesen, die er durch unabhängiges Studium vorbereiten muß. Die Lektion im Schulzimmer wird damit aufgenommen, daß man die mündliche Darlegung des Schülers über das, was er gelernt hat, prüft und kritisiert, indem man besondere Sorgfalt darauf verwendet, daß man die Erklärung des Schülers mit seinen eigenen Worten zu hören bekommt. Dies erfordert Umschreibungen und Erklärungen der neuen Worte und Phrasen, die im technischen und litterarischen Sinne gebraucht werden, im Hinblick darauf daß man die Bereicherung des Geistes mit den neuen Ideen, welche mit den neuen Worten korrespondieren, sichert. Die Mißverständnisse werden verbessert, und der Schüler wird auf den Weg geführt, mehr kritische Genauigkeit bei der Vorbereitung seiner folgenden Aufgaben zu beobachten. Der Schüler lernt ebenso viel aus dem Hersagen seiner Mitschüler als von dem Lehrer, aber nicht dasselbe. Er sieht in den unvollkommenen Erklärungen seiner Mitschüler, daß sie die Aufgabe mit verschiedenen Voraussetzungen auffassen und folglich einige Phasen des Gegenstandes erblickt haben, die seiner Beobachtung entgingen, während sie ihrerseits Punkte verfehlt haben, die er ganz schnell bemerkt hatte. Diese verschiedenen Gesichtspunkte werden mehr und mehr zu seinen eigenen, und der Schüler wächst so zu sagen dadurch, daß er den Geist anderer zu seinem eigenen Geiste hinzufügt.

Es ist klar, daß es andere Unterrichtszweige giebt, die auf einen Platz in dem Studienkursus der Elementarschule Anspruch erheben können,

z. B. die verschiedenen Zweige der Naturwissenschaft, Vokalmusik, Handarbeitsunterricht, Turnen, Zeichnen u. s. w.

Hier wird die Frage einer anderen Unterrichtsmethode angeregt. Es giebt Aufgaben, welche eine vorausgehende Vorbereitung durch den Schüler selbst erfordern, außerdem andere, die ohne solche Vorbereitung aufgenommen und von dem Lehrer geleitet werden können, der bei der Übung einen großen Teil des zu lernenden Stoffes liefert, indem er die Hilfe der Mitglieder der Klasse einreiht, damit alle das neue Material zu ihrer gegenwärtigen Erfahrung hinzufügen können. Außer diesen giebt es mechanische Übungen zum Zwecke der Erziehung, wie Zeichnen, Schreiben und Turnen.

Zunächst ist da zu nennen gewerbliches und ästhetisches Zeichnen, das in jeder elementaren Schule Raum finden sollte. Die Erziehung von Hand und Auge wird dadurch erzielt. Sodann hilft Zeichnen auch bei allen anderen Zweigen, die Illustration erfordern. Wenn es außerdem noch bei dem Studium der vorhererwähnten großen Kunstwerke angewendet wird, so dient es zur Ausbildung des Geschmackes und bereitet den zukünftigen Arbeiter für eine nützlichere und gewinnreichere Laufbahn vor, insofern feinerer Geschmack bei der Vollendung aller Waren höhere Löhne erzielt.

Die Naturwissenschaft beansprucht in der Elementarschule einen Platz nicht sowohl als ein erzieherisch wirkendes Studium neben der Grammatik, Arithmetik und Geschichte, sondern vielmehr als ein bildender Faktor in den Gewohnheiten der Beobachtung und in dem Gebrauch der Technik, durch welche solche Wissenschaften gelehrt werden. Mit einer Kenntnis der technischen Ausdrücke und einiger Erziehung in den Methoden originaler Forschung, die in den Naturwissenschaften zur Anwendung kommen, erweitert der Schüler seine Ansichten von der Welt und erhöht seine Fähigkeit, neue Kenntnis zu erwerben, in hohem Maße. Denn der Schüler, der mit der Technik der Wissenschaft unbekannt ist, muß ohne geistigen Vorteil an den zahlreichen wissenschaftlichen Anspielungen und Punkten der Belehrung vorübergehen, die in unserer ganzen Litteratur, sei sie nun von einem ephemeren oder bleibenden Charakter, mehr und mehr reich vertreten ist. In einem Zeitalter, das sich so stolz des Fortschrittes der Wissenschaft auf allen Gebieten rühmt, sollte von Anfang an in der Elementarschule ein Lehrkursus in den Elementen der Wissenschaften vorhanden sein. Und dies ist ganz leicht möglich; denn jede Wissenschaft besitzt einige Phasen, die dem Leben des Kindes sehr nahe liegen. Diese vertrauten Gegenstände öffnen die Thüren, durch welche das Kind in die verschiedenen besonderen Abteilungen eintreten kann. Die Wissenschaft, behauptet man, ist nichts, wenn sie nicht systematisch ist. In der That kann die Wissenschaft selbst als die Erklärung jeder Thatsache durch alle anderen Thatsachen verwandter Natur definiert werden. Zugestanden, daß dem so ist, so ist es nicht minder wahr, daß die pädagogische Methode mit der bruchstückartigen Kenntnis, die der Schüler besitzt, anfängt und dieselbe nach allen Richtungen systematisch zu organisieren und auszubauen fortfährt. Demnach kann jede Wissenschaft dort, wo sie der Erfahrung des Schülers am nächsten liegt, aufgenommen und ihre Erforschung fortgesetzt werden, bis die anderen Teile erreicht sind. So wird die pädagogische nicht immer die logische oder wissenschaftliche Ordnung sein. In dieser Hinsicht stimmt sie mit der Ordnung der Entdeckung überein, die gewöhnlich etwas ganz Anderes als die logische Ordnung ist, denn diese ist die letzte Entdeckung. Die Naturwissenschaften haben zwei allgemeine Abteilungen: eine, die sich auf unorganische Materie bezieht wie Physik und Chemie, und eine, die sich auf organische Wesen bezieht, wie Botanik und Zoologie. Es sollte ein spiralförmiger Kursus in der Naturwissenschaft gegeben werden, von dem jeder Zweig mit den Phasen beginnen sollte, welche dem Kinde am interessantesten sind. Ein erster Kursus sollte in der Botanik, Zoologie und Physik gegeben werden, um von dem Bau und der Verwendung der bekannten Pflanzen und Tiere und der Erklärung der physischen Phänomene, wie sie das Kind in seinem Spielzeug, häuslichen Maschinen u. s. w. sieht, handeln zu können. Ein zweiter Kursus, der dieselben Gegenstände deckt, aber mehr Gewicht auf die Klassifikation und die Funktionen legt, wird zu der Kenntnis, die es von den früheren Lektionen und seinen jüngst gewonnenen Erfahrungen her erworben, weiterbauen. Ein dritter Kursus von wöchentlichen Aufgaben, die von dem Lehrer wie vorher im Unterhaltungsstil geleitet werden, mit Experimenten und mit einer Vergleichung der bereits in dem Besitz der Kinder befindlichen Thatsachen der Beobachtung wird ihm ausgiebig behilflich sein, die Resultate der Naturwissenschaft sich zu eigen zu machen. Diejenigen von den Kindern, die für die Beobachtung in einer oder mehreren Abteilungen der Natur besonders beanlagt sind, werden angeregt und ermutigt werden, den besten Gebrauch von ihren Gaben zu machen.

  Nach der Meinung Ihres Comités sollte wöchentlich eine volle Stunde zum Zeichnen und die gleiche Zeit für mündliche Übungen in den Naturwissenschaften vorbehalten werden.

  Die mündlichen Aufgaben in der Geschichte sind bereits erwähnt worden. Der spiralförmige Kursus, der in der Naturwissenschaft auf Grund der schnellen Veränderung in dem Auffassungsvermögen des Schülers von seinem sechsten bis zum vierzehnten Jahre für nützlich befunden worden ist, wird auch für den Geschichtskursus am besten sein, der mit biographischen Abenteuern beginnen soll, welche für das Kind Interesse haben und einen wichtigen historischen Charakter besitzen. Diese werden von dem Heimatland erst nach England, dem Mutterland, und dann zu den klassischen Civilisationen fortschreiten (Griechenland und Rom sind — so zu sagen — die Großelternländer der Amerikanischen Kolonien.) Diese aufeinanderfolgenden Kurse mündlicher Lektionen, die der respektiven Fähigkeit des Kindes angepaßt worden, werden viel dazu beitragen, das Kind mit diesem Gegenstande wohlvertraut zu machen. Mündliche Lektionen sollten niemals bloße Vorlesungen sein, sondern mehr gleich Sokratischen Dialogen, systematische Kenntnis aufbauend, teils von dem bereits Bekannten, teils von neuen Forschungen, teils durch Vergleichung von Quellen und Autoritäten.

Der beste Beweis zu Gunsten der wöchentlichen mündlichen Aufgaben in der Naturwissenschaft und allgemeinen Geschichte ist die thatsächliche Erfahrung der Lehrer, die den Plan einige Zeit ausgeführt haben. Man hat gefunden, daß die Aufgaben in der Botanik, Zoologie und Physik dem Schüler beim Lernen seiner Geographie und anderer auf die Natur bezüglichen Aufgaben große Hilfe gewähren, während die geschichtlichen Aufgaben sehr viel zu seinem Verständnis der Litteratur beitragen und das Interesse an der Geographie vermehren.

Die Meinung Ihres Comités geht dahin, daß die Aufgaben in der Physiologie und Hygiene (mit besonderer Beziehung auf die Wirkungen der stimulierenden Getränke und Narcotica), die von den Staatsgesetzen geboten sind, in diesem mündlichen Kursus in der Naturwissenschaft enthalten sein sollten. Handarbeitsunterricht, soweit die Theorie und Praxis im Gebrauch der Werkzeuge für die Holz- und Eisenbearbeitung in Betracht kommt, hat aus einem ähnlichen Grunde, wie derjenige ist, welcher die Naturwissenschaft zuläßt, gerechte Ansprüche an die Elementarschule. Von der Wissenschaft sind nützliche Erfindungen im Dienste aller Arten von Manufakturen und Transportmitteln ausgegangen. Das Kind der Jetztzeit lebt in einer Welt, in der die Maschinerie ihm beständig nahe ist. Ein Erziehungskursus in Holz- und Eisenarbeit nebst einer experimentellen Kenntnis der Physik oder Naturphilosophie macht es für dasselbe leicht, die Handhabung solcher Maschinen zu lernen. Nähen und Kochen haben nicht dieselben, sondern stärkere Ansprüche auf einen Platz in der Schule. Ein halber Tag wöchentlich ein Semester lang, je in der siebenten und achten Stufe, wird zum Handarbeitsunterricht genügen, in dem Nähen und Kochen von den Mädchen, Holz- und Eisenarbeit von den Knaben getrieben wird. Es sollte indes nicht unerwähnt bleiben, daß die Befürworter des Handarbeitsunterrichts in Holz und Eisen diese Zweige für die Mittelschulen empfehlen wegen der größeren Körperreife und der geringeren Wahrscheinlichkeit in der dritten Periode von vier Schuljahren, sich falsche Gewohnheiten bei der Handhabung der Werkzeuge anzueignen.

Vokalmusik hat seit Langem eine wohlbegründete Stellung in allen Elementarschulen erlangt. Die mühsame Arbeit von zwei Generationen besonderer Lehrer hat die Unterrichtsmittel so vereinfacht, daß ganze Klassen im Lesen der Musik so regelmäßige Fortschritte machen können, wie im Lesen der Litteratur. Bezüglich der physischen Ausbildung stimmt Ihr Comité darin überein, daß es irgend eine Art specieller täglicher Übungen, die sich zusammen auf eine Stunde wöchentlich belaufen sollten, geben muß einschließlich der hauptsächlichsten Arten des Turnens und der deutschen, schwedischen oder amerikanischen Systeme physischer Ausbildung, daß dieselben aber nicht als Ersatzmittel für die althergebrachte Erholungspause (Freiviertelstunde) betrachtet werden sollten, welche für die Bewegung der Schüler im Freien eingerichtet worden ist. Systematischer physischer Unterricht hat vielmehr die Ausbildung des Willens als die Erholung zu seinem Gegenstande, und das muß nicht vergessen werden. Von einer schwierigen Aufgabe zu einer Reihe von Turnübungen übergehen, heißt von einer Art von Willensanstrengung zu einer anderen übergehen. Der Erschöpfung des Willens sollte die freie Laune und die wilde Freiheit der Pause folgen. Aber systematische physische Übung hat ihren genügenden Grund darin, daß sie zu einem anmutigen Gebrauch der Glieder verhilft, Muskeln, die nutzlos oder rudimentär bleiben, wofern sie nicht durch besondere Ausbildung in Thätigkeit gesetzt werden, entwickelt und den Lehrer bei der Schuldisciplin unterstützt.

Ihr Comité möchte in diesem Zusammenhange Unterweisung in der Moral und in guten Sitten erwähnen, welche jedes Jahr in einer kurzen Reihe von Lektionen gegeben werden sollte im Hinblick darauf, daß in dem Geiste eine Theorie der Konventionalitäten der guten und reinen Gesellschaft geschaffen werde. Wenn diese Lektionen zu lang oder zu zahlreich sind, so steht zu befürchten, daß sie bei dem Geiste des Kindes Anstoß erregen. Ihr Comité ist natürlich der Meinung, daß die wirklich inhaltreiche moralische Erziehung der Schule vielmehr von der Disciplin als von dem Unterricht ethischer Theorie geleistet wird. Das Kind wird gelehrt, regelmäßig und pünktlich zu sein und seine Neigung zum Schwatzen oder Flüstern zu unterdrücken — in diesen Dingen Tag für Tag Selbstbeherrschung gewinnend. Das Wesen moralischen Betragens ist Selbstbeherrschung. Die Schule lehrt gutes Betragen. Man besteht darauf, daß der Verkehr des Schülers mit seinen Kameraden ohne böse Worte oder gewaltsame Handlungen vor sich geht. Die höheren moralischen Eigenschaften der Wahrheit und Aufrichtigkeit werden in jeder Schulübung gelehrt, die auf Genauigkeit des Urteils Wert legt.

Ihr Comité hat bereits die Wichtigkeit erörtert, auf der siebenten und achten Stufe einige algebraische Prozesse zu lehren, um bessere Methoden bei der Lösung von Aufgaben in vorgeschrittener Arithmetik zu erhalten; die Majorität Ihres Comités ist der Meinung, daß formale englische Grammatik im achten Jahre aufhören und das Studium einer fremden Sprache, am liebsten Latein, dafür eingesetzt werden sollte. Die erzieherische Wirkung auf einen englischen Schüler, welcher eine Sprache aufnimmt, welche wie die Lateinische Flexionen statt der Präpositionen gebraucht, und welche sich ferner vom Englischen durch die Ordnung unterscheidet, in der ihre Worte in dem Satze gestellt sind, ist sehr bemerklich, und ein Jahr Latein stellt einen Schüler weit über den Gesichtskreis eines Schülers, der mit englischer Grammatik fortgefahren ist, ohne Latein aufzunehmen. Aber die Wirkung des einjährigen Lateinstudiums vermehrt das Fassungsvermögen des Schülers nach vielen Richtungen auf Grund der Thatsache, daß ein so großer Bestandteil des englischen Wortschatzes, der in technischen Fächern, wie Geographie, Grammatik, Geschichte und Litteratur gebraucht wird, einer lateinischen Quelle entstammt, und außerdem sind so viele Spuren in der Form und im Inhalt der menschlichen Kenntnis aus Hunderten von Jahren zurückgeblieben, als Latein die einzige Sprache war, in welcher Beobachtung und Reflexion ausgedrückt werden konnte.

Ihr Comité verweist auf das später in diesem Berichte gegebene Programm bezüglich der Einzelheiten, diese verschiedenen bereits empfohlenen Zweige zu koordinieren.

Der Unterschied zwischen elementaren und höheren Studien.*)

Bei der Empfehlung der Einführung algebraischer Prozesse in dem siebenten und achten Jahre als auch bei der eben ausgesprochenen

---

*) Gemeint sind die „secondary studies", die in der Mittelschule, welche hier mit dem tönenden Namen „high school" belegt wird, gelehrt werden. Dr. Harris

Empfehlung, in dem achten Jahre des Elementarkursus Latein einzuführen, steht Ihr Comité vor der Frage des innerlichen Unterschiedes zwischen elementaren und höheren Studien.

Die Gewohnheit hat Algebra, Geometrie, die Geschichte der englischen Litteratur und Latein zum Range der Mittelschul=Studien erhoben; desgleichen auch allgemeine Geschichte, physische Geographie und die Elemente der Physik und Chemie. In einem Mittelschulkursus von vier Jahren kann Trigonometrie zur Mathematik hinzugefügt werden; einige Wissenschaften, deren Elemente in der physischen Geographie erforderlich sind, können getrennt in besonderen Abhandlungen aufgenommen werden, wie Geologie, Botanik und Physiologie. Auch das Studium ganzer Werke englischer Autoren, wie Shakespeare, Milton und Scott, kann stattfinden. Auch Griechisch wird in dem zweiten oder dritten Jahre des Mittelschulkursus angefangen. Aber in den privaten Mittelschulen wird Latein und so auch Griechisch, Algebra und Geometrie früher angefangen. Zuweilen wird Geometrie vor Algebra aufgenommen, wie es in den deutschen Schulen Sitte ist. Diese Anordnungen sind teilweise auf Überlieferung, teilweise auf den Berechtigungen höherer Anstalten und teilweise darauf gegründet, daß die inneren Schwierigkeiten in diesen Studien ihren Platz in dem Studienkursus bestimmt haben. Von denjenigen, welche behaupten, daß es innere Gründe für die Auswahl und Anordnung dieser Studien giebt, begründen einige ihre Schlüsse auf die Erfahrung, die sie bei der Führung der Schüler durch dieselben gesammelt haben, andere auf psychologischer Grundlage. Die letzteren behaupten beispielsweise, daß Algebra sich mit den allgemeinen Formen des Rechnens beschäftigt, während die Arithmetik die besonderen Fälle des Rechnens behandelt. Was sich mit dem besonderen Falle beschäftigt, ist relativ elementar, was sich mit der allgemeinen Form beschäftigt, steht relativ höher. In der Formel $a + b = c$ giebt die Algebra die Form allen Addierens. Dies kann die Arithmetik nicht leisten, ausgenommen in der Form einer Wortregel, welche die Schritte des Verfahrens beschreibt; ihre Beispiele sind alle besondere Fälle, die unter die allgemeine in der Algebra gegebenen Formel fallen. Wenn deshalb die Arithmetik

---

bezeichnet die „high school" selbst als eine „public secondary school", in welcher Schüler und Schülerinnen gewöhnlich nach einem achtjährigen Elementarkursus aufgenommen werden und vier Jahre verbleiben, die etwa — mutatis mutandis — sich mit den Klassen Quarta bis Untersekunda des deutschen Gymnasiums oder der Realschule decken. Freilich sind auch diese „high schools" in den verschiedenen Staaten sehr verschieden. D. Übers.

ein Elementarzweig ist, so ist die Algebra im Verhältnis zu ihr ein höherer Zweig. So muß auch die Geometrie, obwohl sie nicht direkt auf die Arithmetik begründet ist, eine Bekanntschaft mit derselben voraussetzen, wenn sie räumliche Funktionen auf numerische Formen zurückführt, wie z. B. bei der Messung von Oberflächen und Körpern und beim Bestimmen des Verhältnisses des Kreisumfanges zum Radius und der Hypotenuse zu den beiden anderen Seiten des rechtwinkligen Dreiecks. Die Geometrie beschäftigt sich außerdem mit notwendigen Beziehungen, ihre Beweise erreichen allgemeine und notwendige Schlüsse, welche feststehen nicht allein in solchen materiellen Gestalten, wie wir sie in der gegenwärtigen Erfahrung getroffen haben, sondern im Falle aller möglichen vergangenen, gegenwärtigen oder zukünftigen Beispiele. Solche Kenntnis, welche die Erfahrung überschreitet, steht wesentlich höher im Vergleich zu der ersten Bekanntschaft mit geometrischen Figuren in konkreten Beispielen.

In Betreff der Geometrie behaupten einige, daß die sogenannte „erfindende Geometrie" mit Recht in die Elementarstufen eingeführt werden könne. Darunter versteht man die Übung mit Blöcken in Gestalt geometrischer Körper und den Aufbau verschiedener stereometrischer Figuren aus denselben; andere verstehen darunter die Wiederentdeckung der notwendigen, von Euclid erwiesenen Beziehungen durch den Schüler selbst. Die erstere, d. h. die Übung im Aufbauen mit Blöcken, ist in dem Kindergarten gut genug, wo sie beim Zählenlernen behilflich ist, wie bei der Analyse materieller Formen. Aber für Schüler, die zum Gebrauch von Büchern fortgeschritten sind, ist ihr erzieherischer Wert gering. Die ursprüngliche Entdeckung der Euclidischen Gesetze gehört andererseits angemessener zum höheren als zum elementaren Unterricht. In den jüngst in die Elementarschulen eingeführten geometrischen Textbüchern wird so viel originale Beweisführung verlangt, daß der Lehrer wegen der Unterschiede in der angeborenen Fähigkeit für die Mathematik, die sich bei den Schülern derselben Klasse beim Lösen der Erfindungsaufgaben zeigen, in große Verlegenheit kommt. Einige wenige begabte Schüler freuen sich über die Erfindungen und entwickeln sich rasch in der Fähigkeit, während die größere Zahl der Klasse zu viel Zeit darauf verwendet und so die anderen Zweige des Studienkursus beraubt oder sonst in die schlechte Gewohnheit verfällt, sich von andern bei der Vorbereitung ihrer Aufgaben helfen zu lassen. Einige wenige in jeder Klasse bleiben hoffnungslos zurück und werden entmutigt. Das Resultat ist ein Versuch auf Seiten des Lehrers, das Übel dadurch zu verbessern, daß er eine gründlichere Erziehung in den vorhergehenden mathematischen Studien fordert, und infolge dessen werden die Schüler der Mittelschulen in den niederen Stufen des Kursus zurückgehalten, um ihre „erfindende Geometrie" nachzuholen. Viele werden entmutigt und bleiben zurück; eine noch größere Anzahl erreicht höhere Studien nicht, weil sie nicht imstande sind, über die nutzlos vor ihnen errichtete Barrière zu steigen, errichtet von solchen Lehrern, die da wünschen, daß kein Schüler, ausgenommen ein natürlicher Geometriker, zu höheren Studien aufsteigen solle.

Physische Geographie in ihrer wissenschaftlichen Form wird mit Recht zu einem Teile des Mittelschulunterrichtes gemacht. Der Schüler kann in seinem neunten Schuljahr mit gutem Nutzen die wissenschaftliche Technik der Geologie, Botanik, Zoologie, Meteorologie und Ethnologie sich aneignen und in den folgenden Jahren jene Wissenschaften einzeln aufnehmen und fortsetzen, indem er die Methode wirklicher Forschung anwendet. Der Gegenstand der physischen Geographie ist von sehr hohem Interesse für den Schüler, der die Geographie in den Elementarstufen nach einer zu billigenden Methode studiert hat. Sie nimmt die nächsten Ursachen und Gründe für die Elemente des Unterschiedes auf der Erdoberfläche auf, welche ihm bereits durch seine Elementarstudien vertraut geworden sind, und führt sie auf tiefere, einfachere und befriedigendere Grundsätze zurück. Dieses Studium leistet auch die Arbeit, die Wissenschaften, welche sich auf die organische Natur beziehen, in Wechselwirkung zu bringen dadurch, daß es ihren respektiven Nutzen für den Menschen darlegt. Mit dem Blick, welchen der Schüler von der Mineralogie, Geologie und Botanik, Zoologie, Ethnologie und Meteorologie in ihrer notwendigen Beziehung als geographischen Bedingungen gewinnt, sieht er den Umfang und die große Bedeutung jener einzelnen Untersuchungen. Ein Durst wird in ihm erregt, seine Untersuchungen in die einzelnen Gebiete zu verfolgen. Er sieht auch das Grenzland, in welchem von dem unternehmenden Forscher neue Entdeckungen gemacht werden können.

Die Physik, einschließlich der bis zur jüngsten Zeit sogenannten „Naturphilosophie", nach Newton's Principia (philosophiae naturalis principia mathematica,) bedingt mehr Kenntnisse von der Mathematik zu ihrer gründlichen Erörterung, als der Schüler der Mittelschule wahrscheinlich besitzt. Thatsächlich wurde das Studium dieses Zweiges in der Hochschule*) vor dreißig Jahren aus gleicher Ursache unwirksam ge-

---

*) Dr. Harris versteht hier unter „College" die höchste Schule, die es damals in Amerika gab, und die natürlich tief unter unserem Begriff „Hochschule" stand. Heut ist das College von der Universität auch in Amerika deutlich unterschieden und

macht. Es sollte der Beendigung der analytischen Geometrie folgen. Nichtsdestoweniger kann ein sehr ersprießliches Studium dieses Gegenstandes in dem zweiten Jahre der Mittelschule (high school) oder Vorbereitungsschule (zum „college"; preparatory school) unternommen werden, obgleich die Formeln dann nur so weit verstanden werden können, als sie elementare Algebra allein voraussetzen. Der Schüler gewinnt nicht die genauesten Begriffe von den quantitativen Gesetzen, welche die Materie in ihrem Zustande der Bewegung und des Gleichgewichts beherrschen, aber er sieht wohl die Thätigkeit der Kräfte als qualitativer Elemente der Phänomene und versteht recht wohl die mechanischen Erfindungen, durch welche der Mensch sie zu seinem Gebrauch und zu seiner Sicherheit sich unterthan macht. Selbst in den Elementarstufen kann der Schüler sehr viele dieser qualitativen Thatsachen erfassen und die Erklärung der mechanischen Naturphänomene lernen, sowie andere Anwendungen derselben Prinzipien in der Erfindung, z. B. Schwergewicht fallender Körper: seine Messung durch die Wage; die Rolle, welche dasselbe in der Luftpumpe, dem Barometer, dem Pendel spielt; die Kohäsion der Erde, des Thones, Leimes, Mörtels, Zements, ꝛc., die kapillare Anziehung in Dochten, Schwämmen, Zucker, dem Splint der Pflanzen; die Hebevorrichtungen durch den Hebebaum, Zugbaum, die geneigte Fläche, den Keil und die Schraube; die Hitze in der Sonne, Verbrennung, Reibung, Dampf, Thermometer, Wärmeleitung, Bekleidung, Kochen, ꝛc., die Phänomene des Lichts, der Elektrizität, des Magnetismus und die Erklärung solcher mechanischen Mittel wie Brillen, Teleskope, Mikroskope, Prismen, photographische Apparate, elektrische Spannung in Körpern, Blitz, Kompaß, Magnete in Hufeisenform, Telegraphen, Dynamos. Dieses teilweise qualitative Studium von Kräften und mechanischen Erfindungen hat den erzieherischen Wert, den Schüler aufzuklären und ihn von dem Netz des Aberglaubens zu befreien, der ihn in seiner Kinderwelt teils mit Notwendigkeit, teils auf Grund der ungebildeten Erwachsenen umgiebt. Diesen begegnet er zuweilen in Gestalt von Ammen, Dienstpersonal und Händlern, und ihre Beschäftigungen bieten ihm zuweilen mehr Interesse als die der Gebildeten. Die Märchenwelt ist eine Zauberwelt von unmittelbaren Eingriffen übernatürlicher geistiger Wesen, und während diese für das Kind bis zu seiner Schulzeit und in geringerem Grade auch noch für einige Zeit später ange-

---

führt meist in einem vierjährigen Kursus zu dem ersten Grade A. B. (Artium Baccalaureus), der in manchen Fächern über dem Reifeexamen, in anderen unter demselben steht.   D. Übers.

messen ist, ist sie im erwachsenen Mannes= und Frauenalter nur negativ und schädlich. Sie erzeugt verkrüppelte Entwickelung der Kräfte der Beobachtung und Reflexion in Bezug auf Phänomene und bringt das Wachstum der Seele in dem kindlichen Entwicklungsstadium zum Stillstand. Noch ist auch dieses kindliche Stadium von Wunder und Zauber mehr religiös als das Stadium der Entnüchterung durch das Studium der Mathematik und Physik. Es ist auch der Stillstand der religiösen Entwickelung auf der Stufe des Fetischismus. Die höchste Religion, die des reinen Christentums, sieht in der Welt unendliche Vermittelungen, alle zum Zwecke der Entwickelung unabhängiger Individualität; die Vollkommenheit menschlicher Seelen nicht nur in einer Art Frömmigkeit, nämlich der des Herzens, sondern in der Frömmigkeit des Verstandes, die die Wahrheit schaut, der Frömmigkeit des Willens, die weise Gutes thut, der Frömmigkeit der Sinne, die das Schöne sieht und es in Kunstwerken verwirklicht. Dies ist die christliche Idee göttlicher Vorsehung im Gegensatz zu der heidnischen Idee dieser Vorsehung, und das Studium der Naturphilosophie ist ein wesentliches erzieherisches Werkzeug zur Erlangung derselben, obgleich ein negatives Mittel. Natürlich ist die Gefahr dabei, die geistige Idee des Göttlichen durch die dynamische oder mechanische Idee zu ersetzen und so den Geist in dem Stadium des Pantheismus anstatt des Fetischismus zum Stillstand zu bringen. Aber diese Gefahr kann mittels fernerer Erziehung durch die sekundäre zur höheren Bildung vermieden werden, deren gesamter Geist und Methode im besten Sinne des Wortes vergleichend und philosophisch sind. Denn die höhere Erziehung scheint die Wechselbeziehung der mannigfachen Zweige des menschlichen Wissens in der Einheit des geistigen Gesichtsfeldes, wie es unserer Civilisation von der Religion geliefert worden ist, zu ihrem Gebiete zu haben. Durch sie lernt man jeden Zweig, jede Wissenschaft, Kunst oder Disziplin in dem Lichte aller anderen sehen. Dieser höhere oder vergleichende Gesichtspunkt ist zu jeder Vollkommenheit der Erziehung wesentlich, denn er allein verhindert die Einseitigkeit, die sich so oft in den sogenannten „Steckenpferden" breit macht. Er verhindert auch die üblen Folgen, die von dem Einflusse der sogenannten „Autobidakten" („self-educated men") ausgehen, welche meistens elementare Studienmethoden oder in besten Falle sekundäre Methoden anwenden, die zwar die Thatsachen und Beziehungen der natürlichen und geistigen Erscheinungen betonen, aber sich nicht mit ihren höheren Wechselbeziehungen beschäftigen. Thatsächlich kann die vergleichende Methode nicht wohl eingeführt werden, bis der Student einigermaßen vorgeschritten ist. Er muß seinen elementaren Studienkursus, der sich mit der unmittelbaren Anschauung der Welt beschäftigt, und seinen Mittelschulkursus beendigt und sich mit den getrennten formalen und dynamischen Phasen, die hinter den Thatsachen erster Beobachtung in nächster Ordnung liegen, beschäftigt haben. Die höhere Erziehung vereinigt in gewissem Maße diese getrennten formalen und dynamischen Phasen, verbessert ihre Einseitigkeit und verhindert die Gefahr dessen, was man so oft an den Autodidakten bemerkt, welche zu Unrecht irgend eine der untergeordneten Phasen der Welt betonen und sie zu einer Art ersten Grundprinzips machen.

Hier stößt Ihr Comité auf die Frage nach der Anwendung der vollen wissenschaftlichen Methode in dem Unterricht der Wissenschaft in der Elementarschule. Die richtige Methode ist die der Untersuchung genannt worden, aber jene Methode, wenn sie von dem Kinde gebraucht wird, ist nur eine traurige Karikatur der von dem reifen wissenschaftlichen Manne angewandten Methode, der seit Langem die bruchstückartige Beobachtung und Reflexion, die in der Periode der Kindheit vorwaltet, überwunden hat, ebenso wie die Neigung zur Übertreibung der Wichtigkeit eines oder des anderen Wissenszweiges auf Kosten der höheren Einheit, die alle in eine wechselseitige Beziehung setzt, eine Übertreibung, die sich in dem Besitz und der Anwendung eines Steckenpferdes offenbart. Der ideal wissenschaftliche Mann hat sich von Hindernissen dieser Art befreit, seien sie psychologisch oder objektiv. Der von den Astronomen bezeichnete „subjektive Koefficient" muß klar erkannt und aus der Berechnung, die Anfang, Ende und Verhältnisse zeigt, entfernt werden. Eine Möglichkeit vollkommener Specialisierung tritt bei einem wissenschaftlichen Beobachter erst ein, nachdem er dem elementaren und sekundären Stadium des Geistes entwachsen ist. Ein Versuch, das Kind durch Specialisierung in die volle wissenschaftliche Methode hineinzuzwängen, würde einen Stillstand seiner Entwickelung in den anderen Zweigen menschlichen Wissens außerhalb seiner Specialität verursachen. Es könnte die Daten seiner eigenen besonderen Sphäre nicht angemessen zusammenstellen, wofern es nicht wüßte, wie es die bestimmenden Schranken oder Grenzen, die sein Gebiet von den Nachbargebieten trennen, erkennen solle. Die erste Zeit der Wissenschaft war reich an Beispielen von Verwirrung der Nachbargebiete in der Sammlung ihrer Elemente und Daten. Es ist selbst jetzt noch schwierig zu entscheiden, wo die Physik und Chemie aufhört und die Biologie beginnt.

Ihr Comité macht keinen Versuch, das genaue Verhältnis festzustellen, in welchem das Kind in seinen verschiedenen Entwicklungsstufen ohne den leitenden Einfluß seines Lehrers und Textbuches bei seinen Untersuchungen auskommen kann, aber es legt einen scharfen Protest ein gegen den Wahn, unter welchem verschiedene eifrige Sachwalter der frühen Einführung der wissenschaftlichen Methode zu leiden scheinen. Sie ignorieren in ihrem Eifer das Zugeständnis, das der leitenden Hand des Lehrers gemacht werden muß, der beim Kinde die ihm mangelnde Erfahrung schweigend zuführt, seine besondere Aufmerksamkeit auf diese oder jene Phase ruhig hinlenkt und es von übereilten oder falschen Schlußfolgerungen wie von ungehöriger Übertreibung einzelner Thatsachen oder Grundsätze abhält. Hier liefert der Lehrer den erforderlichen wissenschaftlichen Überblick, der dem Kinde fehlt, aber den der reife Wissenschaftler für sich besitzt.

Einige behaupten, daß die wissenschaftliche Geistesanlage nur für die Wissenschaft, nicht aber für die Kunst, Litteratur und Religion geeignet ist, welche letztere etwas Wesentliches besitzen, das die Wissenschaft nicht erreicht, nicht wegen der Unvollkommenheit der Wissenschaft selbst, sondern wegen der Geisteshaltung, die bei der Beobachtung der Natur angenommen wird. In der analytischen Untersuchung herrscht eine Trennung der Teile von einander vor, im Hinblick darauf, die Quellen der Einflüsse zu finden, welche die in dem Gegenstande gezeigten Erscheinnngen hervorbringen. Der Geist unterwirft alles der Prüfung dieser Idee. Jede Erscheinung, welche existiert, kommt aus einer über sich selbst hinausliegenden Quelle, und die Analyse wird im stande sein, die Quelle zu ergründen.

Nun entfernt sich die Geistesanlage, welche auf einen fremden Ursprung alles dessen besteht, das einen Gegenstand ausmacht, von selbst im voraus von dem Gebiet der Religion, Kunst und Litteratur, wie auch der Philosophie. Denn Selbstbestimmung, persönliche Thätigkeit ist das erste Grundprinzip, das von der Religion und stillschweigend auch von der Kunst und Litteratur, der altklassischen sowohl wie der christlichen, angenommen wird. Schon die Definition der Philosophie schließt dieses ein, denn sie ist der Versuch, die Welt durch die Annahme eines ersten Grundes zu erklären und zu zeigen, daß alle Klassen von Gegenständen jenen ersten Grund zur letzten Voraussetzung haben. Dieser Ansicht gemäß ist es wichtig, den Versuch der Anwendung einer streng wissenschaftlichen Methode auf Seiten des Kindes nicht zu sehr zu beschleunigen. In seinen ersten Jahren erwirbt das Kind die Ergebnisse der Civilisation vielmehr als eine Ausstattung von Gewohnheiten, Gebräuchen und Überlieferungen denn als eine wissenschaftliche Entdeckung.

Man kann von ihm nicht erwarten, daß es gegen die Kultur seiner Zeit auftreten und eine und jede ihrer Konventionalitäten herausfordern soll, sich vor seiner Vernunft zu rechtfertigen. Seine Vernunft ist zu schwach. Es ist vielmehr in dem Geistesstadium der Nachahmung als in dem der Kritik. Es wird die vergleichende oder kritische Methode erst mit der Epoche höherer Bildung erreichen.

Wie dem auch sein mag, so viel steht fest, daß der erzieherische Wert der Wissenschaft und ihrer Methode eine sehr wichtige Frage ist, und daß auf derselben die Lösung der Frage, wo die Specialisierung zu beginnen hat, beruht. Der Anfang mit der wirklichen wissenschaftlichen Methode würde auch eine grundsätzliche Veränderung in den Methoden von Anfang an zur Folge haben. Man kann dies ermessen, wenn man erwägt, wie fest selbst der Kindergarten auf dem Symbolismus und der Kunst und Litteratur beruht. Aber nach der Meinung der Majorität Ihres Comités sollte man an die Naturwissenschaft selbst in den frühesten Jahren der Elementarschule vielmehr in Gestalt der Resultate mit einem Seitenblick auf die Methoden, durch welche diese Resultate erreicht werden, herantreten. In den letzten zwei Jahren (dem siebenten und achten) mag einige Strenge der wissenschaftlichen Form und eine Darstellung der Entdeckungsmethode zugelassen werden. Der Schüler kann auch selbst in gewissem Grade diese Methode praktisch anwenden. In der Mittelschule sollte einige Arbeit im Laboratorium geleistet werden. Aber man kann von dem Schüler nicht erwarten, daß er von selbst die wissen=
schaftliche Methode, mit der Natur umzugehen, sich vollständig aneigne, bevor der zweite Teil höherer Bildung — — die Universitätsarbeit — — beginnt. Nichtsdestoweniger sollte dieses gute Ziel von dem ersten Jahre der Elementarschule an im Auge behalten werden, und man sollte sich demselben schrittweise und beständig nähern. In dem Studium der allgemeinen Geschichte erscheint ein anderer Zweig des Mittelschulkursus. Die Geschichte des Heimatlandes wird für ein Elementarstudium ge=
halten. Die Geschichte der Welt ist sicherlich von der Erfahrung des Kindes einen Schritt weiter entfernt. Einige Lehrer halten es mit richtiger Methode für vereinbar, mit den fremden Beziehungen seines Heimatlandes zu beginnen und sich zu der Weltgeschichte durchzuarbeiten. Die europäischen Beziehungen, die aus der Ent=
deckung und Kolonisation Amerikas entsprangen, liefern für eine Menge von Fragen, die der Schüler in der Elementarschule begonnen hat, die einzige Erklärung. Er sollte von diesem Gesichtspunkte aus von dem bereits Gelernten durch das Studium eines neuen konzentrischen

Kreises von Gründen und Ursachen fortschreiten. Dies ist jedoch nicht der gewöhnlich eingeschlagene Gang. Beim Beginn der Geschichte in der Mittelschule wird der Schüler zu der Übergangsperiode zurückgeführt, gerade in eine Zeit, da historische Spuren zuerst sichtbar werden. Durch diese Anordnung wird er von dem Teile der Geschichte losgerissen, mit dem er bekannt geworden ist, und muß sich mit der Periode herumschlagen, welche zu seinen früheren Untersuchungen in keiner Beziehung steht. Man muß indessen sagen, daß allgemeine Geschichte den religiösen Zusammenhang betont, obwohl jetzt in geringerem Grade als früher. Die Weltgeschichte ist eine Idee des großen christlichen Denkers, St. Augustin, welcher der Meinung war, daß die Welt und ihre Geschichte eine Art antiphonischer Hymne sei, in der Gott seine Ansprachen und die Erde und der Mensch die Antworten liest. Er veranlaßte seinen Schüler Orosius, eine allgemeine Geschichte in dem Geiste seiner Anschauung zu schreiben. Es war natürlich, daß die Geschichten des Alten Testaments und besonders die Kapitel der Genesis den wesentlichsten Teil ihres Inhalts lieferten. Diese allgemeine Geschichte war mit der Religion verknüpft und wurde der Erfahrung des Individuums näher gebracht als die Geschichte seines eigenen Volkes. Die Geschichte mit dem Garten Eden, dem Sündenfall, der Sintflut anfangen, hieß mit dem anfangen, was dem Geiste jedermanns am vertrautesten und lehrreichsten war, weil es seine Lebensführung am nächsten betraf. So lieferte die Religion das apperceptive Material, durch welches die frühen Teile der Geschichte erkannt, klassifiziert und zu einem Teile der Erfahrung gemacht werden. — — Jetzt da die Studien in der Archäologie, besonders die in den Nil= und Euphratthälern die Chronologien und die Berichte früher Zeiten verändern und neue historische Daten der Vergangenheit hinzufügen, welche auf die nationalen Bewegungen und Konflikte der Völker Licht werfen, zugleich mit Daten, durch welche der Stand ihrer gewerblichen Civilisation, ihrer religiösen Ideen und die Form ihrer Litteratur und Kunst bestimmt wird, ist die konzentrische Anordnung all dieses Materials um die Geschichte des erwählten Volkes als Kern nicht länger möglich. Die Frage ist darum erhoben worden, ob nicht die Anordnung der allgemeinen Geschichte für die Mittelschule geändert und so eingerichtet werden solle, daß dieselbe zum Zweck des apperceptiven Materials vielmehr mit amerikanischer Geschichte als mit alttestamentlicher Geschichte verbunden werde. Darauf ist beweiskräftig erwidert worden, daß die Idee einer Weltgeschichte, wie sie St. Augustin auffaßte, das edelste erzieherische Ideal, welches je mit dem Gegenstande der Geschichte ver=

bunden worden ist, sei. Zukünftige Auffassungen der allgemeinen Geschichte werden, sagt man uns, diesen Standpunkt nicht verlassen, selbst wenn sie als ihre Grundlage den Standpunkt der Ethnologie und Anthropologie wählen, denn auch diese werden einen Plan in der menschlichen Geschichte darstellen — — — ein erzieherisches Prinzip, welches die Nationen zur Freiheit und Wissenschaft führt, weil der Schöpfer der Natur dieselbe in ihrer fundamentalen Zusammensetzung zu einer Evolution oder progressiven Entwickelung der Individualität gemacht hat. So wird die Idee der göttlichen Vorsehung beibehalten, obwohl dieselbe dadurch, daß man den ganzen Inhalt der Naturgesetze innerhalb des göttlichen Willens als seiner Arbeitsmethode bringt, umfassender gemacht wird.

Diese Erwägungen, sagen uns die Anhänger der Humanitätsstudien, deuten auf den erzieherischen Wert der Geschichte als Gegengewicht gegen die Einseitigkeit der wissenschaftlichen Methode hin. Die Wissenschaft sucht ihre Erklärung in den mechanischen Bedingungen und Impulsen, die sie von ihrer Umgebung empfängt, während die Geschichte ihren Blick auf die Absichten und Ziele der Menschen gerichtet hält und das Werden der menschlichen Handlungen durch die früheren Stadien des Gefühls, der Überzeugungen und bewußten Ideen studiert. In der Geschichte hat der Schüler Selbstthätigkeit, Reaktion gegen die Umgebung statt mechanischer Thätigkeit oder Thätigkeit durch ein Anderes zu seinem Zweck.

Die Geschichte der englischen Litteratur ist ein zweites Studium der Mittelschule. Sie ist mit sehr gutem Recht über den Bereich der Elementarschule hinausgerückt, denn sie besteht in ihrer Lehre hauptsächlich aus den Biographien litterarischer Männer. Die Schüler, die noch kein großes Litteraturwerk kennen gelernt haben, sollten nicht mit litterarischer Biographie belästigt werden, denn in dem Stadium kann die Größe litterarischer Männer nicht gesehen werden. Plutarch erschafft große Biographien, weil er heroische Kämpfe und große Thaten zeigt. Das Heldentum von Künstlern und Dichtern besteht darin, daß sie alles um ihrer Schöpfungen willen opfern. Die Mehrzahl derselben wird von der Hand des Biographen böse mitgenommen, aus dem Grunde, weil gerade die Seiten ihres Lebens beschrieben werden, die sie um der Musen willen verletzt und vernachläßigt haben. Die Propheten Israels lebten nicht in Stadtpalästen, sondern in Höhlen; sie trugen keine feine Kleidung, tafelten nicht reichlich, noch richteten sie sich nach den Vorschriften der feinen Gesellschaft. Sie waren keine Höflinge, wenn sie sich dem König näherten. Sie vernachläßigten alle anderen Institutionen — — — die Familie, produktives Gewerbe und den Staat — — — um der einen, der Kirche willen und selbst diese nicht in Gestalt des hierarchischen Ceremoniells des Volkes, sondern sie pflegten eine höhere und direktere Beziehung zu Jehovah selbst. So ist es bei Künstlern und litterarischen Männern mehr oder weniger der Fall, daß die praktische Seite ihres Lebens vernachlässigt oder unsymmetrisch ist. Wenn dies aber nicht der Fall ist, so wird es prosaisch und ereignislos befunden werden und kein Licht auf ihre unvergleichlichen Schöpfungen werfen.

Sollte aus diesen Gründen nicht die gegenwärtige Verwendung litterarischer Biographie, wie sie in den Mittelschulen besteht und allmählich ihren Weg in die Elementarschulen findet, entmutigt und die ihr jetzt gewidmete Zeit dem Studium litterarischer Kunstwerke geweiht werden? Man wird zugestehen müssen, daß die Enthüllung der Schwächen der Künstler auf die Jugend einen unmoralischen Einfluß ausübt: z. B. giebt einer vor, ein Dichter zu sein, und rechtfertigt Leichtsinn und Sichgehenlassen durch das Beispiel Byrons. Diejenigen, welche diese Ansicht teilen, sind der Meinung, daß wir die unmoralische und fehlerhafte Seite des Lebens nicht erhöhen sollten, indem wir sie zu einem Studienzweig in der Schule erheben.

Wechselbeziehung durch Studiensynthese.

Ihr Comité wünscht eines anderen Sinnes Erwähnung zu thun, in welchem der Ausdruck Wechselbeziehung der Studien zuweilen gebraucht wird. Dieser Sinn wird von den Verfechtern eines künstlichen Mittelpunktes des Studienkursus aufrecht erhalten. Sie verwenden z. B. De Foe's Robinson Crusoe als Leseübung und verbinden damit die Lektionen in Geographie und Arithmetik. Aber von den Kritikern dieser Methode ist behauptet worden, daß dabei stets die Gefahr vorhanden ist, die litterarischen Züge des Lesestoffes unter dem Beiwerk der Mathematik und Naturwissenschaft zu vergraben. Wenn das Material zu anderen Zweigen in Verbindung mit den litterarischen Übungen gesucht werden soll, wird es die Aufmerksamkeit von der poetischen Einheit ablenken. Andererseits kann die Arithmetik und Geographie nicht frei und umfassend entwickelt werden, wenn beide auf die Gelegenheit warten müssen, die sich in einem Gedicht oder einer Novelle für ihre Entwickelung darbietet. Eine Wechselbeziehung dieser Arbeit ist, statt eine tiefere Wechselbeziehung zu sein, wie sie sich in allen Teilen des menschlichen Wissens durch die Universitätsstudien findet, vielmehr eine hohle, un=

interessante Art der Wechselbeziehung, die uns an das System der Mnemotechnik oder des künstlichen Gedächtnisses erinnert, welches die Ideenassoziation der Thatsachen und Ereignisse mit ihren Ursachen und der Geschichte ihrer Entwickelung vernachlässigt und nach unwesentlichen Wortspielereien, Witzen oder zufälligen Einfällen sucht mit der Absicht, das Gedächtnis zu stärken. Die Wirkung dieses Vorganges ist, die Kraft des systematischen Denkens zu schwächen, das sich mit wesentlichen Beziehungen beschäftigt, und dafür ein chaotisches Sicherinnern zu setzen, welches Dinge durch falsche und scheinbare Beziehungen nicht von Dingen und Ereignissen, sondern von den sie bezeichnenden Worten zusammenbindet.

Die Wechselbeziehung von Geographie und Arithmetik und Geschichte in der Einheit und durch die Einheit eines Dichterwerkes ist im besten Falle eine künstliche Wechselbeziehung, die der wahren, objektiven Wechselbeziehung im Wege stehen wird. Sie ist ein ephemeres, für Schulzwecke errichtetes Gerüst. Der Unterricht sollte solche nur für den Augenblick errichtete Gerüste möglichst vermeiden, und wenn überhaupt gebraucht, sollten sie nur für den Tag gebraucht werden, nicht für das Jahr, wegen der Gefahr, in dem Geiste des Kindes ein Begriffszentrum zu errichten, das mit dem wahren, von der Civilisation erforderten Begriffszentrum nicht übereinstimmen wird. Die Geschichte von Robinson Crusoe hat für das Kind als eine Aufgabe in der Gesellschafslehre, die ihm die Hilflosigkeit des isolierten Menschen und die Verstärkung, die ihm durch die Gesellschaft geleistet wird, darlegt, ein tiefes Interesse. Sie zeigt die Wichtigkeit der Arbeitsteilung. Alle Kinder sollten dieses Buch in den späteren Jahren des Elementarkursus lesen, und einige nützliche Erörterungen können in der Schule bezüglich seiner Bedeutung daran geknüpft werden. Aber De Foe beschrieb darin nur den Abenteuergeist, den er in jener Epoche bei seinen Landsleuten vorfand, als England nach der Niederlage der Armada seine Laufbahn der Eroberung auf den Meeren begann, die mit der Kolonisation und dem Handel der Welt endete. Die Liebe zum Abenteuer dauert unter allen Anglo-Sächsischen Völkern bis heute fort, und mehr als bei anderen Nationalitäten findet sich bei den englisch sprechenden Bevölkerungen eine innige Freude daran, von Grund auf Civilisation aufzubauen. Aber dies ist nur eine Phase des anglo-sächsischen Geistes, folglich ist die Geschichte Crusoe's nicht ein geeigneter Mittelpunkt für ein einjähriges Studium in der Schule. Sie läßt Städte, Regierungen, den Welthandel, die internationalen Beziehungen, die Kirche, Zeitungen und Bücher außer Acht und thut ihrer nicht einmal Erwähnung.

Ihr Comité möchte in diesem Zusammenhange auf die Wichtigkit, des pädagogischen Grundsatzes der Analyse und Trennung, als der Synthese und Wechselbeziehung vorausgehend, aufmerksam machen. Eine strenge Trennung der Elemente jedes Zweiges ist notwendig, um einen klaren Begriff dessen, was in einem besonderen Lehrgebiet individuell und eigenartig ist, zu gewinnen. Sonst wird man von jedem seinen besonderen Beitrag zu dem Ganzen nicht erhalten. Daß in der Art Wechselbeziehung, die in jedem Zweige alle Zweige zu lehren versucht, eine große Gefahr liegt, wird von diesem Gesichtspunkt aus klar zu Tage treten.

III. Das Schulprogramm.

Um für die mannigfachen in diesem Bericht empfohlenen Zweige in der Elementarschule Raum zu finden, wird man notwendigerweise mit der für das Schuljahr bestimmten Zeit, die mit Ausschluß der Ferien und Feiertage etwa 200 Tage beträgt, sparsam umgehen müssen. Fünf Tage wöchentlich und fünf Stunden wirklicher Schularbeit oder etwas weniger täglich, wenn man die Pausen zur Erholung abrechnet, ergeben fünf und zwanzig Stunden wöchentlich. Es sollte möglichste Abwechslung der Lehrstunden und Schulübungen (das Wort „recitation" wird in den Vereinigten Staaten für die Lektion gebraucht, welche von dem Lehrer geleitet wird und die kritische Aufmerksamkeit der ganzen Klasse verlangt) stattfinden. Die Studien, welche das klarste Denken erfordern, sollten gewöhnlich am frühen Morgen aufgenommen werden, so die Arithmetik in der zweiten halben Stunde des Morgens und die Grammatik in der halben Stunde, die direkt der Erholungspause im Freien am Morgen folgt. Einige, welche häusliche Arbeit verhindern, oder ihr Maß wenigstens kontrollieren wollen, halten es für ratsam, die Rechenstunde der Grammatik folgen zu lassen, so daß der zu Hause vorbereitete Zweig Grammatik statt der Arithmetik sein wird. Die Erfahrung lehrt, daß, wenn mathematische Aufgaben zur Lösung nach Hause mitgenommen werden, zwei schlechte Gewohnheiten entstehen, nämlich in einem Falle läßt sich der Schüler von seinen Eltern oder anderen helfen und verliert so im gewissen Maße seine eigene Kraft, Schwierigkeiten durch wackere und beharrliche Angriffe ohne fremde Hilfe zu überwinden; das andere Übel ist eine Gewohnheit, lange Stunden in der Vorbereitung einer Aufgabe zu verbringen, die in dreißig Minuten gelöst werden sollte, wenn alle Geisteskräfte frisch und bei der Hand sind. Ein Durchschnittskind kann bei der Vorbereitung einer Rechenaufgabe drei Stunden zu-bringen. Ja, bei den wiederholten Bemühungen, eins der sogenannten „Rätsel" zu lösen, kann eine ganze Familie den ganzen Abend dazu verwenden. Eins der unangenehmen Resultate des folgenden Tages ist es, daß der Lehrer, welcher die Aufgabe leitet, niemals die genaue Fähigkeit und das Maß des Fortschrittes seines Schülers kennt; bei der Schulübung prüft er die Kenntnis und Vorbereitung des Schülers plus eine unbekannte Quantität Vorbereitungsarbeit, die von Eltern oder anderen entlehnt ist. Er erhöht sogar die Länge der Aufgaben und verlangt mehr häusliche Arbeit, während die Aufgabe bereits die eigene Fähigkeit des Schülers übersteigt.

Die Lehrstunden sollten so geordnet sein, daß sie solche Übungen, welche Erholung von geistiger Abspannung gewähren, zwischen solche gelegt sind, die an die Denkkraft große Anforderungen stellen. Solche Übungen, wie Singen und Turnen, Schreiben und Zeichnen, auch wohl Lesen sind ihrer Natur nach eine Erholung von denjenigen Lehrstunden, welche das Gedächtnis, die kritische Aufmerksamkeit und den Verstand anstrengen, wie die Arithmetik, Grammatik und Geschichte.

Ihr Comité ist zu keiner Übereinstimmung gekommen in der Frage, ob Schüler, welche die Schule früh verlassen, einen von dem Studiengange derjenigen verschiedenen Kursus haben sollten, welche zur Mittelschule und zu höherer Arbeit übergehen. Auf der einen Seite wird behauptet, daß die, welche die Schule früh verlassen, einen praktischen Kursus haben müßten und ihnen die Studien erspart werden sollten, die ihrer Natur nach zur Vorbereitung für den Mittelschul- und höheren Unterricht zu dienen scheinen. Solche Studien, wie beispielsweise Algebra und Latein, sollten nur dann aufgenommen werden, wenn der Schüler dieselben lange genug fortsetzen will, um den Kursus der Mittelschule zu vollenden. Darauf wird auf der anderen Seite erwidert, daß es am besten sei, einen Kursus für alle zu haben, weil jede Schulbildung im besten Falle nur eine Einweihung des Schülers in die Kunst des Lernens ist, und daß, wo immer er in seinem Schulkursus aufhört, er mit Hilfe der öffentlichen Bibliothek und des häuslichen Studiums fortfahren sollte, sich in der Wissenschaft und Litteratur weiter zu bilden. Es wird ferner behauptet, daß ein kurzer Kursus in höheren Studien, wie Latein und Algebra, anstatt nutzlos zu sein, vielmehr von höherem Werte ist als irgend welche Elementarstudien, die sie etwa ersetzen möchten. Die ersten zehn Lektionen in Algebra geben dem Schüler die Grundidee von dem allgemeinen Ausdruck der arithmetischen Lösungen mittelst Buchstaben und anderer Symbole. Ein sechsmonatiges Studium dieser Wissenschaft

giebt ihm die Fähigkeit, die Methode beim Feststellen der mannigfachen
Bedingungen einer Aufgabe, in der Gesellschaftsrechnung oder beim Feststellen eines Wertes, der auf mehreren Umwandlungen der gegebenen
Data beruht, anzuwenden. Man behauptet sogar, daß die ersten wenigen
Lektionen in irgend einem Zweige einen relativ höheren Erziehungswert
haben als eine gleiche Anzahl der folgenden Lektionen, weil die Grundgedanken und Grundgesetze des neuen Studiums an den Anfang gestellt
sind. Im Lateinischen z. B. lernt der Schüler in der ersten Woche
seines Studiums die ihm fremde Erscheinung einer Sprache kennen, die
durch Flexion das leistet, was seine eigene Sprache durch Präpositionen
und Hilfszeitwörter leistet. Er ist noch mehr erstaunt zu finden, daß
die Wortordnung in einem Satze im Gebrauch des Lateinischen ganz
und gar verschieden ist von der, an welche er gewöhnt ist. Er beginnt
ferner in den lateinischen Worten viele Wurzeln oder Stämme zu erkennen, welche gebraucht werden, um unmittelbare sinnliche Gegenstände
zu bezeichnen, während sie in seine englische Sprache aufgenommen
worden sind, um seine Unterscheidungsschattierungen in Gedanken oder
Gefühlen auszudrücken. Durch diese drei Dinge werden seine Beobachtungskräfte in Bezug auf Sprache so zu sagen mit neuen Fähigkeiten bewaffnet. Nichts, was er bisher in der Grammatik gelernt hat,
ist so radikal und weitreichend, als was er in der ersten Woche seines
Lateinstudiums lernt. Die lateinische Wortordnung in einem Satze weist
auf eine verschiedene geistige Anordnung in dem Fassungsprozeß (Begriffsvorgang) und Gedankenausdruck hin. Diese Wortordnung wird
durch Deklinationen möglich gemacht. Das heißt so viel als Präpositionen
den Wortendungen beifügen, welche sie so in adjektivische oder adverbiale
Bestimmungswörter verwandeln, während die getrennten Präpositionen
des englischen durch die Stellung in dem Satze ihre grammatische Beziehungen andeuten. Diese Beobachtungen und die neue Einsicht in die
Etymologie englischer Wörter, die eine lateinische Ableitung haben, sind
gewissermaßen geistige Samenkörner, welche wachsen und das ganze
Leben lang Frucht tragen werden in einer besseren Beherrschung der
Muttersprache. Dies Alles wird schon in einer sehr kurzen Zeit, die dem
Lateinischen in der Schule gewidmet wird, gewonnen werden.

Zeitdauer für jeden Zweig.

Ihr Comité empfiehlt, daß je eine Stunde von 60 Minuten
wöchentlich in dem Programm für jeden der folgenden Zweige acht Jahre
lang angewiesen werde: physische Ausbildung, Vokalmusik, mündliche

Übungen in Naturwissenschaft (einschließlich Hygiene unter diesem Titel), mündliche Übungen in der Geographie und allgemeinen Geschichte, und daß dieselbe Zeitdauer wöchentlich vom zweiten bis zum achten Jahre dem Zeichenunterricht gewidmet werde, ebenso auch dem Handarbeits= unterricht während des siebenten und achten Jahres, und daß derselbe in Nähen und Kochen für die Mädchen, in Holz= und Eisenarbeit für die Knaben bestehe.

Ihr Comité empfiehlt, daß Lektüre wenigstens eine Stunde lang täglich während der ganzen acht Jahre gegeben werde, wobei es sich aber von selbst versteht, daß in dem ersten und zweiten Jahre zwei oder mehr Stunden im Lesen täglich gegeben werden sollen, weil in dieser Zeit die Lektion notwendigerweise sehr kurz ist wegen der Unfähigkeit des Kindes, fortgesetzt angespannte Aufmerksamkeit auf den Gegenstand zu richten, und weil dasselbe nur geringes Vermögen hat, sich der Vor= bereitung der Aufgaben selbst zu widmen. In den ersten drei Jahren sollte das Lesen auf Stücke in dem mündlichen Stile beschränkt werden, aber ausgewählte Stücke aus den Klassikern der Sprache in Prosa und Poesie sollten dem Schüler von Zeit zu Zeit vorgelesen und Erörterungen solcher Züge der ausgewählten Lesestücke daran geknüpft werden, wie sie für die Schüler von Interesse sind. Nach dem dritten Jahre, glaubt ihr Comité, sollte sich die Leseübung auf ausgewählte Stücke der englischen klassischen Autoren erstrecken und die Arbeit zwischen (a) Aussprache, (b) die grammatischen Eigentümlichkeiten der Sprache mit Einschluß des Buchstabierens, der Definitionen syntaktischer Konstruktion, Interpunktion und prosodischer Figuren und (c) den litterarischen Inhalt geteilt werden; der letztere sollte die haupt= und nebensächlichen Gedanken, die gemalten Seelenstimmungen, die beschriebenen Handlungen, die Stilmittel umfassen, um einen starken Eindruck auf den Leser hervorzubringen. Ihr Comité wünscht die Wichtigkeit des letzten Punktes — — den des litterarischen Studiums — — — besonders zu betonen, welches letztere in der Periode vom vierten bis zum achten Jahre mehr und mehr von der Zeit der Schulstunde von Stufe zu Stufe beanspruchen sollte. In dem vierten Jahre und vorher sollte der erste Punkt, — — — der der Aussprache — — am wichtigsten sein. In dem fünften und sechsten Jahre sollte der zweite Punkt, — — — der des Buchstabierens, Definierens und Interpungierens — — — ein wenig über die zwei anderen Punkte vor= herrschen. Vom fünften bis zum achten Jahre sollte Lesen ganzer Geschichten ge= pflegt werden, wie Gulliver's Reisen, Robinson Crusoe, Rip Van Winkle, Die Lady vom See, Hiawatha und andere Geschichten, die in Stil und

Stoff der Fähigkeit des Schülers angemessen sind. Eine Stunde wöchentlich sollte der Konversation über die hervorstehenden Züge der Geschichte, ihre litterarische und ethische Tragweite gewidmet werden.

Ihr Comité stimmt in der Meinung überein, daß beim Lehren der Sprache Vorsorge getroffen werden solle, daß sich der Schüler durch Schreibübungen und Originalaufsätze stark mache. Zuerst wird der Schüler nur seinen mündlichen Wortschatz anwenden, aber wie er die technischen Vokabularien der Geographie, Arithmetik und Geschichte beherrschen lernt und sich das höhere litterarische Vokabularium seiner Sprache aneignet, so wird er entsprechend seinen Sprachgebrauch erweitern. Täglich von dem ersten Jahre an soll das Kind eine Aufgabe oder einen Teil einer Aufgabe schriftlich vorbereiten. Ihr Comité hat unter dem Titel mündliche Grammatik (von dem ersten bis zur Mitte des fünften Jahres) eine Phase dieser schriftlichen Arbeit eingeschlossen, die dem Studium der litterarischen Form und der technischen Formalitäten des Aufsatzes gewidmet ist in solchen Übungen wie Briefschreiben, geschriebene Revuen der verschiedenen gelernten Zweige, Berichte der mündlichen Aufgaben in Geschichte und Naturgeschichte, Umschreibung der Geschichte und Prosastücke der Lesebücher und schließlich Aufsätze oder geschriebene Essays über geeignete vom Lehrer aufgegebene Themata, die aber aus den in der Schule gelernten Gebieten der Erkenntnis gewählt werden sollten. Alle Umschreibungen der Poesie sollten in Bezug auf den guten oder schlechten Geschmack, der sich in der Wahl der Worte zeigt, sorgfältig geprüft werden; Parodien sollten niemals gestattet sein.

Ihr Comité glaubt, daß der alte Stil im Aufsatzschreiben zu formell war. Er wurde von dem anderen Arbeitsgebiet des Schülers zu fern gehalten. Anstatt einen geschriebenen Bericht von dem zu geben, was der Schüler in der Arithmetik, Geographie, Grammatik, Geschichte und Naturwissenschaft gelernt hatte, versuchte er künstliche Beschreibungen solcher Themata wie „Frühling", „Glück", „Beständigkeit", „Freundschaft", oder sonst etwas außerhalb der Sphäre seiner Schulstudien Liegendes.

Ihr Comité hat sich bereits dahin ausgesprochen, daß ein guter englischer Stil nicht sowohl durch das Studium der Grammatik als durch Vertrautheit mit großen Meisterwerken der Litteratur erworben werde. Wir empfehlen besonders, daß Schüler, welche die vierte und fünfte Stufe der Lesebücher mit den aus den großen Autoren ausgewählten Leseproben begonnen haben, schriftliche Umschreibungen der poetischen oder Prosamuster des Stils machen sollten, wobei sie ihren eigenen Wortvorrat beim Ausdrücken der Gedanken so weit als möglich gebrauchen und von dem Autor die Worte und Phrasen der Untersuchung borgen sollten, wo ihre eigenen Hilfsmittel sie im Stiche lassen. In dieser Weise lernt der Schüler sehen, was der große Autor geleistet hat, die Sprache zu bereichern, und geeignete Mittel des Ausdrucks dafür zu liefern, was vorher in Worten nicht dargestellt oder zum mindesten nicht in so glücklicher Weise dargestellt werden konnte. Ihr Comité glaubt, daß jede Lehrstunde in einer Hinsicht ein Versuch ist, die Gedanken und Belehrung der Lehrstunde in des Schülers eigenen Worten auszudrücken, und in dieser Weise als eine Anfangsübung im schriftlichen Aufsatz angesehen werden kann. Die regelmäßige wöchentliche schriftliche Übersicht der wichtigen in den verschiedenen Zweigen gelernten Gegenstände ist nur gründlichere Übung im Aufsatzschreiben, wobei sich der Schüler bemüht, sein Wissen zu sammeln und es systematisch und in angemessener Sprache auszudrücken. Interpunktion, Buchstabieren, Syntax, Orthographie, Auswahl der Worte und Stil sollten aber in Verbindung mit den anderen Lektionen außer der eigentlichen Sprachstunde nicht zum Gegenstande der Kritik gemacht werden. Aber der Schüler wird nichtsdestoweniger aus den schriftlichen und mündlichen Schulübungen Sprache lernen. Die mündlichen Grammatik-Lektionen von dem ersten bis zur Mitte des fünften Jahres sollten sich hauptsächlich mit dem Sprachgebrauch beschäftigen und schrittweise die grammatische Technik einführen, wie sie erforderlich ist, um richtige Formen und Verletzungen im Gebrauch der Sprache genau zu beschreiben.

Ihr Comité glaubt, daß einige Gefahr besteht, in den ersten vier Jahren bei diesen mündlichen und schriftlichen Sprachübungen des Schülers Zeit zu verlieren, dadurch daß man seine Arbeit auf den Ausdruck gewöhnlicher Alltagsgedanken beschränkt, welche zu den Gegenständen der anderen Lektionen in keiner Beziehung stehen, besonders wenn der Ausdruck auf den Wortschatz der Konversation beschränkt ist. Solcher Unterricht ist streng und gerecht verurteilt worden als ein Unterricht im sogenannten Geschwätz und Geplauder vielmehr als in einem edlen Gebrauch der englischen Sprache. Es ist klar, daß der Schüler einen edlen und würdigen Stoff für den schriftlichen Aufsatz haben sollte, und was ist für seinen Zweck so gut als die Themata, die er in seinen regelmäßigen Lektionen zu beherrschen versucht hat? Die Leseübung wird Stoff für den litterarischen Stil, die Geographie für den wissenschaftlichen Stil und die Arithmetik für den geschäftlichen Stil bieten; denn alle Stilarten sollten gelernt werden.

Ihr Comité empfiehlt, daß ausgewählte Listen von schwer zu buchstabierenden Worten aus den Lesestunden angefertigt und durch häufiges Schreiben und mündliches Buchstabieren während des vierten, fünften und sechsten Jahres zu eigen gemacht werden.

Ihr Comité empfiehlt, daß der Gebrauch eines Textbuches in der Grammatik mit der zweiten Hälfte des fünften Jahres beginne und fortgesetzt werde bis zum Studium des Lateinischen in der achten Stufe und daß demselben eine tägliche Übung von fünfundzwanzig bis dreißig Minuten zu widmen sei. Für Latein empfehlen wir eine tägliche Übung von 30 Minuten für das achte Jahr. Für die Arithmetik halten wir Arbeit mit Zahlen von dem ersten bis zum achten Jahre in einer Lektion täglich für genügend, aber der Gebrauch des Textbuches im Rechnen sollte nach unserer Meinung nicht vor dem ersten Viertel des dritten Jahres beginnen. Wir empfehlen, daß die Anwendung der Elementaralgebra auf die Arithmetik, wie vordem erklärt, für die reine Arithmetik im siebenten und achten Jahre substituiert werde und zwar in einer Lektion täglich.

Ihr Comité empfiehlt, daß Orthographie als ein besonderer Zweig in den ersten sechs Jahren mindestens drei Stunden wöchentlich gelehrt werde.

Geographie sollte nach der Meinung Ihres Comités mit mündlichen Übungen in dem zweiten Jahre und mit einem Textbuch im dritten Viertel des dritten Jahres beginnen und mit täglich einer Stunde bis zum Schluß des sechsten Jahres fortgesetzt werden und im siebenten und achten Jahre mit drei Stunden wöchentlich.

Die Geschichte der Vereinigten Staaten mit dem Gebrauch eines Textbuches empfiehlt Ihr Comité für das siebente und die erste Hälfte des achten Jahres, täglich eine Lektion, die Verfassung der Vereinigten Staaten für das dritte Viertel des achten Jahres.

Das folgende Schema wird die Stundenzahl der Woche für jedes Viertel jedes Jahres zeigen:

Lesen. Acht Jahre mit täglichen Lektionen.

Rechtschreiben. Sechs Jahre, zehn Lektionen wöchentlich für die ersten zwei Jahre, fünf für das dritte und vierte, drei für das fünfte und sechste Jahr.

Buchstabierlisten. Im vierten, fünften und sechsten Jahre vier Lektionen wöchentlich.

Grammatik. Mündlich mit Aufsätzen oder Diktierübungen, das erste Jahr bis zur Mitte des fünften Jahres, Textbuch von der Mitte des fünften Jahres bis zum Schluß des siebenten Jahres. Fünf Lektionen wöchentlich. (Aufsatzlehre sollte unter diesem Titel enthalten sein. Aber die schriftlichen Prüfungen der verschiedenen Zweige sollten unter dem Titel Aufsatzlehre stehen).

Latein, Französisch oder Deutsch. Achtes Jahr, fünf Stunden wöchentlich.

Arithmetik. Mündlich im ersten und zweiten Jahr, Textbuch im dritten bis zum sechsten Jahr, fünf Stunden wöchentlich.

Algebra. Siebentes und achtes Jahr, fünf Lektionen wöchentlich.

Geographie. Mündliche Übungen im zweiten Jahr bis Mitte des dritten Jahres, Textbuch von der Mitte des dritten Jahres, fünf Lektionen wöchentlich bis zum siebenten Jahre und drei Lektionen bis zum Schlusse des achten.

Naturwissenschaft und Hygiene. Sechzig Minuten wöchentlich, acht Jahre.

Geschichte der Vereinigten Staaten. Fünf Stunden wöchentlich im siebenten und in der ersten Hälfte des achten Jahres.

Verfassung der Vereinigten Staaten. Im dritten Viertel des achten Jahres.

Allgemeine Geschichte und Biographie. Mündliche Übungen sechzig Minuten wöchentlich, acht Jahre.

Physische Ausbildung. Sechzig Minuten wöchentlich, acht Jahre.

Vokalmusik. Sechzig Minuten wöchentlich, acht Jahre.

Zeichnen. Desgl.

Handarbeitsunterricht, Nähen und Kochen. Einen halben Tag wöchentlich im siebenten und achten Jahre.

Ihr Comité empfiehlt Lektionen (Schulübungen) von fünfzehn Minuten Dauer im ersten und zweiten Jahre, zwanzig Minuten im dritten und vierten Jahre, fünfundzwanzig Minuten im fünften und sechsten Jahre, und dreißig Minuten im siebenten und achten Jahre. Die Ergebnisse dieses Programms zeigen für das erste und zweite Jahr zwanzig Lektionen wöchentlich von je fünfzehn Minuten, außer sieben anderen Übungen, die je zwölf Minuten täglich im Durchschnitt beanspruchen; die Gesamtzeitdauer, die das Kind in unausgesetzter Aufmerksamkeit, welche es den Schulübungen zollen muß, beharrt, ist zwölf Stunden wöchentlich oder durchschnittlich zwei Stunden und vier und zwanzig Minuten täglich.

Zweige.	1. Jahr	2. Jahr	3. Jahr	4. Jahr	5. Jahr	6. Jahr	7. Jahr	8. Jahr
Lesen	10 St. wöchentl.		5 Stunden wöchentlich					
Schreiben	10 St. wöchentl.		5 St. wöchentl.	3 St. wöchentl.				
Buchstabierlisten				4 Stdn. wöchentl.				
Engl. Grammatik			Mündl. mit Aufsatz-Lektionen		5 Lektionen wöchentl. m. Textbuch			
Latein								5 Lekt.
Arithmetik	Mbl., 60 Min. wöchtl.		5 Lekt. wöchentl. m. Textb.					
Algebra							5 Lekt. wöchentl	
Geographie	Mbl., 60 Min. wchtl.		*) 5 Lekt. wchtl. m. Textb.			3 Lekt wchtl		
Naturwissenschaft und Hygiene			60 Minuten wöchentlich					
Ver. Staaten Geschichte							5 Lekt. wchtl.	
Ver. Staaten Verfassung								5 Lekt
Allgemeine Geschichte			Mündlich, 60 Minuten wöchentlich					
Phys. Ausbildung			60 Minuten wöchentlich					
Vokalmusik			Desgl., in 4 Lektionen eingeteilt					
Zeichnen			60 Minuten wöchentlich					
Handarbeitsunterricht oder Nähen und Kochen						einen halben Tag wöchentlich		
Zahl der Lektionen	20+7 tägl.	20+7 tägl.	20+5 tägl.	24+5 tägl.	27+5 tägl.	27+5 tägl.	23+6 tägl.	23+6 tägl.
Gesamtstundenzahl der Übungen	12	12	11⅔	13	16¼	16¼	17½	17½
Länge der Übungen	15 Min.	15 Min.	20 Min.	20 Min.	25 Min.	25 Min.	30 Min.	30 Min.

Für das dritte Jahr zwanzig Lektionen wöchentlich von je zwanzig Minuten und fünf allgemeine Übungen, die fünf Stunden wöchentlich oder eine Stunde täglich im Durchschnitt erfordern, was im Durchschnitt eine Zeitdauer von zwei Stunden zwanzig Minuten täglich für Schulübungen ergiebt.

Im vierten Jahre erhöhen sich die Schulstunden zu vier und zwanzig (wegen der vier Extrastunden im Buchstabieren) und die Zeit der Schulübungen zu dreizehn Stunden; der tägliche Durchschnitt beträgt zwei Stunden sechs und dreißig Minuten.

In dem fünften und sechsten Jahre steigt die Zahl der Schulübungen auf sieben und zwanzig wöchentlich auf Grund des Hinzufügens der formalen Grammatik, und die erforderliche Gesamtstundenzahl ist 16¼ Stunden per Woche oder ein Durchschnitt von 3¼ per Tag.

---

*) Beginnt im zweiten Halbjahr.

Im siebenten und achten Jahre sinkt die Zahl der Lektionen auf drei und zwanzig, indem zwar Geschichte neu hinzukommt, dagegen Schreiben und besondere Übungen im Buchstabieren aufhören und die der Geographie gewidmete Zeit auf drei Stunden wöchentlich zurückgeht. Aber dafür ist die Klassenübung auf eine Zeitdauer von dreißig Minuten erhöht. Handarbeitsunterricht nimmt einen halben Tag oder 2½ Stunden wöchentlich in Anspruch. Die Gesamtzahl ist 19 Stunden wöchentlich oder 3¾ per Tag.

Das vorausgehende Schema zeigt alle diese Einzelheiten.

IV. Methoden und Organisation.

Ihr Comité stimmt darin überein, daß die der Elementarschularbeit gewidmete Zeit von acht Jahren nicht vermindert werden solle, aber es hat — wie vorhin dargethan — empfohlen, daß im siebenten und achten Jahre eine modifizierte Form von Algebra anstatt vorgeschrittener Arithmetik eingeführt werde, und daß im achten Jahre die englische Grammatik dem Lateinischen weiche. Dies schafft nach seiner Meinung einen angemessenen Übergang zu den Studien der Mittelschule und ist darauf berechnet, den Schüler wesentlich in seiner Vorbereitung für jene Arbeit zu unterstützen. Bisher ist der Übergang von der Arbeitsleistung der Elementarschule zu plötzlich gewesen, insofern der Schüler auf einmal drei formale Studien begann, nämlich Algebra, physische Geographie und Latein.

Ihr Comité hat es für nötig befunden, die Frage der Lehrmethoden in zahlreichen Fällen zu besprechen, während es die Frage der wissenschaftlichen Werte und Anordnungen erwog, weil der Wert und die Zeit des Anfanges der verschiedenen Zweige in so hohem Maße von der Lehrmethode abhängt.

Die folgenden Empfehlungen bleiben indes für diesen Teil seines Berichtes vorbehalten:

Wir empfehlen, daß die Specialisierung der Arbeit des Lehrers vor dem siebenten oder achten Jahre der Elementarschule nicht versucht werden sollte und auch dann nicht in mehr als in einem oder zwei Gegenständen. In der Mittelschule erwartet man, daß ein Lehrer einen oder höchstens zwei Zweige lehre. In der Elementarschule ist es wenigstens für die ersten sechs Jahre im ganzen besser, daß jeder Lehrer seine Schüler in allen Zweigen, die sie lernen, aus dem Grunde unterrichte, weil er nur in dieser Weise die Erfordernisse der Arbeit gleichmäßig zu betonen imstande ist, indem er dieselbe derart in Wechselbeziehung setzt, daß kein Lehrzweig auf Kosten des andern ungehörige Aufmerksamkeit erhält. In dieser Weise bereiten die Schüler alle ihre Aufgaben unter der direkten Aufsicht desselben Lehrers vor und zeigen durch ihr Aufsagen derselben, welche Mängel der Lernmethode in der Vorbereitung vorhanden waren. Die ethische Erziehung ist unter diesem Plane viel erfolgreicher, weil der persönliche Einfluß des Lehrers oder der Lehrerin viel größer ist, wenn er oder sie ganz genau den ganzen Umfang der Schularbeit kennt. In dem Falle besonderer Lehrer ist die Verantwortlichkeit geteilt und die Gelegenheit für die besondere Bekanntschaft mit Charakter und Gewohnheiten vermindert.

Mit einem Lehrer, der die Vorbereitung überwacht und alle Aufgaben abhört, ist eine weit bessere Gelegenheit vorhanden, die zwei Arten der Aufmerksamkeit zu pflegen. Der Lehrer teilt seine Schüler in zwei Klassen und hört die eine ab, während die andere Klasse sich für die nächste Aufgabe vorbereitet. Die Schüler, welche abgehört werden, müssen dem einen aus ihrer Zahl, der die ihm vom Lehrer zugeteilte Aufgabe erklärt, scharfe Aufmerksamkeit schenken — sie müssen scharf aufpassen, um Fehler oder Auslassungen wichtiger Daten zu bemerken und zugleich die Bemerkungen des Lehrers zu hören. Dies ist eine Art der Aufmerksamkeit, die vereinigte kritische Aufmerksamkeit genannt werden kann. Die Schüler, die mit der Vorbereitung der nächsten Aufgabe beschäftigt sind, arbeiten selbständig, indem jeder für sich das Buch studiert und seine Thatsachen und Gedanken zu beherrschen sucht, sie miteinander vergleicht und sich bemüht, seine Mitschüler, die vor sich gehende Schulübung und den Lehrer zu vergessen. Dies ist eine andere Art Aufmerksamkeit, die nicht vereinigt ist, sondern es ist eine individuelle Anstrengung, für sich allein ohne Hilfe eine vorgeschriebene Aufgabe zu beherrschen und allen zerstreuenden Einflüssen zu widerstehen. Diese beiden Disziplinen in der Aufmerksamkeit sind die beste formale Erziehung, welche die Schule gewährt.

Ihr Comité hat bereits eine Art falscher Wechselbeziehung erwähnt, bei welcher der Versuch gemacht wird, alle Zweige in jedem zu studieren mit einer falschen Anwendung der Maxime Jacotot's „alles ist in allem" („tout est dans tout").

Ein häufiger Irrtum dieser Art ist die Gewohnheit, jeden Lehrgegenstand zu einer Sprachübung zu machen und die Arithmetik, Geographie, Geschichte, Litteratur oder was es auch immer sein mag, zu unterbrechen, indem man die Aufmerksamkeit des Schülers ohne Zusammenhang auf etwas in seinem Ausdruck, seiner Aussprache oder auf irgend einen fehlerhaften Gebrauch des Englischen lenkt. Auf diese Weise wird das ganze System der Schularbeit in eine Reihe grammatischer Übungen verwandelt und die Kraft des kontinuierlichen Denkens über den objektiven Inhalt der verschiedenen Zweige dadurch geschwächt, daß man eine verderbliche Gewohnheit des Selbstbewußtseins beim mündlichen Ausdruck schafft. Während Ihr Comité nicht zu behaupten wagt, daß man dem mündlichen Ausdruck in allen Lehrzweigen bis zu einem gewissen Grade keine Aufmerksamkeit zuwenden soll, ist es doch der Meinung, daß dieselbe auf die Kritik der Schulübung wegen mangelhafter technischer Genauigkeit beschränkt werden sollte. Die technischen Worte sollten in jedem Lehrzweige besprochen werden, bis der Schüler mit ihrer vollen Bedeutung vertraut ist. Das fehlerhafte Englisch sollte deshalb getadelt werden, weil es Verwirrung des Denkens oder Gedächtnisses verrät, und sollte in diesem Sinne verbessert werden. Aber vereinzelte Sprachformen (Solecismen) sollten schweigend von dem Lehrer für die Besprechung in den regelmäßigen Sprachstunden notiert werden.

Die Frage der Versetzung der Schüler hat von Zeit zu Zeit sehr viel Aufmerksamkeit erregt. Ihr Comité glaubt, daß in vielen Elementarschulsystemen durch zu große Formalität beim Ausfinden, ob die Schüler einer bestimmten Klasse die Arbeit bis zu einem gewissen willkürlich fixierten Punkte vollendet haben und vorbereitet sind, den nächsten Abschnitt der Arbeit aufzunehmen, großer Schaden angerichtet wird. In der früheren Zeit unserer Stadt-Schulsysteme, als das Amt des Schulsuperintendenten zuerst geschaffen wurde, hielt man es für nötig, den abgestuften Studiengang in Arbeitsjahre einzuteilen und bestimmte jährliche Prüfungen abzuhalten, um sich zu vergewissern, wie viele Schüler zur nächsten Stufe oder Jahresarbeit versetzt werden könnten. Alle, die bei dieser Prüfung durchfielen, wurden zurückversetzt, um noch ein Jahr in der Repetition der Jahresarbeit zuzubringen. Dies war zur Bequemlichkeit des Superintendenten so eingerichtet worden, der — — — wie man sagte — — — keine Prüfungen abhalten könnte, um den Bedürfnissen der Individuen oder besonderer Klassen zu entsprechen. Aus dieser Anordnung resultierte dann natürlich der große Mißstand des hier sogenannten „marking time".*) Schüler, welche ihre Jahresarbeit beinah vollendet hatten, wurden mit Schülern zusammengesetzt, die bisher um ein Jahr

---

*) Der militärische Ausdruck „marking time" bedeutet das „Tempo der Schritte markieren, ohne fortzuschreiten." Die vorgeschritteneren Schüler werden durch ein thätiges Nichtsthun getäuscht, bis die Zurückgebliebenen nachkommen können.

D. Übers.

hinter ihnen waren. Entmutigung und Demoralisation bei dem Gedanken, einen bereits einmal gelernten Kursus wieder aufzunehmen, veranlaßte viele Schüler, die Schule vorzeitig zu verlassen.

Dieses Übel ist in fast der Hälfte der Städte beseitigt worden, dadurch daß man die Schüler versetzt, sobald sie die Arbeit einer Stufe vollendet haben. Die beständige Tendenz des Klassifizierens, unvollkommen zu werden wegen der Verschiedenheit im Fortschritt der verschiedenen Schüler auf Grund der Altersungleichheit, der Reifestufe, des Temperaments und des Gesundheitszustandes macht häufige Veränderung im Klassifizieren notwendig. Dies kann leicht gethan werden durch Versetzung der wenigen Schüler, welche die Mehrzahl ihrer Kameraden weit hinter sich lassen in die nächst höhere Klasse, die durch einen Zwischenraum von weniger als einem halben Jahre von ihnen getrennt ist oder getrennt sein sollte. Die begabten, in dieser Weise versetzten Schüler müssen sehr fleißig sein, um die Arbeit zu leisten, die in der höheren Klasse in dem halben Jahre bereits geleistet worden ist, aber sie sind fast immer imstande, dies zu thun, und bedürfen gewöhnlich in zwei Jahren wieder einer Versetzung nach der höheren Klasse.

Der Charakter des Prokrustesbettes in den alten Stadtsystemen ist durch diesen Plan beseitigt worden. Einige andere Mißstände außer den schlechten Versetzungssystemen, die mangelhaften Organisationen entspringen, bleiben zu erwähnen. Die Schulgebäude werden oft mit abergläubischer Sorgfalt ausschließlich für besondere Stufen der Schüler reserviert. Das Hauptgebäude, das für Mittelschulzwecke*) errichtet worden ist, wird, wenn es auch nur halb gefüllt ist, nicht dazu benutzt, die Grammärschule**) zu entlasten, welche oft so überfüllt ist, daß sie die Klassen nicht aufnehmen kann, die von den Elementarschulen versetzt werden sollten. Es ist in solchen Fällen vorgekommen, daß dieser Aberglauben so weit vorherrsche, daß die Schüler in dem Elementarschulgebäude bei bereits beendigten Lehrgegenständen weiter beharren mußten, weil sie nicht nach der Grammärschule wegen Raummangels versetzt werden konnten.

In allen guten Schulsystemen erhalten die Schüler neue Arbeit, wenn sie die alte beendigt haben, und die begabten Schüler werden nach höheren Klassen versetzt, wenn sie ihre Kameraden so weit hinter sich ge=

---

*) high school, cf. p. 34, Anm. I.
**) Die grammar school deckt sich etwa mit den vier höheren Stufen der deutschen Elementarschulen, wenn sie auch bei der Abwesenheit der Einheit in den verschiedenen Staaten der Union etwas verschieden ist. Die Schüler rangieren etwa von zehn bis vierzehn Jahren. D. Übers.

lassen haben, daß die Arbeitsquantität, die für die Durchschnittsfähigkeit der Klasse fixiert worden ist, ihnen nicht genug zu thun giebt.

Zum Schluß möchte Ihr Comité zur Erklärung beifügen, daß es beim Beleuchten der Einzelheiten seiner Empfehlungen in diesem Bericht wiederholt abgeschweift ist in dem Bestreben, die Gründe klarzulegen, auf welchen seine Schlußfolgerungen beruhen, und in der Hoffnung, daß solche Einzelheiten eine noch tiefer gehende Erörterung der Erziehungs= werte der für die Elementarschulen vorgeschlagenen Lehrzweige und der Methoden, durch welche jene Zweige erfolgreich gelehrt werden möchten, hervorrufen wird.

Um das Interesse an dem Gegenstande zu erhöhen, empfiehlt Ihr Comité die Veröffentlichung ausgewählter Stücke aus den Berichten, die von eingeladenen Hilfscomités und von Freiwilligen eingesandt worden sind, von denen viele sehr wertvolle Anregungen enthalten, die in diesem Berichte nicht erwähnt worden sind.

William T. Harris, Vorsitzender,
Vereinigte Staaten Kommissär des Erziehungswesens,
Washington, D. C.

www.ingramcontent.com/pod-product-compliance
Lightning Source LLC
Chambersburg PA
CBHW030353170426
43202CB00010B/1365